Voices From Our Galaxy

Voices From Our Galaxy
A Bright Star Press Book
First Edition 2000
Second Edition 2005
Copyright © Elaine Thompson
All Rights Reserved

ISBN 0-9538441-0-2
©Elaine Thompson 2000
First Published in Great Britain.
2nd Edition 2005
Bright Star Press
elaine.thompson@ukonline.co.uk
www.elaine-thompson.com

To order additional copies, please contact us.
BookSurge, LLC
www.booksurge.com
1-866-308-6235
orders@booksurge.com

Illustrated by
ELAINE
J THOMPSON

VOICES FROM OUR
GALAXY
A Multidimensional Journey

A Bright Star Press Book
United Kingdom 2000
2006

Voices From Our Galaxy

TABLE OF CONTENTS

This Book Is Dedicated To All Of You Who Look Into The Night Sky With Wonder And Awe At The Beauty Held There.
To Those Who Have Had Their Own Extra-terrestrial Experiences.
To Those With Enquiring Minds Who Constantly Search For The Truth, And Are Open To The Vast Amount Of Evidence That Shows We Are Not Alone In This Or Any Other Galaxy.

INTRODUCTION

There have been times in my life when I have been quoted as a medium with extraordinary telepathic ability. I only know that life can be more than just the reality we see in front of us. Through my contact with beings from other worlds, I have seen that the future for us as a human race is going to be more than we ever dreamed of; and that the possibilities and realities of such a future are manifesting right here in the now.

Man has been looking to find that we are not alone since the beginning of civilised time. Nicola Tesla listened to Mars in the hope of hearing Martians. Frank Drake, the Godfather of SETI (search for extra terrestrial intelligence) was inspired by this 'need to know' that grips us all.

In recent history, the cold war ignited a race between the cosmonauts and the astronauts to be the first to find life on other worlds. Now, with the aid of our ever improving technology, Epsilon Andromeda is big news, as the first star to be found with orbiting planets just like our own solar system. The tenth planet has been discovered, and I suspect the eleventh and twelfth will not be far behind. Our previous concepts as to what conditions are required for life are being constantly challenged. As human beings, we all want to know what is beyond us, and this account of my experiences begins to open the door to possibilities beyond that which we already know.

***

My story begins as far back as my memory goes, when as a three-year-old child I had an astonishing encounter with a 'woman in blue' from an Andromedan Starship. This review of my early life covers the strange occurrences that shaped my destiny up to the present day. There are many surprises along the way, beginning with my golden memories of the very essence of long ago childhood. As we all know as we grow up in this world, life can turn out to be bittersweet and well punctuated with sudden and unexpected events.

After several surprising encounters with beings from other worlds, in 1996 I began to communicate regularly with Extra Terrestrials from the star systems of Arcturus, Andromeda, Sirius and Lyra. I was asked to contact them on a regular basis, and as a result, received the information in this book.

My friends the Extra Terrestrials showed me their concerns for the human race. I was allowed to see, communicate telepathically, and emotionally feel many different races, and was privileged to be able to paint them. As a result, there are full colour plates of these ET's for you to see. I have had many people write to me and tell me that they 'know' and recognise these Star Beings. With every letter I get, I feel that my job has been worth while.

I know that bringing this information to the world is an essential part of the ET plan; humans need to be familiar and less afraid of the unknown. This book is an account of my Extra Terrestrial and spiritual world contacts given with Love. What I experienced and was shown visually proved to me beyond doubt, that life in our Galaxy and beyond is absolute fact.

1
Where it all began

I remember......the leaves of the old apple tree rustled in the night air. Reflecting the moon's light and whispering softly, it dominated the inky darkness of the garden. Like the swirling dress of a ballroom dancer drenched with sparkling rhinestones, the stars flashed their brilliance across the velvet of the night.

Suddenly the air became still as the deepest ocean. No sound, no movement around a small house, nestled amongst dozens of clones. At the second story back bedroom window, I see myself as a child gazing through the metal-framed window and beginning to climb upon the sill, my soft chubby fingers grasping at the catch. With determination, I opened the glass, allowing the warm night air into the darkness of the bare room.

With an innocence only found in the spirit of the very young, I looked up at the shining moon with wonder, listening to the melody of the night and watching the moonlight play on my hands.

Softly I began to sing. My song was a little song, a simple melody from my own soul.

'Baby moon, it's time for bed, time to rest your sleepy head.'

Around and around the words went, like painted horses on a merry-go-round, bringing satisfaction to my heart. Leaning out of the open window as far as I could, my eyes met the moon as it came completely into view, shedding its light on me more fully. The moment of beauty it created as the moonlight lit up my long blond curls and set a sparkle to my deepest blue eyes passed unseen, as the seconds marched forward. Mesmerised, I gazed up at the glowing, shining orb and sang on, my baby voice sweet and beguiling in its simplicity.

And suddenly there was a Star.

It seemed to have always been there, but now its appearance captured the whole of my vision, diverting my attention away from the hypnotic beauty of the moon. Slowly it had cruised into view from behind the roof of the house, filling the night sky with its brilliant radiance.

And then all was filled with The Light.

Blue and shimmering, it extended from the star like a searchlight from a lighthouse; and within the mist and scattered reflections was a woman. She seemed to flow like liquid mercury; blue-black hair reaching to her waist framed her face like curtains of shining tourmaline. Clothed in a flowing dress of cobalt blue, she wore a cape as dark as a black hole, that rose with the night air and settled around her shoulders. Her weightless body rode the beam until she was standing in front of me at the window. Now suspended in the air, she emanated a peace that could not be defined.

She held out her hand, palm open, and something sparkled there, golden and inviting. My eyes lit up and an unspoken question welled up in my mind.

'What is it?'

In that timeless moment, lifetimes passed.

In reaching forward to take it, instantaneously it was gone. I felt a brilliant heat spring up in my body, and I turned my eyes slowly to gaze at the front of my glowing night-dress.

'Where is it?' my mind whispered, and the woman spoke at last. No sound hit the air, only the telepathic communion of minds.

'Courage it is, and it now lives in your heart. You will need its power in your life if you are to survive'.

She spoke no more.

Blue light effervesced around her, and in the twinkling of an eye the brilliant star-ship, hanging still as a Christmas bauble, drew her back, enfolded her and was gone.

The night seemed cold now, as the craft streaked away, and the moon no longer held the same attraction as it had before.

Suddenly I heard the banging of footsteps on the stairs outside my room. Momentarily frozen, I stared as the door burst open and my father, understandably fuelled by the rage of fear, uttered a shout and grabbed me violently. Fearing I was in danger of falling out of the window, he threatened to board it up with nails and a blanket if I ever touched the handle again. Scooping me across to the bed, he thrust me back under the heavy blankets, totally unaware of the enormity of the event he had missed, and tucked me tightly in. He then stormed out of the room, leaving images of the iridescent woman in blue and his angry face indelibly imprinted in my mind.

As a child, I felt that my life had been spent in happy aloneness; I didn't feel neglected, but rather felt an inner solitude that came with an as yet unknown purpose. The night enfolded me, and the warmth that had sprung up in my heart grew until it enveloped my tiny body, trickled into my mind and plummeted me into deep dreamless sleep.

***

Golden Childhood

Time passed.

I was said to be a child of extremes; they called me 'Good as Gold', never any trouble to look after and yet more curious and meddlesome than a basket full of kittens.

Unknown to me, I was *a child with a mission.*

I grew, and became as all other children, a chrysalis waiting for the right season to emerge. Then there came onto the stage of my life two dear souls called Erika and Stefan, he was a professor, she was a violinist.

My mother was employed by them, and could be found daily with sleeves rolled, washing and cleaning the endless fragile crystal. She swept and dusted the silent crevices; sweet traces of lavender wax lingering under her nails from endlessly polishing the dark heavy furniture that dominated the rooms. And hour after hour the 'golden haired' child, as I was called, spent time in the upper rooms listening distractedly to the strains of violin practice sessions.

The woman and her husband were German Jews of aristocratic lineage, who had escaped the war by virtue of their diplomatic connections and position. I quickly became their favourite, sitting quietly at Erika's feet, soaking up the music, amusing myself day after day with her jewellery box and its sparkling contents.

The house held a stillness that was hard to define, and everywhere was the smell of juniper oil from the heavy wood polish. To the right of the sunny entrance hall was a study where I was allowed on the special occasion of her husband Stefan being at home. The walls were filled floor to ceiling with ancient leather bound books with gold embossed spines, enclosing a cosy room crowded with heavy antique furniture. On top of the leather-inlaid desk was a small brass lamp that was turned on in order to highlight the treasures that he would show me. From behind a secret panel would come an old leather case, and as the contents spilled out into the lamplight, I stared, enchanted by the glint of dozens of golden Krugerands. His lilting German accent burrowed into my mind as he described the coins to me, asking if I liked them, and showing the engraved pictures on back and front. There were medals and silky ribbons in another compartment, and with patience, he would recount tales of his forefathers and the heroic deeds they performed to win the honours that he treasured so much.

But the thing that held the most excitement for me was on the third library shelf behind the desk. In its yellow cover, over four inches thick was a copy of Grimm's Fairy tales. Too high for me to reach, it needed the small wooden library ladder before it was in my hands. Stories would be read to me, until the wondrous day came when I was able to read for myself.

Erika had many musical visitors. Very often a string quartet would practice in the dining room around the great black Beckstein that dominated the atmosphere with expectancy. Celebrated pianists would accompany on occasions, and I was allowed to stay not only because I was so quiet, but also because I would sit very still, totally absorbed in the music and conversation. Armed with a silk covered cushion, my favourite place was under the piano, leaning with my back against one of the intricately carved legs.

In a child's world that overflowed with sensory input and images, I felt enraptured as I listened; my hands tracing the fat curves and ridges of the wood, down to the claw feet and polished brass castors. Here I could listen and observe without being noticed. The Beckstein became the natural object of my curious attention, and amused and pleased with my interest, a gift was given. Here, I was in a world that considered music as a way of life, and so it was arranged with my mother's grateful consent, that I should have piano lessons from the age of four.

Dutifully the learning began, and my talent began to emerge. Twice weekly after infant school had spilled out, you could see me struggling to carry my large leather music case, whilst being escorted by bus to the home of the music tutor. Although overworked and hard pressed to find enough time, my mother gladly dedicated herself to further my learning until I was old enough to go to my lessons alone.

Piano lessons were held in a dark gloomy house, with a dedicated but unloving spinster dolling out the scales and arpeggios as my penitence twice a week. At such a young age, I found learning was easy and natural to me, and as I progressed, Erika gave me the most wonderful gift of a piano of my own.

As time went on, I began to discover the discipline and pain that comes with expected dedication. To be made to practice scales when the sun shone and the days were long seemed futile and trying to me, and the memory of the hard and sharp ruler that was used on my knuckles when I made mistakes began to bite into my happiness.

The memory of the woman from the starship came only in my dreams now, but I always had a fascination with the night sky that grew stronger day by day.

***

The Sunshine Man

My sixth year dawned and the last vestiges of winter were forgotten as the longer spring days stretched out their enticing arms to welcome me. As my head filled with thoughts of playmates and freedom, the enforced lessons became even more tiresome.

Cowslips and celandines flaunted their shades of yellow in the hedgerows, heralding a promise of meadows brimming with delight when summer arrived in full glory.

With the freedom that comes with being old enough for school now, the local fields and houses became a place of investigation and discovery. Starry periwinkles bloomed on the waste ground in the next road, and my adventures became keener trying to find the right pile of bricks to stand on so that I was tall enough to see the elusive blue flowers hidden in the sea of green. At the top of the street was a small lane that led to great tracts of grassland, flowing way up and over a hill crowned with tall trees and hedgerows.

The 'Sunshine Man' put in his regular Sunday appearance throughout that long hot summer. He would appear as if from nowhere and take his place on the corner of the street, seated on a tiny three-legged stool. Fellow children gathered around, scrabbling about to seat themselves on the dusty pavement, eyes popping wide at the sight of his knarled weather-beaten face and the ravaged grey strewn beard that seemed to explode from his chin. When we were all ready, he would pull from under the many layers of tattered clothing a small hand accordion. His hands sported fingerless gloves, and with a nimbleness to challenge Nureyev, he would begin to play. We children sang and clapped to the strains of 'Jesus wants me for a sunbeam' and 'Nick–knack Paddywack', swaying cross-legged to the lilting harmonies. Today, he would be shunned as a tramp, and warned off. Then, on those hot summer afternoons, parents watched with approval, as their children were entertained and amused for an hour or two. Concepts were different then.

July matured into September, heralding the prospect of an autumn laden with mouth puckering blackberries from the lanes. Rosehips decorated the briars like scarlet painted fingernails, and crisp scented apples leant over the hedgerows from orchards down the lanes, inviting you to climb the banks and feast.

Like a charmed captive, the mid-day sun shone unfailingly with a ferocity and stillness that is only remembered from summers long past. Born of working class parents, I took for granted that everyone's father was away for most of the week; that everyone's mother slaved night and day at whatever job they were lucky enough to find, just to make ends meet. My dear father was a warm and wiry man, coming home at weekends from wherever his job took him. Sometimes he had burns and blisters on his arms as big as my small hands, earned from the hot asphalt that he worked with, laying flat roofs on buildings. He would take me to one side as a special treat, and show me the tools of his trade with pride. Hand crafted wooden floats of all shapes and sizes were stored in a tar encrusted canvas carry all. I loved to run my fingers over the polished wood, feeling the smoothness, smelling the familiar aroma of bitumen. They conjured up scenes awash with glossy black pools of tar, smoking and acrid to the nose; his gang of men, sleeves rolled and trousers tightly belted, black faced and sweating over the perfection of the mix.

He was only at home on the weekends, and when shaved and brushed, he became once again the father that I adored. He was a gentle man with a spectacular sense of humour for all things ridiculous. Often on a Sunday afternoon, you would find him on all fours, leaping around the front room playing ride-em-cowboy games, or pretending to eat sweet wrappers, swearing that the brightly coloured foil was tastier than the sweet itself. Wide eyed and totally taken in, I would watch him dress up in an old round motorbike helmet and carrying a feather duster, pretend to be a roman soldier. Once, he made me believe that there were little balloon men who flew around the room, calling out for more air, more air! But more than anything, the stories he told me captured my heart the most. He would turn ordinary everyday things into fantastic make-believe like the Jabberwocky and Alice in Wonderland. He would join me in my own faraway realm, making me feel at home with all things ridiculous, and then teach me how to laugh about it.

*****

My Garden of Delights

My mother seemed to be always in the kitchen, cooking glorious food you could smell from the bottom of the street. Golden Bramley apple pies, sweetly sharp and spicy, revealed plump raisons speckled with cinnamon as the crisp sugary pastry melted in your mouth. There were always jugs of sunshine yellow custard, heavily skinned like clotted cream, and crisp skinned roast Sunday lamb. My job was to collect the fresh mint from the garden, and I would watch, soaking up the wondrous smells, as my father finely chopped it, mixing sugar and vinegar to make mint sauce.

And on Mondays it was washing day. The fragrant smell of hard bars of green fairy soap and Persil suds lingered in my memory. I remember the smell of fragrant steam as it enveloped my face, inhaling and storing the memories as I peered into the huge copper boiler containing the bubbling sheets. Hot and soapy sheets and towels, heavy as lead to lift, were boiled and then rinsed in the deep china sink with the blue bag. Sometimes, I was allowed to stand on a stool and poke at the billowing sheets with the boiler stick, making a game of trying to get them all under the water. The bubbles held magic, each with their rainbow of colours. I would stare intently at them as they divided into a million different sizes, some reflecting my face, others the edges of the kitchen windows. But always other realities beckoned to me from around hidden corners.

I spent hours in the garden watching my father digging, mopping his brow as the sweat dripped off his nose. With insatiable curiosity my eyes followed the strong muscled arms pulling at the relentless couch grass, waiting to see the small grubs he called leatherjackets that appeared in every spade full of soil turned over.

The garden was full of fruit bushes; gooseberries so hard and prickly you had to bite off the hairs, but when they turned rosy, such a delight to steal. Black and red currants, plums and apples, raspberries and damsons, all jostled for room in the small garden, flanked on the other side of the path by ranks of potatoes, onions and various rows of crisp green vegetables. When the washing line running down the centre of the garden was full, I discovered a game that made me shriek with laughter and gasp for breath. The billowing sheets would almost knock me off my feet as I beat and pushed at them with my little arms, getting the occasional wet sheet wrapped around me, filling my nose with a glorious aroma of summer breeze dried cotton. My excuse for getting tangled was that I was on my way up the garden path to get to the chickens, or that I needed to stand on the rhubarb tump to see who was out in the other gardens around. I had a favourite hen that was docile and quiet, and, after overcoming my first fears, I would tentatively feel underneath the warm feathery breast for new laid eggs. My heart was always captivated by the hen's bright eye looking at me curiously when I rummaged around in the deep straw. I was always careful to talk nicely and thank the hen for her eggs, and as a ritual, I would sing 'Chick chick, chick chick, chicken, lay a little egg for me, I want one for my tea' as I approached the old wooden hen house. As carefully as a tightrope walker, I would slowly carry my precious bounty back to my mother, each warm brown egg filling my hand completely.

***

Missing time

With the first flush of autumn the heavy sweet aroma from the old apple tree outside my window called to me. So it was that with a stolen apple in one hand, and heavy music case in the other, I once again dawdled and dragged my feet in the direction of the main road. It was four fifteen in the afternoon, and I was bidden once again to piano lessons.

I leant against the low red brick wall by the corner bus stop. The metal bar on the case dangled as I bit into the crisp flesh of the apple. Juice running from the side of my mouth, I stepped to the kerb and craned my neck into the road. There at last was the bus, trundling down over the hill in the distance. The day had been long and humid, and my thoughts were elsewhere. Mentally I was lying at the foot of the apple tree lost in the cool shade and hypnotic sway of the branches. The bus pulled up at the stop, and dropping the apple core over the wall for the snails to feast on, I got on. I was allowed to go on my own now, and feeling myself to be 'a big girl', I climbed to the top floor where an empty seat invited me half way down the bus. My favourite occupation was looking into other people's houses and gardens. So with my forehead pressed up against the window, I stared intently through the glass for a glimpse of where other people held their realities, as the bus pulled away for the fifteen minute journey.

From nowhere a man appeared in the seat in front of me. His heavy black wool coat, collar turned up, smelt damply of rain. It registered somewhere deep in my sub-mind that he must be very hot to have such a coat on, and to be ignoring the humid weather. I stared at the back of the seat, smelling the dank odour of cigarette ends and wondering what woman had stubbed out the lipstick stained ones that spilled out from the overflowing ash tray. Faster than an intake of breath, the man turned in his seat and touched the centre of my forehead with his middle finger. Our eyes met for a millisecond, and it was over. Starting back in my seat at his sudden touch, I became afraid and jumped up, grabbing my open music case to go downstairs. I clattered down to the platform below, intent on getting off the bus no matter where the stop was. Relieved and surprised, I saw that I was at my stop. Jumping quickly onto the pavement, the shock of what I found threw me into confusion.

It was dark, and it was raining.

Stepping to the front of the bus, I saw pouring rain falling onto the black oily tarmac. Bright steaming headlights from an oncoming car illuminated a pool of water washing across the pitted surface of the road. The warm heavy rain spattered onto my bare arms in thunderous plops. The gloomy front door of the music teacher was right by the bus stop, and my feet carried me faster than a startled rabbit up to the bell. The door opened and a diminutive figure dressed in Victorian mode, peered at me. It was apparent to all except me that I was late. One and a half hours, to be exact.

'And you'll have to wait until Emily has completed her lesson before I can begin with you, and where have you been, and why are you late? Tsk, come in child, and get dry. I'll turn on the gas fire for you, and fetch you a towel.'

Where had the time gone? At what point had I entered into a timeless dimension? An hour and a half had kaleidoscoped into zero point and I was without memory.

At that age, I didn't even try to figure it out, my mind not able to grasp it as being not possible, or wrong in any way. I was more concerned with the disapproval of my music mistress, and what my mother would say about my lateness. But by the time the lesson was over, the whole incident was erased from my memory, only to be brought forward in later years under hypnosis.

And so it was.

***

Near death experiences

At seven, books became the tallship that carried me to other worlds. I merged my soul into the realm of fairies and folk tales, devouring book after book at a rate of three or four a week. Travelling high into the fields and meadows behind the house, I took my little feet over the hill and down the stony lane to the tiny library. I made my pilgrimage almost daily, pestering the harassed librarian time after time for new book arrivals. When nothing was forthcoming, I would re-read with a hunger born of a desperate need to find myself somewhere in the magic of the pages.

My life revolved around books and music, music and books. Imperceptibly, my own universe was beginning to form. My personal melody was taking shape with its enchanting lilt woven between the lines of the fairy tales and the bars of the music. It seemed as if I spent timeless periods when I was not fully present in this world, and when I saw a halo of colour around a classmate, or golden light around the headmistress at morning service, it passed as a normal thing. The awareness that I was in any way different didn't reach me until the river of time had flowed on for a few more miles.

Childhood marched on, leaving tell-tale markers along the way in my book of life. Apart from the strange encounter with missing time and the woman from the star ship, there were two experiences that took me close to death. The first incident occurred when I was just three years old. I remember playing outside in the dusty road on a manhole cover with three or four children from the street. With my tiny fist full to overflowing with brightly coloured marbles, and without seeing any danger, I put several in my mouth. Within moments, I had done the inevitable, and had swallowed a marble. I must have inhaled quickly as it became lodged in my tiny throat. I was later told that I was blue and almost unconscious before an older boy from up the road took fright and literally dragged me to the back door. My mother, as always, was in the kitchen with the door open. The tentative knocking caught her attention, and turning from the sink, saw before her a small boy struggling to hold my body upright. In a flash, she took in the blue colour of my face and the eyes turning upwards into unconsciousness. She flew into action as the boy stuttered out the story. In one swift movement, she turned me upside down, put her fingers down my throat as far as she could and hooked out the offending marble. It was both the cause and the saving grace that my chubby throat with overly large tonsils had blocked the marble from going any further. This quick action from my mother saved the day and my life, and, almost as if it had never happened, became just a small bump in the road to my future.

***

Into the depths of the sea

My second brush with death came at ten years when the sea stretched out its hand to try and claim me.

Happily on a rare seaside holiday with my mother, I had ventured out to sea on a plastic lilo sun bed, wanting to paddle towards a cliff face that held all kinds of tiny silvery shells and amethyst treasures. With my legs dangling either side of the airbed, playful waves rocked me up and down. With the wind stinging my skin, and the hot sun burning into my back, I aimed my fragile craft for the cliff face. Reaching my goal,

I entered the cool dark shadows where swaying seaweed floating like mermaid hair brushed with longing against my legs. The bed tipped and swayed as the waves slopped and slapped against the dark shell encrusted rock. Here were shells gleaming with mother of pearl, sitting snugly in veins of weed encrusted amethyst. I was wishing I could dig them out to take home with me, so I paddled closer until I almost touched the rock.

Images embedded themselves deeply into my mind from the next moments that were almost my last. With the rise and fall of the water, I had caught a wave sideways, and gone over backwards like a diver rolling into the deep. With my mouth open in surprise, my last memories were watching the bubbles of air rising to the surface from my lips as I sank slowly into the cold dark ocean.

Then there was no more.

Then an unknown man entered onto the stage of my life, surely sent by Angels to become the saviour of one small life. Only this vigilant soul, seemingly sent to watch over me, had seen me disappear into the deep waving fields of seaweed from his watchpoint on the shore. God gave him the accuracy and speed to find his mark. Into the water and faster than an arrow he swam, out towards the empty bobbing sun bed; then diving again and again with speed and sureness until his hands found my limp body. Like a scrap of wet paper he drew me to the surface and began the swim to safety; my consciousness only returning when I was given mouth to mouth resuscitation.

Once again I was back in the realm of the living, lying on the hot sand with my eyes stinging and my throat raw from coughing. As my gaze began to focus, I saw his legs, but as I turned to struggle to my feet, wobbling like a new-born calf, he was gone. He had disappeared as if the air had swallowed him up, leaving me with the gift of my life as proof that he had been there.

***

Family fortunes

During my tenth year, a surprising twist of fate occurred.

The early morning was warm but thunderously overcast, punctuated occasionally with half-hearted showers that threatened to storm but didn't. The resident song thrush could be heard, tap-tapping a snail shell on a large flat stone in the border by the apple tree. The creak of the metal gate heralded the postman. Beaded with perspiration, he had dismounted from his bike and clambered up the steps to the front door, his jacket gently steaming. Amongst various others, *The Letter* lay innocuously waiting with no indication of the havoc and excitement it was about to create. My father had not yet gone off to work, so he was unshaven and still in his vest and trousers when he gathered up the mail to peruse.

Moments later there were shrieks and screams coming from all over the house. The full implication hit dad first, then mum and my two elder sisters joined in, rushing around like the house was on fire. A cheque had arrived from 'Littlewood's Football Pools'; There was a win amounting to the grand total of four hundred and thirty nine pounds; in those days past, a fortune! Oh, how they hugged and kissed, shrieked and whooped, and bounced from bed to bed in absolute delight!

I looked on in curious appeal at the sudden flurry of wild excitement. What had happened? Without any concept of more than five pennies (if I was a good girl) the furore was somewhat of a mystery to me.

When the entire hubbub had died away, and with nobody wanting to tell me anything really important, my interest faded and I rejoined my own world like the outgoing tide flowing towards the horizon.

Later that day, my mother and father sat with the family in grand consultation on to how to make the very best of the money. This event and the consequent decisions were to change the lives of all concerned.

In the year that followed, I graduated from junior school, surprising everyone with honours results. I was always a daydreamer, and no one expected me to surpass all the other kids around me in the exams, and as a result, winning a scholarship to public school. The teachers were astounded that the tests had brought out in me a grasp of maths and an indication of a computer quick mind that they had not seen before. By now, my parents had decided that they needed to 'better' their status, and had used the winnings to buy a little lock up shop in a better part of town. What came with it was a prefabricated bungalow just down the road, and something that made my heart soar. No further than a short run, (if you ran fast) was a place that was to become my vital world. If you had asked me where it was, I would have told you to walk past the next bungalow, go around the corner for a count of twenty steps, and there you will find 'The Gate'. From my very first step inside I was in a realm that only childhood dreams are made of.

***

2

A Forest of Dreams........

A forest, with its steep wooded slopes thickly intense with undergrowth lay beyond The Gate. The day I took my first cautious steps there, the heavy odour of wood anemones hung in the air, challenging my city nose. Cool and enticing, it called me down a sloping pathway littered with treasure stones. Magical ferns and unknown flowers drew my attention as my pace slowed to take in every varied blade of grass and every tree root. Such wonders in so much abundance had never been mine alone before. As I wandered, I explored every crevice and glade, speaking in my mind to the tree spirits and fairies that I knew lived there. There were tree entangled cliff faces and hidden dells; winding paths lined with cuckoo pint and wild garlic; darkest green mossy stones smelling of forest peat; and twigs covered in sphagnum moss that protected the minute worlds of plant life held there.

Each step took me ever downwards, and I was now close to reaching the lush green valley at the bottom. So deep it was that to me, the trees touched the sky and enclosed me forever in its magic. But the pearl in the oyster of this forest was a jewel to set in my crown of imagination. In places lazy and shallow, in others fast and exciting, a queen of a river had her throne there.

All through the summers to come I found my solace there. Day after day, I bared my feet and entered the water, searching for shining treasure. Time stood still as I watched the minnows dart amongst the rocks and pit their skill against the current. My heart and soul danced its joy in rhythm with the silky green weed that flowed in the current like a water nymph's hair. Hour after hour I lay in the dappled sunlight, lulled by the wind in the tall trees and the serenade of blackbird, robin and thrush. Coming home at dusk sometimes wet and muddy with my pockets bulging with treasure trove, my heart was full and my contentment complete.

And this was how it was.

***

The Golden ET

One such hot and languid afternoon I was lying on a large raised stone platform, close to the bend in the river by the old green bridge. The waterfall under the iron construction sang its usual song and the heat of the day had made me lazy. An electric blue kingfisher flashed up and down the river, ignoring me as I chewed thoughtfully on a long stalk of grass. My mood was cat like in its contentment, my inner satisfaction so great that it just had to rest a while on the warm stone to absorb even more of the beauty around me.

I was lost in my own world as I stared into the distance, mesmerised by a heat haze over the fast flowing water. This was a timeless day when dragonflies flashed red and gold in the sunlight, mayflies hovered in the air over the still places in the river, and chestnut blossoms fell like snow into the water, floating their way down stream and into oblivion.

And as naturally as the birdsong or the breeze, a Being was there, standing in front of me. About four feet tall, his eyes met mine as I lay flat on my stomach with my legs bent at the knees and my feet crossed. Raising myself to a sitting position, wide-eyed but unmoved, I took in the whole scene.

About fifty feet in the air above the little being was a slim, pear shaped golden craft. It shone in the sunlight, radiating shafts of light onto the ground, and was completely smooth like a polished golden egg. 'Big enough for one person' I thought, as my eyes refocused on the little being. His skin colour was tawny gold, and his eyes, which glittered large and almond shaped, smiled at me from a strange shaped head. He reminded me of the elves and fairies that dwelt in my beloved books, but with a difference. Without any visible clothing, his skin looked like the soft folds of chamois leather. His arms and legs were long and slender, and his belly was round and low. He had the longest fingers I had ever seen, and as he held out his hand to me, I saw he was offering a buttercup glowing with a radiance that took my breath away. I peered closer. Three fingers and a thumb with bulbous ends held the glowing flower. I met his eyes and suddenly my soul was flooded with the most exquisite feeling of love I could ever remember. It transfixed and charmed me, and the depth of feeling emanating from this little creature momentarily overwhelmed me. There was no fear in the presence of so much love, and asking me mentally to take the flower, I did. His mind reached out to join mine in a communion of respect and peace, and somewhere deep in my brain new knowledge joined the ever growing data bank that was as yet still hidden.

With a smile in his eyes, he stepped backwards and a flight of golden steps dropped down from the ship, stopping at his feet. Without turning, he floated up the stairway, telepathically sending his farewell to me with a promise of another meeting someday, somewhere. Then he was at the portal, the steps were swallowed back into nothingness, and the doorway melted into polished gold again.

I was aware of some kind of forward motion, but it was so fast that it gave the illusion of instantly disappearing. And it all felt as natural as falling off a log, as if I knew about all this already, and there was nothing on this Earth to make a fuss about. Scanning the sky to see if there was any trace of the craft, but knowing in my heart that there wouldn't be, I decided to go home for tea.

***

Out of my body and into the ether

Public school with all its prestige delighted my mother, and managed to grab my interest for the first year. As a new teenager, I felt that the uniform with its regulation blue velour hat and heavy serge gymslip was totally uncool, and a constant source of embarrassment. I wore it with a grumble, and as time went on the novelty of having to wear 'required' clothing with both indoor and outdoor shoes really began to wear off with a vengeance. In my private life, the piano lessons continued to drone on and on and just before my thirteenth birthday I found myself being hustled by my diminutive piano teacher into entering a music festival. Only moments before I was to play did I discover that it was a competition. I was still very naive, and I had no idea that I would be up for judgement in front of so many people. This was to have a devastating effect on me.

The day dawned, and the first thing to go awry was my music teacher insisting that I attend in my school uniform. I felt uncomfortable and awkward, and wasn't sure what was expected of me. Sure, I knew all the nuances of the piano piece perfectly, and, already accustomed to rigorous piano exams, I thought that all I had to do was go somewhere and play it. The concept of an audience of hundreds of people and a panel of judges had never entered my mind.

I was taken to the venue by car, which was an ancient Rolls Royce provided by my benefactress Erika. The cracked leather seats smelled of polish and this was the first time I had ever seen glass between the front and back seats of a car. We duly arrived at a vast ornately carved stone cathedral, and I was ushered through a set of carved double doors that would rival the best stately home. I found myself faced with the long walk down the central isle, so I took a deep breath, and with all eyes on me, started the slow walk through the vast audience towards the enormous grand piano. This was when a mind-numbing fear overtook me. The impact of so many people in such a grand auditorium threw me into my first experience of stage fright. It was as if I was not even in my body as I sat down to play. The music, required to be there but unread, drooped silently against the ebony gleam of the rest. Bowing my head, I tried to compose myself to begin. Searching around for some signal as to when I should play, I saw a panel of judges all looking at me intently; a man with grey hair and moustache nodded at me, and mouthed the words 'you may begin'.

My eyes glanced at the keyboard, and then seemed to glaze over. My performance was to be as I had been taught, flowing and note perfect; yet I was held in a trance as if some automatic pilot had taken over my hands.

Taking one last look at the music, I slowly phased out of conscious awareness and found myself rising above the small body sitting there at the huge grand piano. I took flight in the acoustic heights of the cathedral hall to bask in the rainbows from the stained glass windows. Like some ethereal ghost leaving my body to play its melody, I was momentarily free. The time became no time, and as the music rose all around me, I took in the rainbow colours of the tones as they floated upwards. As the dying finale faded away, I re-entered my body like a wraith drifting over a marsh, and conception of where I was came once again into wobbly focus. It had seemed like a lifetime, and then it was over.

Bewildered and not understanding what had happened, my child mind felt the fear again, and reacted accordingly. As the last notes died away, the audience roared their appreciation with applause. I got up, turned like an automaton, and walked out the way I had entered looking neither left nor right. I was told later that I had been beaten into first place by one point. I never heard any of the others play, and had no idea of what went on. What I was left with was the feeling that I had been set up, judged, and found to be wanting. Even though my performance had been stunning, I had still failed by just one point. Because of this I felt all the hard work and hours practising were wasted time. The lasting legacy imprinted on me was that I felt so worthless I could never again bring myself to play whilst anyone was watching me, not even for my parents.

***

A new body

Feeling betrayed by my teacher, I began to balk at the lessons, and this heralded the beginning of my struggle to find myself. Things went, according to my mother, from bad to worse. Nothing I could do was good enough, and so I began not to care anymore. When not allowed out, I buried myself in books night after night, seldom spending time in the communal family living room. Privately, I was growing into my teenage years with all the fire of a racehorse that would not be ridden by anyone.

I was blonde and startlingly pretty, my puppy fat having melted away after an illness I contracted from my father. The memories of him lying in bed, eyes yellow with jaundice, were linked with the haze of my own fever. All I could remember was not being able to eat for two weeks, and my struggle with the first meal from my mother of scrambled eggs in a bowl. When I was eventually allowed out, my teetering steps took me slowly to the play area close to the local junior school. It was a hot afternoon, the atmosphere was still and silent, and the trees around the playground were heavily laden with spring blossoms. Sniffing the air, I found my sense of smell to be acutely sharp. The small park was deserted, and I sat down on a swing to rest awhile. An old iron maypole was the centrepiece of the playground, and its double-handled bars clinked in the breeze from their long chains, inviting me to swing. Without much strength, I wandered across and took up the worn wooden hand bars, intending to swing just a little. My steps gathered speed, and as I lifted off the ground, I found myself flying higher than I thought was possible!

Lighter than thistledown I floated around the pole, squeaking with delight at this new found freedom. As a child, I had never given much

19

thought to my body or my weight. Suddenly the awareness of this lighter than air feeling brought me in totally in touch with my self in a way I had not experienced before. Elated, I swung on, never wanting the flying to end. During the long illness, I had shed over thirty pounds of body weight, and it revealed a growing woman-child whose face I almost didn't recognise when I looked in the mirror.

Between twelve and fifteen I discovered boys, and fell into my first puppy love with the boy next door. As my hormones kicked in, the pangs of the unrequited love I held for him stung me to the core. So, my beloved forest became more of a place for joint adventure with him and 'the gang' as they called themselves, me being the only tomboy amongst five or six of the local lads. Try as I might to attract him, his only interest remained staunchly with the boys, the Boy Scout group, and the antics of his mates.

Pushing as hard and as far as I could into personal freedom, I managed to retain a kind of grubby innocence liberally sprinkled with fierce individuality.

All the ingrained teachings from my early years at Sunday school and religious education at public school went out of the window. I became a trendy atheist and didn't believe in anything. Stubborn and headstrong, I began to identify with the 'hippies', and as my hair grew longer and my choice of clothes got blacker, my mother despaired of what to do with me. I was almost leading a double life. During the day I was a well-groomed young lady at public school, and at night, a felt like a rebel with no idea where I was going. In the winter evenings, moody and alone, I would pour over my books. In summer, I reached for my guitar, put on my oldest sloppiest clothes and sat on the front doorstep singing songs by Bob Dylan. My mother was beside herself with concern about what the neighbours might think. I however, didn't give a hoot. Inside, I was my own master, and so when none of my gang of friends identified with this new culture with the same fervour, I remained unconcerned. I went out into the hidden places in town, where only the hip people hung out, seeking out others to identify with. This was leading me slowly but surely along a path that was definitely not marked in my book of destiny.

At sixteen, Divine Intervention played an Ace.

***

Divine contact

Days had been more tedious than usual, and I suffered with indignance the same old 'going to school' rigmarole as if it were beneath me. It was not as if I hated the staff or didn't get on with any of the other girls, I just wanted to be somewhere else--anywhere else! My health had taken a downward turn, and I suffered regularly with bronchitis. From fourteen onwards, I had been afflicted with the most terrible allergy to dust and pollen, and spent a lot of my time sneezing and wheezing in the chalk dusty classrooms or in the school library. This added, on the whole, to making school a begrudgingly tolerated experience.

Solace came in afternoon lessons twice a week, when I indulged my vocation in the art room and the pottery studio. In the airy heights of the top of the building, I painted and drew my fantasies, addicted to the colours and the textures of the art materials. As a legacy of my childhood, I had a passion for collecting 'things'. Bits of knarled wood, shining stones, leaves and my personal objets d'art, all made their way into my richly fruitful collages. Maths, history and religious education bored me beyond reason, but I had an aptitude for languages and the written word both in French and English. A compulsive poet, I poured out my private emotions in heartfelt script. All my newly experienced feelings found their avenue of expression on every page that was available to me. In contrast, Latin lessons seemed like purgatory and felt like a big waste of time. My mind was usually to be found elsewhere, daydreaming the hours away until home time.

On my daily route home I would stop at the magazine kiosk and with my bus change buy a personal place to retreat to. Within the world of Superman comics, I could fly and possess the super powers I so often dreamed of.

And still I did not recognise that the auras I could see around people and the bright colours that illuminated the walls wherever I looked where unusual. I still had no knowledge of what these things were, but that was about to change.

It was on one ordinary day in the summer of my sixteenth year that a milestone in my life was vividly marked. Coming home from school, with my heavy satchel slung over my arm, I got off the bus and made my way as usual up the road to the little shop my parents ran. It was like an Aladdin's cave, with ranks of sweet jars glittering in the sunlight by the big window. In the cool interior, cigarettes such as Woodbines, Senior Service and pouches of fragrant tobacco formed the backdrop to my father's familiar position behind the old ornate ringer till. Newspapers, hardware, knitting wool, lemonade and paraffin, all jostling for attention, were paraded on shelves around the walls. Unusual items were tucked away in every corner, and every inch of available space was filled with extraordinary things. Liver salts and little twists of 'Bile Beans' in tins sat next to pipe cleaners, boxes of odd buttons and rolls of postage stamps.

In earlier years, it had been my delight to go with my father on a Saturday to the wholesalers. At the wholesalers, there were 'outers' (boxes) of Black Jacks and Fruit Salad chewy sweets at four for a penny; liquorice boot laces and jewelled jars of shining chocolates; and bars of Rowntrees 'Five Boys' with their faces grinning at me from the red wrappers. These were all selected from the wooden shelves and loaded onto the rickety old trolley; up to the counter to pay the bill, and then on to the next. The Saturday round took us to the Newspaper Warehouse, where all the comics I ever dreamt of were there for me to sneak a look at whilst my father made his orders.

At Christmas time, the Toy Wholesalers were all mine. They were literally bursting with tinsel and baubles, the shelves calling out to me with shining marvels, and my job was to select or reject from this Aladdin's cave of wonders. There were dolls and miniature kitchen sets, tiny toyshops and teddy bears; tin toys that whirred and clanked, china tea sets and rubber animals, all to be put on sale in *my* shop for Christmas!

Held in the remembering, I saw fond visions of the giant walking talking dolls, each with different coloured hair and dress, each with a pull string that made them talk. These took over the space normally held for knitting wool, patterns and haberdashery. I can feel myself smiling as the picture changes, and there before my eyes are the enormous boxes of Christmas chocolates with their beautiful covers. There were village scenes at harvest time, stage coaches in the forest, winter landscapes with snow, and log fires with kittens, all finished with a ribbon and a huge triple bow in one corner. They always held pride of place on the top most shelves of our little shop with the largest box at the centre as the special Christmas Raffle prize.

Retrieving my mind from its momentary reverie, my thoughts turned to the frozen chocolate bars my father kept in his 'lolly' cabinet. It was one of his better ideas, and the local kids loved it. They would spend ages gnawing at the rock hard Mars bars and Milky Ways, instead of the chocolate being all gone in two minutes. The old ice cream freezer thrummed and wobbled noisily as I ducked past under the counter and headed into the tiny stock room. The familiar smell of bleach and soap powder made my sensitive nose wrinkle, and with a sigh I laid down my heavy school bag under the table where kegs of vinegar were stored. The ever-ready kettle stood waiting for me, steaming fiercely. Plonking myself down on an ancient wooden chair, I eagerly accepted the steaming mug of tea my mother offered me. We chatted small talk for a while, it being interspersed with my mother popping in and out to serve the occasional customer with a quarter of tea or a small bag of loose chocolate pieces, called 'mis-shapes'.

The time was almost five o'clock, and I became impatient for the peace that home held. Picking up the bulging leather satchel, I begrudgingly promised my mother that I would start on my homework the minute I got in. Walking out of the coolness of the shop I emerged into the bright, eye screwing sunlight. Home was no more than a few hundred yards away, punctuated with regularity by old, green painted iron lampposts.

As I crossed the dusty road, the familiar paving stones that were home to so many weeds and grasses, went unnoticed. I found the heat of the summer sun too much for my fair skin and heavy uniform. Sparrows, taking their dust baths in the gutter came under my scrutiny, and I remember wondering just how hot they felt with all those feathers. I reached the first lamppost, passed it and plodded on, weary but eager to get to the cool of my room and shed the uniform I hated so much.

Suddenly I became aware of a figure walking beside me. From the corner of my eye I could see a man, dressed in a white flowing robe that glowed like a floodlit pearl. The simple garment was belted at the waist, accentuating the easy gait of his walk. His bearded face, the epitome of gentleness and compassion, was framed with golden chestnut hair that curled loosely to his shoulders, glinting bronze and rich in the sunlight.

From my bible studies over the years, I knew it was Jesus. Slowly, my consciousness took in His whole Presence.

His heavenly eyes, eclipsing the blue of sky and sea, drew me deeply into an exquisite Love, held me there, and suspended time.

His hands, held out in welcome, invited my soul to join His in the unison of Oneness. It was as if He captured my spirit like the wind, with all power and strength, and then set me free. He radiated absolute purity and grace from the crown of his head down to the brown toes of his sandaled feet.

Light enveloped me, and a wave of ecstasy passed through me, tingling my skin like a slow electric shock. I felt myself physically rise from the ground by about two or three inches. Weightless, my body seemed to glide effortlessly as we walked the pathway side by side.

He looked into my eyes, and, joined with Him, I became All That Is. Inside my mind a flower opened, and his words took form.

'I AM WITH YOU ALWAYS'.

The words became One with me, and every cell in my body responded to the promise.

The vision of His Presence seemed to have been there forever, with only some small part of my mind registering that two lampposts marked the actual distance we walked together. And as I reached this final marker, the vision dissolved into some other dimension, and He was gone. Like the suddenness and shock of a cold shower, I was back on the ground again, but only physically. My spirit was flying and my heart felt as if it could burst open and engulf the entire universe.

And strange as it may seem, I held this miracle within me, and didn't tell a soul until some years later, when the events that were shaping my life began to take on meaning.

***

Extra Terrestrial contact again

As I slowly said goodbye to childhood, that sixteenth year was marked a second time by the appearance of beings from another world. The sultry sun of summer slipped away in favour of a glorious autumn, flaming her colours across the canvas of the days. Early mornings and evenings came fresh and chilly as the sun bowed in and out. Days shortened, and as the nights drew in and friends were few, I returned once again to the power of the written word.

Evening swept its darkening skirts about the house, enclosing it in an early winter's glow. It was raining. The golden lamplight shone strongly into my bedroom, illuminating the rain falling fast on the windowpane. Dreaming between the lines of the Greek mythology book I was reading, my eyes took in the droplets as they trickled and ran one into the other. Lazily I shifted from one elbow to the other as I gazed at the glass. I marvelled at how the droplets were attracted to one another, and as if by magic, they leapt together becoming tiny rivulets tracing a path ever downwards. Mesmerised and fascinated I watched until the room was no more and I was one with my mind and soul.

And as naturally as rolling off the bed, I found myself suspended in space above the lamppost, glowing orange outside the house. Then my consciousness divided, and I saw myself simultaneously in three places at once. My main awareness was high above the old clock tower across the wooded valley. Hanging in the dark night sky was a spaceship pulsing with silvery blue energy, and this is where I found myself, talking to the woman in blue from my childhood.

The woman looked unchanged, except that I could now see more detailed aspects of her and the surroundings. Her eyes hooked my attention immediately. They were such amazing eyes, larger than humanoid, almond shaped and black as the night; yet they radiated softness, reflecting the flashing lights that twinkled all around her from the instrumentation panels in the ship. The alien woman took me to a screen and pointed. I could see myself leaning against the window in my bedroom, watching the rain as if in a trance; and travelling between this part of me and the ship, was a bright stream of lights. I heard sounds like a computerised fax download and saw a twisting coil of red, yellow and orange light streams that were focused directly onto my temple. I knew that they (the extra-terrestrials) were placing information into the deepest levels of my brain for later use. The screen flickered and formed another picture. This time I saw my suspended self, hanging in the air like a ballerina spiralling in a slow pirouette; my legs were crossed at the ankles, arms extended fully above my head with hands clasped around each other. My eyes were closed, and a look of blissful unawareness was on my face as I slowly turned in space above the lamppost as if hanging from a wire.

My attention turned to the woman.

Our minds melded together and my unspoken question was answered.

'We have come from the Andromedan Galaxy. We are here on your planet in readiness to assist the human race. When the time comes for you to fulfil your destiny, we will meet again. There is nothing more for you to know now'.

My eyes took in the insignia that held the cloak around the woman's shoulders. It was shaped like a butterfly bow with arcs at either end. She was wearing a silvery suit over her long slender body, standing well over six feet tall. It was at this point that I realised that this woman had no hair, and that the long black hair I could see was only an illusion. I knew that this pretence was for my benefit, as it had been when I was a child, in order not to frighten me. The meeting was over as swiftly as it began, and once again I was alone in the bedroom with my book, feeling as if I had just woken from a long sweet sleep. The memory of this event burrowed its way deeply into my sub conscious, allowing me to continue on with life as if nothing had happened.

My mind was now filled with choices and decisions as to what to do with my life. Exams were over that summer, and I had gained a place at the Royal College of Art in London. The next days brought a bitter blow to me; no amount of pleading could change my argument. My mother had pulled rank on me, and declared that at sixteen, I was too young to be alone in London, so with this finality, the hopes of an art career slid forever into the chasm of impossibility. I felt that perhaps time was my friend, and so I decided to stay at school to do my advanced level exams, hoping against hope that one or two years would make a difference. They did, but in a way that no-one expected.

***

First opening to the Spirit World

See me at the kitchen table now. Two makeshift candlesticks adorn the corners, and it's the middle of a quiet Sunday afternoon. My best friend from school is with me, and out of our boredom has been born a game; this game is going to impact my life more than we realise. The scene is set, the die is cast.

The letters of the alphabet form a crude paper semicircle across the table. My closest school friend Jo, who was as dark as I was fair, sat next to me with her right hand held captive by my hand over a plain upturned glass. The magic of the Ouija beguiled us both. Jo was wide eyed and feeling a bit scared. Her mother had died when she was quite young, and her strict but loving aunt had raised her. Was it possible we could contact her? Daring to challenge, we called upon the mother to speak. The glass began to move, squawking as it scraped across the table to the letter Y, signifying that yes, there was somebody there. With painful slowness, the letters came one after the other, and as her mother's name was spelled out, Jo stiffened in her seat, fear rising, and began her denial. The accusation of 'You're doing that' followed, and she yanked her hand away from the glass, upsetting it in her haste.

'What's the matter?' I laughingly replied. But for Jo, it was no laughing matter. She jumped up from the table, yelling that it was all rubbish, and made her excuses to return home. What happened next defied logical understanding, and Jo had no idea what a narrow escape she had just had. I watched my friend depart, and hurried back to the kitchen table, eager to find out more. In truth, I knew I had exerted no energy at all on the glass, and could feel the power under my hand as it moved. Innocently intrigued, I began again, and a friendly ghost of someone long gone began to engage me in banal conversation. I could see no harm in that, and so I began to ask simple questions, and simple replies came quickly and without hesitation.

As the candles flickered lower, the glass gained speed, and now it was becoming so violent in it's movements that it began to push letters off the table. I could barely keep my hands on it, finally losing my grasp as it whizzed around, now out of control. I was alarmed at the sheer power of the force, and in a moment of swift decision, I jumped up, blew out the candles and hastily swept the remaining letters off the table.

But the presence I been communicating with would not go away, and not knowing what to do next, I sat quietly in my room and said a prayer to God. But the situation needed more than prayers, it needed experience, strength and wisdom. The nights that followed were restless and fearful for me. I could hear a constantly chattering voice inside my head, wheedling and whining, complimenting and threatening, and although I fought it with my mind, it was with me all the time, day and night.

Throughout this strange and unbelievable situation, one major thing quickly emerged. I found that I could control the voice in my head if I remained unafraid and focussed in the moment. It only took a matter of time before I was free, and my mind became clear again. I then realised that I might be able to help others who found themselves in this situation.

So, with faith in a higher power, I quietly sat in my room, eyes closed in meditation and prayer, and asked for help from Jesus. This was the prelude to my first conscious link with the higher spirit world, and my two guides. I realised that if I made my mind still and free from thought, I could sense and see spirit people held in a white light, bringing feelings of peace and love. I was extremely cautious at first, so I tested them out, and they tested me. I would see image after image in my mind; sometimes beautiful gardens, scenes of galleons at sea, things wonderful and strange to behold. Then as suddenly as they came, they would disappear to be replaced by gruesomely horrible faces, skulls, and things that looked as if they had come from hell. Initially, I reacted with shock, and closed down my mind immediately; jumping up from my reverie and finding something to do that occupied my mind. But before very long, I got angry and decided to face these images and challenge them.

'Show me your worst', my mind yelled defiantly, and like a sunburst after rain, the images dissolved slowly and were replaced with beauty again. This was my learning, my test. The object was to measure my level of fear, and I triumphed, passing the test well.

I began to talk to the two souls that showed themselves to me, one a Chinese man, the other a Red Indian. Dressed in traditional costume, and sporting a long thin moustache, the Chinaman presented himself as somewhat of a philosopher. With his hands tucked in his voluminous sleeves, nodding and smiling, he would impart wisdom with a few words or a sentence or two.

Sometimes my mind would be full of anything and everything, and I was not sure whether the words were his or mine. This is when I would talk to my other guide, and ask for help to make things clear. The Red Indian was a tall, strong, and usually bare chested warrior, wearing thin leather strips around the tops of his arms. His long dark hair flowed free, and he carried only one feather at the back of his head pointing downwards. I would always see him silhouetted against a backdrop of white clouds over a mountaintop, so I christened him White Cloud. He sent images and short picture stories instead of words into my mind.

One day I saw a huge circular object coming down towards me from above. From a distance, it looked like a huge dinner plate, and as it drew closer, I saw that one section was broken. Watching intently, it slowly became clearer, and as it turned over I could see that it was the bottom of a horse's hoof. Travelling upwards now, the scene expanded, and the whole horse came into view. In this unusual way, I found I could receive messages and pictures from them without the bias of my own mind interfering. It became quite an exciting adventure, as I never knew what was coming next. Sometimes the things they showed me were like puzzles, sent for my mind to unravel after I had finished talking with them. It was a voyage of discovery both into another world and into my own abilities. One woman and her husband, both dedicated to helping others in this way, confirmed to me the existence of my guides, helping me to feel secure in my own findings. Then, happening as if overnight, I began to feel heat and tingly sensations pouring out from my hands, and I instinctively knew that I had access to a power that could give healing to others.

Then came a new guide that I had not seen before. He was an old Red Indian warrior, coming to show himself in complete regalia. His face was painted, and he wore a grey and red feathered war bonnet that reached almost to the floor. On one occasion he spoke to me with words that were to become the driving force in my work with the spirit world. I asked him about the terrible problem I had had with the entity I contacted with the Ouija board.

'Lost spirit entities should not be a problem. Your worst enemy in this avenue of work is your own fear; remove the fear, and the problem will dissolve'.

My mind was flooded with the knowing that this was a most profound truth. I knew that the key lay in the emotion of fear; when fear is present, anything can manifest, and your fear will feed it. You create your own fears and then they can rule your life. I knew that the answer for anyone faced with the kind of problem I had experienced, was to face the fear and use love and compassion instead of trying to fight it. With this accomplished the way forward becomes clear. It allows other more evolved spirits to come closer, helping lost souls to go to where they belong.

In this valuable lesson came a wisdom that applies to the whole world. Fear is the absence of Love. When Love is totally present, there can be no fear. In this, I saw a lesson for the whole of mankind. When Love prevails amongst humanity, there can be no war, only peace.

3
Stepping out.......

In the years that spread out between sixteen and twenty-one, I entered the arena of life and found romance, work and enough of my ego to ensure I was carefree and independent. My intended career in the Art world had never manifested, and so I opted to leave school at almost eighteen just before my 'A' level exams. With my creative flair leading me by the nose, I had discovered that I had a talent as a hairstylist. Long or short, it presented a challenge I could not resist. A good friend of the family ran her own hairdressing salon, and had given me a Saturday job from the age of fourteen, shampooing and cleaning up. So when there was enough time, I was allowed to practice on clients for free, and I proved to be so talented, that pretty soon I had clients of my own. So when the mirage of art school dissolved before me, I eventually abandoned my studies and went to work full time as a hairdresser.

My mother was again distraught, telling me I had wasted my prized public school education, and thrown away all my chances of ever amounting to anything. She held visions of me succeeding as a doctor or a lawyer, and reminded me time and again that I could have been a concert pianist.

So many could's and should's! I told my mother firmly that my 'Book of Destiny' did not contain the words, 'might-have-been', only 'And so it was'.

The boys that had been in 'the gang' had matured and were dating my friends, but I walked my own path on my own terms and would not commit to serious relationship with any of them. There was one however, that drew me back time and again in between all the casual dates with the other boys. I always looked on him as just a friend, and I didn't care how he felt. I allowed the fiery racehorse in me the freedom to run unfettered by any man, and the more he pursued me the more elusive I became.

***

Sadness and sorrow

At nineteen, I eventually left the hair salon to try my hand at running my own business, selling and dressing wholesale wigs and hairpieces to the trade. This brought me into contact with hospitals; with children and adults who had forms of cancer and leukaemia and had undergone chemotherapy; especially those who had lost all their hair. The job of fitting them with wigs left me distraught and in tears at times, as some poor children suffered not only with disease, but sometimes with unbelievably insensitive parents.

One woman had brought in a delicately frail china doll of a girl about five years old, and asked for a thick brown wig to be styled with Shirley Temple ringlets. I asked what the child's natural hair was like, and she produced a photo. I tried my best to hide my shock and then to dissuade her mother. The fine silky blond hair that the child had lost was a million miles away from what her mother was asking for, and she would not be dissuaded. On the fitting day, the little girl sat in front of the mirror and sobbed silently, her tiny body shaking with distress. Despite this, still her mother ignored her, saying she would get used to it eventually.

On another occasion, a small child had arrived in the back of a station wagon, containing six other raucous children and a dog. Their mother was harassed beyond belief, and after the fitting, the poor child got back into the car and was immediately the butt of jokes and teasing from all of them. One tried to pull the hair off, and got a clout, but what remained with me was the look directed straight at me from the child's eyes as they drove away. With her bottom lip trembling, a single tear escaped onto the child's cheek; her eyes turned to me and were filled with such a pitiful pleading for help that I felt sick to my stomach with compassion and helplessness.

Not long after this, I suffered a nervous breakdown. Whether it was the stress of the job or a side effect of some pills the doctor had prescribed to help me lose weight, I never knew, but it happened one day at the wig boutique.

I often spent time with an older man who ran a hairdressing salon upstairs. We would talk for hours, mainly about his mother and the problem she was to him. He often felt suicidal, and so I found myself in the role of counsellor and confidant. All this added to the grief I felt for both the children and adults suffering from the effects of chemotherapy, and one day I walked out of the shop and could not go back. I got home and began pacing the floor, up and down, up and down, my mind full of distress and hopelessness. All I knew was that I felt like a caged animal, and would burst into tears at the drop of a hat. It took six weeks before I began to come around to anything like normality. I was never able to go into that shop again; even passing by on the bus made me feel sick and icy cold.

When I was fully recovered, I began the search for a new career.

Now well into my twentieth year, I joined the busy world of beauty, cosmetics and perfumery, and went back into the public eye once more. I spent a short period in London promoting a cosmetic house, and found it was an exhausting, exciting time. I met colourful people from all walks of life, and stood on the department floor till my feet were screaming. I dined out at the Savoy, and enjoyed the opera. Life was full and life was rich, and I lived it without a care in the world.

***

Death calls again, I get third time lucky

At twenty-one years old, I brushed past the doors of infinity once again. Over the past few years I had felt odd pains on and off in my abdomen, and I had always thought that perhaps it was indigestion. I passed them off lightly, but this time, I woke up one morning with the nagging ache in my abdomen yet again. I drank my morning tea and promptly felt sick, so I lay down on the couch thinking it would pass. I thought that maybe I could go into work a little late, but within hours, the acute discomfort was becoming unbearable. I was wracked with such gripping pain that I was unable to move or drive my car. I called my father home from the shop, and he took me quickly to the local surgery. My wonderful doctor examined me and thanks to his immediate response, within one hour, I was being wheeled into the operating theatre with peritonitis or burst appendix. He told me that had there been any delay, I would have been dead within hours.

So there I was, the day after my operation, lying in a hospital bed surrounded by an absolute deluge of flowers. It was like the inside of a florist shop, with exotic lilies, roses and carnations enclosing me from every side. Well wishers from every aspect of my busy life had sent bouquets, because not only did I have my full time job, but also an evening job as a barmaid in the local pub as well. I did this as a fun thing more than out of necessity, and it kept me up to date with anything and everything that happened in the local area. So the flowers had poured in from my workmates, landlord, pub customers and family.

It was three in the afternoon, and I was dozing amidst the riot of blooms, when the ward doors swung open, and there, covered from head to foot in dust from work, and clutching a bedraggled bunch of red roses stood the young man I had known for so long in my teens, and run so hard from.

Rising especially early, he had gone to work at five in the morning to be finished by mid-day. I found out that he had driven miles and miles at breakneck speed to be by my side for the afternoon visit, clutching his offering of now bent and drooping roses. As he walked in through the swing doors I saw his eyes take in the riot of flowers all around me. Our eyes met, and the happy expression on his eager face fell into sudden embarrassment and shyness. As he walked towards me, with the roses now behind his back, the warmth of his smile overpowered my heart with an avalanche of love.

I welcomed him to me, and as I looked into the deep green of his eyes, there came in a brief second the dawning realisation that here was a man I truly loved, and that if he asked me 'Will you?', I most definitely would.

And so we did.

One month before my twenty-second birthday, we were married.

It was a fairy-tale wedding with sleek black limousines, all the men in silver and black morning dress and top hats, complemented by bridesmaids and pageboys decked out in emerald green velvet with buttercup yellow sashes. My father's pride in me was unmistakable, and I thought he would burst from smiling so much as he escorted me down the aisle to give me away.

There was undeniable magic in the air that day. Standing at the altar of the old gothic church, we took our vows in love and quiet reverence. The sunlight streamed in through the stained glass windows, casting rainbows of iridescent light onto my snowy white gown. Two peacock butterflies suddenly appeared, fluttering in from the bright sunshine outside. They fluttered up the aisle, finally coming to rest on the beautiful flowers either side of us at the alter; with one butterfly landing on my side, and one on his. It was a miraculous and perfect finish to the stunning floral displays.

My mother cried, as all mothers do, and the opening night of my personal play was underway.

***

4

The Agony and the Ecstasy....

The following year for me was spent in happy discovery. Having a home of my own as a creative journey was only outweighed by my growing devotion to my new husband.

As I took on the new role of wife, the gloss that surrounded my career in cosmetics and perfumery began to wear thin, and I decided that I needed a change from the nine to five rat-race.

I got a job that meant I could leave my make-up and high heels in the bedroom, and live in my favourite jeans and sweater. I was totally at home with both working outside, and the comfort of being able to work in casual clothes. The days when I gazed enviously out of the department store doors at people enjoying the sunshine were over. No more aching feet, and no more customers always being right. My job was delivering laundry and dry cleaning, driving a daily route with a company van. At my own pace, I drank in the pleasures of the quiet suburbs and the green peacefulness of the countryside around the town. This new job gave me the freedom to stop and shop, and allowed me precious alone time, providing I got the job done on time. The route I drove gave me a fixed routine, and in no time, I had the timing of deliveries down to perfection. Then one bright afternoon in summer, I saw something that fired my excitement and brought back memories that lay so deeply hidden.

Weaving in and out of the traffic making my deliveries, I came to the last but one stop before I was to head around the outskirts of the town for the depot.

A bright silver object appeared in the sky, catching my attention as I headed for the dual carriageway. I pulled over into a bus stop and got out of the van; running round to the passenger side, I opened the door and climbed up on the runner board to get a better view. I couldn't believe it! There, cruising above the houses at no more than low helicopter height was a spaceship! I stared at it, incredulous that no-one else seemed to notice its presence! It was oval and sleekly silver, with a full complement of glittering windows around the circumference, reflecting the sun as it tacked slowly from side to side in the afternoon sky. As it turned, I could see aerodynamic fin-like shapes on the sides. It was so close! Shielding my eyes to get a better view, I watched it for at least ten minutes, noticing the incredibly slow movements it made. It seemed to glide effortlessly above the houses, almost as if it were looking for something, or observing with interest. The sky was clear and cloudless, and the craft glittered and flashed with reflected sunlight as it tacked slowly left, then right. Suddenly, at what must have been faster than light speed, it shot away into the distant clear blue sky and disappeared. Incredulous at what I had seen, I spent the next few days phoning the police, the newspaper and the local aerodrome, checking to make sure there had been no mistake in my sighting. I drew blanks at every turn except from a journalist at the local newspaper office, who told me that there had been sightings of UFO's earlier that week over France. Other than that, my story fell on deaf ears, with no-one wanting or willing to believe me.

***

And now we are three

Three years into our marriage, our wonderful baby daughter was born. So now I was a mother as well as a wife, and my life was changing even more rapidly than before. It seemed as if my happiness was complete; I had a wonderful husband, a home of my own, and now a perfect child to make the perfect picture.

As a new mother, I had trouble at first with feeding my daughter; this was a legacy of the archaic nursing home where baby Kate had been delivered. The sister in charge had a strict regime, and insisted that the babies be allowed to scream and cry until the regulation four hours were up until the next feed time. When Kate got colic at four days old, the only help I received was a telling off from the sister for eating grapes. I had no idea that it was wrong, and it only served to undermine my confidence even more. The final labour had taken thirteen hours, and I needed surgery plus a forceps delivery in the end. Poor Kate's head was shaped like a watermelon when she eventually arrived, adding extra worry to the distress I felt already.

My husband John's first visit brought the life back into me, and we sat together in the last rays of evening sunlight sharing love with our new baby until it was time for him to go home. In those days, my stay at the nursing home was almost two weeks; giving me wonderful time to rest, but setting a pattern of feeding that proved to be unworkable once I got the baby home. Hoards of our family members came to visit us, and as every mother knows the more peace and quiet you get, the better. In the end, I got so stressed, that after six weeks, I couldn't feed the baby myself and I became obsessed with thoughts of failure. Baby Kate, however, had other ideas.

She was sturdy, strong and as pretty as a picture with a dimple in her chin exactly like mine. As time went on, she began to show signs of the true Taurean that she was. Stubborn and independent, she never slept at all during the day, and demanded all of my time, energy and patience.

Oh, but the joy she gave us was immeasurable! Her first attempted word was 'cucumber' and the antics she got up to made us laugh till our sides ached. John naturally adored her, and took as many of the baby chores from me as he could. Bath time was the absolute favourite for both of them, causing such loud shrieks of laughter from both Kate and her dad that it sounded like someone was being murdered! The bathroom was always inches deep in water by the time they had finished, but nobody cared about the watery mess, for these times were precious and filled with fun and love.

My John was an amateur football player and kept himself strong and fit playing for two clubs twice a week during the season. Katie and me were regulars at the matches and we got to know all the team players really well. Kate became like a club mascot, being the youngest person at seven months ever to watch them play. They all loved her and the care and attention she got after each game merged us and the team into one big extended family.

The clairvoyance that was part of my life was becoming stronger, but I spent little of my time paying attention to it. My guides were always there if I needed them, and occasionally they would drop a message in loud and clear, when I least expected it. Twice I experienced the strange phenomenon of clear clairaudience.

The first time it happened was whilst I was in hospital for a minor check-up; there was a woman in the bed next to me who was very upset and would shout and disturb the others on the ward. That night, I was abruptly awakened by the bed shaking, as if someone had fallen against it. A male voice spoke loudly but gently in my ear and said, 'Tell her I was thinking of her when I died'.

I was mildly annoyed to be woken in the middle of the night, and I turned to see if the woman in the next bed had really fallen over my bed, and was talking to herself or sleepwalking. I was brought into full consciousness by the realisation that there was no one there, and everything was still and quiet on the ward. It wasn't until the next morning that I found out exactly what it was all about.

A woman in the bed opposite me was in for a mastectomy, and was recovering from surgery. She was maybe sixty-five or so years old, and had been telling her story to us all the previous day. Widowed for some time, she had at last found love again with a man friend that now lived with her. She sounded so happy as she told me about their plans to be married, and to take a holiday as soon as she was able to leave the hospital. Inadvertently, a young nurse had come onto the ward that morning with a message for her, not knowing the circumstances.

'Are you a friend of Mr X?' she asked in innocence. When the woman replied that she was, the nurse said bluntly that Mr X had passed away the previous night. The nurse did not realise just how much this meant to the woman, and so her matter of fact attitude in breaking the news stunned the woman into severe shock.

Her future happiness had just disappeared forever, and she broke down and began to cry. I listened and watched as the scene unfolded, and knew that the voice that had come in the night to wake me was from the man who had died. I waited for the right moment, then gently and with compassion, delivered the message.

On the other occasion, it had been an encounter with the old grandmother who lived next door to me. The old lady was 'Gran' to everyone, and I had spent many happy hours in the house next door with gran and her boisterous family. One bright Christmas morning, she died peacefully in her bed. It was an expected passing, and although the whole family was in grief, there was quiet joy that gran, who had been almost blind for many years, was now happily with her maker.

On the Boxing Day, I was next door as usual for a morning cup of coffee. All the family were in the kitchen, and I needed to go to the bathroom. So I walked into the quiet hallway and headed for the front door and the bottom of the stairs that led upstairs to the toilet. Suddenly, with complete clarity and strength, gran spoke to me.

'Chin up, chicken, its not as bad as you think', said the familiar voice I knew so well. The words had come, clear as a bell, from halfway up the stairs. I turned my gaze upward and there, grinning like a Cheshire cat was Gran, albeit somewhat more transparent than usual.

At first, I rushed back into the kitchen, demanding to know if anyone had spoken or heard the voice, not really believing that I had both seen and heard gran so clearly. The family stood open mouthed at the news that Gran was 'around' so soon, and they all flowed into the hallway like the incoming tide to see if they too could see her. We were all shedding happy tears as I gave the twinkle-eyed message to her daughter Barbara. As we hugged and kissed each other we laughed and cried, and none of the family was really at all surprised at this little appearance by such a strong character as gran.

***

Life and death, time is so short.

My daughter Kate continued to grow like a flower in the sun, and as the May blossoms filled the air with their sweetness she had her first birthday. With hair as fair as ripe corn and eyes as blue as the first bluebells, she was the star in our show. As always, she charmed her daddy into complete compliance. John's devoted adoration overflowed for her in the same way as it did for me.

All was peaceful in our world.

And then the hand of fate dealt me a situation that could not be possible. It was June 23rd, six weeks after Kate's first birthday party, and the day dawned hot and sunny. The weather had been exceptionally good that month, and the gardens were bone dry and in need of some rain. John had volunteered to dig over a neighbour's vegetable patch, ready for planting, because the old lady's garden was overgrown, and she needed some help.

We sat down to a Sunday roast with all the trimmings, and after John had eaten and enjoyed, he spent all afternoon in the hot sun at his volunteer task. With his shirt off and tanning nicely, he laboured on until way past teatime, coming home just before dusk. He brought the spade he had been using in for repair, having bent and buckled it on the unforgiving rock hard soil. I knew he felt tired and hot, so I suggested that we go for a drink later that evening with our friends from two doors down. Our neighbours had a boy the same age as Kate, and so we organised a foursome knowing that the toddlers would be company for one another.

The pub garden had a sand pit, swings and a slide for the children, and as the laughter rang out and the evening wore on, I noticed that John was exceptionally quiet. When the children asked him to play with them on the slide, he declined and asked me to do it. Knowing he must be worn out, I did, and dismissed his pale face and tired eyes as a temporary thing. The children were lively, demanding to be pushed and swung, exchanging 'tiny talk' that made everyone nod and smile with parental pride, and occasionally offering a funny situation that resulted in hoots of laughter. As the twilight stars came out and a chill began to touch the sweet spring air, we decided to go home for supper.

The children were still lively and full of mischief, but we all knew that pretty soon both would be sound asleep.

John sat next to my neighbour Kathy on the sofa as they jokingly recalled the antics of the children in the pub garden. Kathy got up to go to the kitchen to pour some coffee, leaving everyone in mid laugh.

At this point, John fell over sideways onto my lap, bringing about even more gales of laughter from everyone.

I disengaged my trapped arms and pushed at him playfully. 'Get up, silly' I admonished, as he lay there unmoving.

But he didn't get up, then or ever again.

I struggled out from underneath him and standing quickly, I pulled him up to a sitting position. I could see his eyes had rolled back in his head, and that he had no control over his bodily functions at all. I heard the command to phone the ambulance leave my lips as we pulled him onto the floor. At first I thought that he must be having an epileptic fit, perhaps brought on by the strenuous work in the heat of the day, or maybe the beer that evening. But in my heart, alarm bells were ringing, and some part of me knew he was dying.

My instincts took over, and I began to give him mouth to mouth resuscitation. His lungs filled and his voice sighed as I breathed my will to live into him. Over and over I repeated the breath in a desperate attempt to gamble with God for his life.

All the neighbours rushed to the scene to help, as if some great magnet was at work, irresistibly willing them to give assistance. Some said that everything was going to be ok, and they threw tentacles of help around me, slowly pulling my life giving breath away from his lips, telling me reassuring lies in an attempt to be kind. Leave it for the ambulance men they said. Wanting to believe, I allowed myself to be taken away from him. And as if by some miracle, the ambulance crew were there within two minutes, sirens wailing and oxygen tanks at the ready. As they applied their skills to his seemingly lifeless body, I was ushered protesting into the hallway and then shepherded out through the front door into the stinging cold night air. Time stood still for me, and those moments outside froze and burned themselves into my mind like a branding iron.

Still believing that he could be saved, I turned towards the doorway only to find it blocked by a six foot man wearing a red and white emergency uniform. There stood the paramedic with tears in his eyes, telling me that he was so sorry that they couldn't save him, and that my beloved John was gone. The paramedic held up his arms to enfold me, and also to stop me from going back into the house.

'NO!'

This was too quick! It *could not* be happening like this. My mind screamed to the heavens that it was not happening at all. Anger rose in my throat and I called upon the strength that was now overflowing in my body. The burly paramedic could not hold me back, and I pushed my way past the crowd and into the room where he lay. Kneeling by his side I gently took his head into my hands. My eyes closed in prayer and communication with his spirit.

'If this is to be, then let it be, but if there is just **one** chance for him, then let it be now'.

I sent the words to God like a thunderbolt cracking open a stormy summer sky.

I waited. And then I knew.

I kissed him gently on the lips and said my goodbye to his soul. As my lips touched his, his lungs filled, and with my breath his voice sighed in acknowledgement that it was done.

For a moment, I thought that he still lived, and I screamed out for help to save him again. But it was my breath and not his. This final kiss had deceived me, and the cruel hand of destiny triumphed. Overwhelmed with searing pain and the black night of grief, I let him go.

At only twenty seven years old, his soul had left the arena of my life, and the void, greater than the infinity of space, was utterly unbearable. They held a post mortem, and I just couldn't believe it when they told me cause of death was a heart attack.

One week later under an overcast and grey sky, I stood at his graveside to be with him as he was buried in time honoured fashion. With my daughter Kate and both of our families gathered around, I sobbed as his mortal body was committed to the Earth. The words I had engraved on the headstone vowed that for me, 'Love dies not with Death', and with all of my being, I knew it was true. As I look back now, I remember that the following six months were totally erased from my memory, as grief took its pound of flesh. There wasn't a day that went by without I shed tears for him, and try as I might, I couldn't contact him as my grief always got in the way of clear communication.

I couldn't connect to his spirit or think about him without breaking down, and it took three years of tears and ten years of my life to assuage the grief.

***

5

The Journey goes on......

The call of the spiritual world and my attunement to it became even stronger now, as I knew this was where my beloved John was. But no amount of trying would allow me to talk to him. Always too overcome with grief, my mind could not reach him. There were others who could, and did, and they brought me bright islands of solace to punctuate my bleak ocean of existence. One clairvoyant I saw gave me such strength in a message that it reminded me for a short while that John was indeed, not far away. I was told that there was a gift for me from John, and that I should go home, pull back the wardrobe and look in the old safe that was hidden in the wall. This safe was a leftover from the last owners of the house, and as we never had much money, it was never used. In fact we had even wallpapered over it. Eager to see what this could be, I drove home as fast as I dared. I deposited Kate in her playpen, and rushed upstairs to the bedroom; I emptied the clothes quickly onto the bed, and then set about heaving the heavy double wardrobe away from the wall. I could see that the wallpaper around the safe door had been cut finely, so I left it to rummage in the dressing table drawer for the key. Hardly daring to breathe, I pierced the keyhole, opened the door, and there inside was a wad of money wrapped in a piece of paper. With shaking hands I unfolded the note and read it.

'If you find this, I want you to know that I have been secretly saving for us to have a holiday'.

I counted the notes, and in all there was two hundred and fifty pounds. I was incredulous that this message had been so accurate. Now totally convinced that the clairvoyant had really been talking to John, I began to cry and laugh at the same time. This much needed money was a miracle! My heart was full and empty at the same time; feeling his love and at the same time agonisingly bereft without his presence.

Despite this proof that he was always close, the days that followed remained empty and full of pain. Had it not been for the sunny smiles and love from my daughter, suicide would have been my answer. I remembered the words that Jesus had spoken to me that afternoon when I was sixteen. 'I am with you always', he had said, but they held no gift of comfort now.

Gone were his touch, his smiles, his humour, and his strength. Everything that is held within love for another had vanished, and the lesson that was there for me to learn was masked in painful emotions that would not cease. I longed to feel his arms around me, and paced the living room night after night in lonely distress.

One winter's night I became so totally hysterical with crying, I had an out of body experience. I found myself standing in the room looking at my body lying on the sofa. In my hysteria I was howling like an animal, and the shock of seeing this from the other side of the room was like a cold shower. As fast as it had happened, it was over. Back in my body once more, I sat up realising that I could not go on like this any more. I walked into the hallway and called the Samaritans, and spent the next two hours talking away some of my pain.

Four hard years passed, during which my beloved father died. He was just three months away from retirement when he was diagnosed with cancer; within those three months, he was dead. Again, I was devastated; calm when it happened for my mother, but on the day of his funeral, I cried all day because I just couldn't stop. I found the inner strength to be strong for my mother and younger sister because we had a common wound to share, and I knew the wound well.

My life went on, and I had to take whatever work I could find, fitting in my hours around anyone who would take care of Kate. My mother came to the rescue many times and showed her love by sacrificing her time and energy over and over again. I had to take on the role of mother and father, so I had no choice but to become a jack of all trades. I learned to fix the car and mend the roof; I dug and planted, mended and sewed, decorated and repaired.

Then five years on, a man entered the stage of my life and I thought he was someone I could lean on, someone I could love again, and one who would love me and my daughter in return. With him I discovered the will to live again, but not in the way I expected.

***

Life's little lessons

Life teaches us many things, and if we ignore the lessons then they become harder and more frequent. Once married, this new man taught me to fight for what I believed in, to stand on my own two feet, and be once again proud of it. But within six months, a side of his personality that I hadn't seen began to emerge, and he changed back and forth from being strong and quietly gentle, to an angry someone I hardly knew.

Over time, it felt to me as if he became like a desperate man clinging to my back, beating me with words and jabbing at me with the stick of testing. Through the eleven years we stayed together, both our emotional states changed as rapidly as the sun playing hide and seek with the rain. It was a difficult marriage to say the least, but it taught me many things.

From the beginning of our marriage, I longed for another child. It had been my original intention to have a large family, and no sooner than we had taken our vows in the registry office, I knew that another new soul was to join me on Earth. In my heart, I knew that all wasn't right then, and had I known just how difficult the relationship was going to be, my choice to marry him might have been a different one. But then, I believed that we all make choices before we come down to this Earth, and in order to learn, human beings sometimes have to touch the fire before they will accept that it's hot.

Soon after my pregnancy had begun, I began to feel stressed and ill. On the one hand, I was absolutely overjoyed that I was pregnant, but at the same time, feeling desperately unhappy with my life. I became so depressed one day that I found myself at the bathroom sink, tears streaming down my face, with an open razor in hand ready to make the final cut. My husband was so concerned he took me to the hospital, where I was interviewed by a psychiatrist.

The doctors labelled me 'hormonal' and said that 'it' would pass and I would be all right in a few months. What was I expected to do whilst these 'few months' were passing? The time became an incessant roller-coaster of highs and lows that came and went within hours of one another. What I did do, was to fight the demons of emotion as they tried to grab me, telling myself constantly that this person I saw in the mirror was not the real me. In the fifth month my emotions started to settle down, and finally after a rollercoaster of emotions, I was delivered of a beautiful baby boy. My labour was intense, painful and short, and it was all over within two hours. Alexander had come into the world like an express train, and in this small bundle of angelic potential I found renewed joy and faith that things could be better.

What I could not see was that all I suffered in my relationship to his father represented the fire in which the strongest steel is forged. Life, the universe and everything were preparing me for my destiny.

Many issues became bones of contention in the daily round of my life and marriage. My new husband had a daughter of his own from a previous marriage, and he couldn't help but have divided loyalties over the children. This caused us both pain; and arguments and friction burned at every corner like a fire beacon on a hilltop. I bore it and fought back, defending and acquiescing, all the time taking my learning on the chin.

Then one day I had a phone call saying my new husband had had an accident. A large crate containing an engine had fallen on him, and his back was injured. He ended up in plaster from hip to chest, and I now took up the role of nurse. The company disputed his accident claim, and there was a lot of bad feeling over the whole affair and as a result, his work there was finished.

This event seemed terrible, but in a way, was perfect. After a period of recovery he needed to find a new career and the only job to suit him was out of the city, and into the heart of the countryside.

Moving out of the house I now owned was a big decision for me, and it scared me more than I can say. How would I survive, living in a tiny village far out of the city I knew so well? I felt that I was leaving everything behind that I loved, to go to the ends of the Earth. In reality it was the most wonderful thing I ever did. In this new house in the tiny village, I found the quiet solitude my soul was longing for. It was as if I was permanently in the beloved forest from my childhood. Walks with the children filled my heart with joy again, and animals I had never seen before slowly appeared one after the other to surprise and delight me. Nightingales sang their sweet medicine to me across the woods at midnight. Night after night I would go out into the cool air of the garden and look to the panoply of glittering stars, always asking, always needing to know more.

This was a time of recuperation for my ravaged spirit, bringing me closer to the guides who had waited so patiently for me to be ready.

***

Lucy comes calling

There was a family who lived in a farmhouse one field away, and they kept a few sheep and various breeds of pigs. One day, hearing a knock at the door, I opened it to find my neighbour with a small box in her arms. The box seemed to leap about, and with a wide grin, she asked me if I could be a Good Samaritan, and take care of the mysterious animal inside. Explaining that she already had two orphaned lambs in the kitchen at home, she went on to ask if I could find the time for the runt from a litter of pigs.

What a challenge! The box was opened and inside it was a tiny black piglet with one pink ear. She was so small you could have sat her on a dinner plate. My children gathered around, and of course were captivated. There was no choice but to fall in love with her, so in she came and we christened her Lucy.

Lucy lived the first few weeks of her tiny life in a wooden crate packed with straw in the kitchen. We checked her bristly skin for ticks and other bothersome creatures and then washed her gently until she was shiny clean. She was as noisy and demanding as a baby, loving the attention we showered on her, and learned really fast. I taught her to lap up special feed from a dish on the floor, and even taught her to use the cat litter tray in the corner. What an intelligent animal! She had enormous strength and determination. We put her to sleep at night in the straw filled crate, closing down the top with a couple of large stones. This kept her content and quiet until morning feed time arrived. Lucy loved to run free around the house and garden, and in the evenings, she liked nothing better than sitting on the sofa watching the television, as long as she was next to an adult. If I knelt on the floor, she would rush into my arms, ears flapping, making tiny barking noises and cuddle as close under my armpit as possible. She would follow me around the garden, digging merrily away at the lawn, making furrows with her nose. She even played tag with our dog, rushing across the garden, nipping at his hind legs, and then running full pelt in the other direction, barking with glee.

The dog, who was our family favourite, had been my first 'baby'. Long before even Kate was born, he had been there, loyally by the side of my beloved John. One day when I was on my route for the dry cleaning company, I stopped at the city dogs' home, and spotted him amongst a litter of abandoned puppies. He was beautiful, and it was love at first sight. He was my best friend, and his tolerance of all the other animals we kept was saintly. He became a mother figure to Tomas the belligerent cat who was the next arrival and then caretaker to all the others in turn. The countryside certainly gave us all the delights any child could ever dream of.

We had a massive cockerel with a harem of hens and chicks in the back garden, a rainbow of loud show budgerigars in an aviary and of course Lucy the pig with her amazing intelligence and playful games. All this and much more became a memorable part of their growing up. Lucy went from strength to strength, growing fatter and happier as the days went on. When she was just six weeks old she was able to lift the cover of her crate, which was now held down at night with two enormous concrete blocks. She was becoming so strong it was time for her to live outside, and I began to worry about how we could keep her. In the real world, a large pig in the garden, however wonderful, is not a practical thing. The children of course, wanted her to stay forever, and a thankful solution came when the farmer's wife sold the rest of the litter. She knocked on the door once again, and asked if Lucy was all right, and did we want to keep her any longer?

She told us that a woman had come to buy the whole litter, and learning that there was one more, thought that her thirteen year old daughter would adore having the housetrained Lucy as a pet pig. So her future was assured; nobody was going to turn this delightfully tame pig with the very best manners into bacon, and so she earned by the fluke of being the smallest, the right to live the longest. I marvelled at the intelligence of this small animal as she left with the farmer's wife, and thought about all the poor pigs that are artificially reared and never see the light of day. Lucy had been clean, bright and clever; obedient and gentle and a pleasure to have around. My eyes were opened to yet another aspect of the old adage that seeing is believing, and this was just one of the many wonders I found during my life in the village.

***

A ray of spiritual hope

I searched around for somewhere or someone I could share my spiritual experiences with, and eventually found a woman who ran a tiny spiritualist church from her own home. I couldn't wait to join, not knowing what I would find, but hoping for some guidance. The woman who ran the church was a small bundle of inexhaustible energy and wisdom, bustling around me like a mother hen. She quickly recognised my abilities, and suggested that I come and join their weekly development circle in order to learn more about control and direction of the mind.

So every Wednesday I drove twenty miles to attend the spiritual circle, and slow but sure, I began to polish the gifts I had to a brighter shine. There were times though, when the stresses of my busy life took their toll on me, and I found sitting still with a quiet mind almost impossible.

During one such period, I had been arriving each week with so many worries on my mind that I was permanently fidgety and uncomfortable. My husband was often late from work, arriving home long after I was due to leave. The position he held allowed him to come home when he wanted, but my requests for him to be there for the children often fell on deaf ears. He would always agree, and then find some reason when he eventually got in, to justify his lateness. Sometime he wouldn't turn up at all, and when I phoned he would tell me he was at a social club having a few pints. Always I felt that this was a way he exercised control over me, always making me late for whatever it was I wanted to do.

One night, I took my place as usual and tried to calm myself whilst the meeting was opened, breathing deeply until the session began. Try as I might, my mind would not be still. Thoughts about the day, the shopping list, the children and anything else you could think of, persisted incessantly and would not leave me alone. This struggling with my mind had gone on for weeks, and I was beginning to feel depressed and alone in my endeavour to link with my guides and get anywhere.

This night things came to a head and reaching into the turmoil of my racing mind, I began to call to them asking, 'Where are you? Why can't I reach you? I don't believe you're really there!'

Within a few moments my internal vision just opened up like a television screen, and a clear blue sky like the brightest of sunny days appeared. Suddenly, up popped a cherub in the clouds, on a rose garlanded swing complete with tiny golden wings and smiling rosy face; then came another, and finally a third! How they laughed and played with each other! Fascinated, I watched the scene unfold, and there, appearing out of the blue, came a huge bank of snowy white clouds. Then the clouds began to part in true cinematic style like a Busby Berkley musical. Time slowed to a standstill and I sat transfixed as a white marble staircase formed, curving and unfolding upwards into the heavens beyond. I watched mesmerised and in awe as magnificently shining Angels dressed in the most delicate colours began to appear on either side of the staircase, some blowing golden horns, some singing.

Then All Powerful golden haired Seraphim with dazzling white wings came in, emanating pure strength and radiant light. I was transported to another world as this vision became my world and captivated my very soul. The music I was hearing was beyond belief. A heavenly choir of Angelic Beings was singing to me alone, ringing out the most exquisite harmonies in graceful unison. Tears began to roll down my cheeks as a feeling of humility overtook me.

As if this were not enough, a sudden blinding white light appeared at the foot of the stairs, and out of the shining rays stepped the Virgin Mary. Her radiant figure was clothed in an ice blue robe with a creamy white covering resting over her golden brown hair. Slowly she raised her eyes, and gazed directly at me. Her smile was beyond description. The love of all humanity was pouring from the depths of her sacred soul into my heart. With gentle words, the Holy Mother reached out and touched me with a flowing river of compassion.

'We Have Not Forgotten You'.

My soul resonated until it rang in total harmony, and I broke down weeping with gratitude and joy that my prayers had been answered. The group sat in stunned silence as I told them, between sobs, the vision I had seen. They were all so taken aback that no one really knew what to say. Never before had any of the group seen such a thing, and with a confused awkwardness prevailing in the silence, they concluded the evening with prayers, and went their separate ways.

So it was with renewed fervour and clarity, I started once again to concentrate my attention on my guides and the realms they occupied. This felt like a fresh start, and I found myself receiving messages for people more frequently than ever before. Now began a time when people sought me out for help and guidance with their losses and grief over loved ones. I began to see the basic concepts that I held in my mind stretch and change further and further.

***

An country haven for my soul

For eight years I lived in the idyll of the village, slowly building my strength and determination to survive. With its quaint thatched cottages resting idly side by side with busy farmyards, it oozed floral charm and rural peacefulness. Nestling in the arms of a wooded valley, my house was surrounded on three sides by steep escarpments crowded with oaks and pines, beech and hawthorn. The landscape was managed by the forestry commission allowing the old English forest safe keeping.

I often saw deer, foxes and even badgers walking their pathways close to my garden. On my evening walks past the orchards with the children, barn owls flew past like silent ghosts, and little owls sat like statues in the apple trees. In my neighbours garden I saw my first woodpecker, dressed brilliantly in red and black. Nightingales came in their season, and night after night I would wait for their enchanting midnight song to roll across the valley, weaving its soothing magic around me. I revelled in the sights and sounds surrounding me; each new day was like a balm to my soul, bringing air that was always fresh and clean and filled with glorious aromas from field or farmhouse.

Once Alex and Kate had got over their initial fear of change, they took to country life like ducks to water. Thirty-two children attended the tiny village school at the top of the hill, and so the community spirit was close and protective amongst mothers and youngsters. Everyone knew everyone else, and whilst you couldn't have any secrets, you were never alone either. Alex was just two years old when we arrived, and once he was old enough for nursery school, I created a small hairdressing business from home to help make ends meet. All the locals came, farmers and housewives alike, glad to have somewhere close to go, and eager to exchange all the local gossip. Only a chosen few got to know about my abilities, but those I did tell soon started asking me for clairvoyant readings as well. During the time spent in the village my children blossomed and grew like sunflowers, thriving on the rare gift of country life. But despite the beauty and calm of my surroundings, I was often restless and deeply unhappy. My frustration and longing for the fulfilment I couldn't seem to get from my marriage prompted me to take up art classes and yoga. Yoga became my mental and physical discipline, and the art classes awakened the long buried talent passed by at sixteen. I astounded even myself when after six months a friend and I organised an exhibition of our work in the local library, and much to my delight I sold my first oil paintings! Encouraged, I entered a poetry competition at the local arts and craft exhibition and again, to my great surprise, I took first prize. I met the judge at the presentation, and found out it was local author Leslie Thomas. I was flattered by his praise, and I dared to ask him for advice about my writing skills. It was then that a seed was planted that in later years would come to fruition. Write about yourself, he told me, it's the subject you know best.

Despite my busy life I was still plagued by the nagging voice in my mind reminding me constantly that there had to be more in the spirit realms that I had yet to discover. I wanted to reach out and touch more people, so with unerring determination I began to rise to the challenge. One night I went back to my home town to visit an old friend. We spent part of the evening watching a video about tropical islands, small-talked about possible holidays, and then sat for a while talking about my guides. I left feeling warm and content with my visit.

It was on the way home that I began to dream a little, with the car almost driving itself. With the windows down and the warm night air blowing the cobwebs in my mind away, a plan began to form in my mind. I realised afterwards that it must have been my guides prompting me, but at the time, I felt that my mind was just free flowing. It came to me again that I needed to meet more people, and knowing that there were so many grieving people out there who needed help; I became determined to put myself in a position to give it.

I arrived home a little after midnight, flying into the house with the new plan roaring its immediacy in my head.

'We must move house, and buy a guest house, then all the people who need clairvoyant help and want to see me will just come through the door!'

My husband was *not* enamoured with the idea at all. We eventually went to bed at two thirty in the morning after a heated argument. He goaded me by saying I was lazy and would never get up in the mornings to give the guests breakfast. I was hurt and insulted by his remarks, but what he actually did was to fire my intention and determination to prove him wrong even more. His final parting shot was that if I could clean out our enormous attic of all its contents within two days and have nothing left at the end, then he would say yes and move.

What a task!

Symbolically, it was a clearing out of all the old past memories from my mind, and a demonstration of my willingness to begin again with a clean slate. I bore his challenge like a cross, and the weight of it made me strong. When something is right, then the pathway towards it is easy. When you resonate with what is good for you, like attracts like stronger than a magnet. I found a map, and drew a circle on it encompassing a fifteen-mile radius around the place where he worked. I knew that this was the right area, but had no idea where I was going to end up. What I discovered to my complete amazement was that just two miles away from my tiny village was a small town that was hailed as the Spiritual Centre of England. *How had I missed it?*

I had been unaware because the time had not been right. Things began to fall into place like clockwork, and during a quiet meditation one day as I was asking my guides to show me where I was supposed to go, I had a vision of a large house on a hill. The exterior was cream and it had many rooms inside. This is it, I thought, this is my house. Excitedly, I began to look for places that were similar, but none appeared, so I drove around the small town, looking to see if I could find it. There were two places that came close, but both were occupied, not for sale, and would have been far too expensive for me anyway.

Then on the market came a charming cottage with six bedrooms, brimming full of character. There were curved bay windows with old-fashioned bull's-eye glass panes, and an old open fireplace for crackling log fires in the winter. Glossy oak beams supported the ceiling and gave me a feeling that made me warm and content. It stood on the top of a hill overlooking a valley, and when I saw it, I knew that here was my beginning.

I puzzled a while over the fact that it was not the house I had been shown by my guides, but let that go as the excitement of moving crept closer. Negotiations were underway and looking good, when things began to get difficult. The house owner was asking for more money than had been agreed, saying that the place that they were buying had gone up in price, and it couldn't be helped. It was a testing time as I attempted to borrow more money, and it seemed as if my vision might be slipping away. The cottage was so beautiful, that I summoned all my reserves to go for it. Finally it came right, and our moving day was set; but first I had to bridge a gap of two weeks from moving out to moving in. My mother came to the rescue once again, offering me and the children a place to stay.

After I had packed everything, the journey up to my mother's house was fraught with difficulties but not without its funny moments. My car was a really tiny car that we nicknamed Dolly, and in it I packed myself, two children, three cats and a large dog. The dog spent the journey on the floor with his ears down groaning intermittently, and Thomas the cat howled for an hour and a half without letting up. We had a tiny ginger cat called Jenny in the basket with Thomas, and within ten minutes she was promptly sick, then emptied her bowels all over him; then the third cat, Sylvester who was loose in the car, spent the journey leaping from seat to seat in an attempt to get out. We had to keep the windows closed, and so the smells and the noise were horrendous. The final straw that dissolved us all into hysterical laughter was when the indicator arm on the car fell off in my hand. We were stuck at a junction with no way to show which way we were going. We couldn't open the window because of the cat, and so we just sat there, panicking at first, and then roaring with laughter at the comical situation we were in. Alex bounced up and down between the cats and dog, screeching with boyish glee, causing the car to rock alarmingly from side to side, and with tears of laughter rolling down our cheeks we managed to pull away from the crossing without causing any danger.

It was a good job my husband was not there. His appreciation of the ridiculous was never very good, and so we had avoided a potentially awful journey and turned it into one that was fun and full of laughter, despite the noise and the smells!

My husband couldn't join us at my mum's house, so he found temporary accommodation close to his work because the daily journey was too far. It was a somewhat cramped, make do and mend situation, but for two glorious weeks it represented a haven of peace away from friction with my husband. We were all full of excitement and anticipation about what was to come next, and I was so happy to be under the care and protection of my mother once again.

6
Forwards into the future,
Backwards into the past........

Moving day arrived, and surrounded by packing cases, we began to settle into the new atmosphere. I felt such exhilaration at being let loose in a cottage with so much potential. As we began to unpack and set up house I let my creative talents run wild, filling every nook and cranny with armfuls of wild flowers and shining brasses. I found an old wooden armed cottage suite, and upholstered it with country material that shone with bright red peonies and green ferns, finally setting it in a cosy corner under the old oak beams. I made floral cushions and drapes to match, and soon the richly warm 'olde worlde' atmosphere began to emerge. I had crystals hanging in every bay window, casting rainbows out to touch the rooms with a sprinkle of magic. My mother came to cast a maternal eye over the completed cottage, and with a smile, she gave me her seal of approval.

We took a trip into the town, and I was intent on showing my mum some of the places that held the unique spiritual magic. The first stop was the ancient Abbey, and whilst we took our time wandering amongst the manicured lawns and timeless ruins, I talked about everything that had happened since we moved.

Strolling in peaceful company with one another, we soaked up the energy and strength of the ancient trees, overlooking a tranquil fresh water pool that was awash with dusky pink water lilies.

I was growing hot and tired, so we headed for shade where I leant my back against the Abbey walls to rest. With my mother sat beside me, I closed my eyes, and a vision started to unfold in my mind. Recently, I had found that I had a new ability that was called psychometry; when I touched an object with my hands I could somehow 'read' the history that was imprinted in its energy. This now seemed to be happening as I leant against the wall. Moments in time held in the stones began to open in my mind like a great sail unfurling in the wind. The scene opened with a view of the Abbey in its original glory; and inside, shadow and sunlight danced together, illuminating the rising motes of dust. Under ornate stained glass windows hung many flags bearing different coats of arms, and standing in a pool of rainbow sunlight were two figures. The first was a tall man dressed in a fine leather jerkin and woollen hose, wearing a ceremonial chain across his chest and shoulders, and a circlet like a simple crown on his head. The second figure was a beautiful woman with long red hair, wearing a floor length green dress made of fine soft wool. A golden belt circled her waist and plunged to a point over her abdomen. Two young pages were in attendance, carrying small wicker bowls full of flower petals. Somehow I just knew that there was a May Day celebration coming, and they were in the Abbey to discuss their part in it.

My vision shifted to outside of the great wooden doors, and I saw a knight, who was wearing a sword at his side and chain mail on his chest, arrive at great speed on the biggest Shire horse I had ever seen. He reined his sweating steed to a halt and ran into the great building, kneeling at the feet of the man and giving him a message. They all headed for the great Abbey doors at the far end of the aisle, and as they opened I saw a wonderful vista of green fields and apple orchards in the distance. It was at this point that my mother interrupted me to ask a question about what was going on, breaking my concentration. As suddenly as it had appeared, the vision dissolved like a soap bubble popping, and was gone.

I laughed at the wonder of it all. Where had this come from? It had been so real and so solid that it seemed as if I had stepped back in time as a silent witness to history. The energy was so strong it had seeped into my body through the contact of my back against the wall, and amazed me once again.

Life was full again for a while, and as autumn gracefully gave way to the first chill of winter I found I was joyfully expanding in all directions with the sole exception of my marriage. My problems had been numerous from the start, and in March of the following year, I gave yet another 'final ultimatum' of six months as the last chance for us to work things out. Then strange and curious events that were to help give me the final push towards choosing to be free, arrived out of the blue and shook my world yet again.

***

Back in the Second World War

My husband was a tall man, six feet six in his bare feet, and he always presented himself in a very military manner. He had a fascination with anything German, and had often expressed a wish to visit Germany. He was a man with many biases, one of which was a peculiar and profound dislike for French people. As he had had no dealings with either France or Germany, it seemed to me to be a strange way of thinking. I found many of the things he did to be so totally opposite from the way my thoughts and beliefs went, that this made living with his ethos exasperating in the extreme.

One day I had a phone call from an old friend of mine from London. Tom had visited me many times and I eagerly looked forward to his arrival. We spent many happy hours in debate about spirituality and clairvoyance, and cosy afternoons around the log fire talking about his work as a medium and healer.

I had been feeling tired and distressed with the constant indecision about my marriage, and so Tom offered me a session of Shiatsu bodywork treatment combined with healing. In the past, I had felt some discomfort over a quite a period of time with my left leg. It always seemed to be aching and uncomfortable, with a kind of 'bone pain' that I found hard to describe. The session was uncomplicated, and everything was ok until Tom began work on the upper section of my left leg. Relaxed and in an almost altered state, I suddenly found myself with incredible visions flowing through my mind as if some internal television had been turned on.

I saw myself in a dark basement room, and I knew that I had been transported mentally to somewhere in France. The outside facade of the big old building I was in appeared grandiose with stone carvings. There were decorated columns at the main entrance, and at roof height there was a carved shield flanked by two stone lions facing each other. I saw many windows, all of which had dark green louvered wooden shutters.

Once again in the basement, I saw myself being interrogated. It became obvious that the time period was the Second World War and that my captor was a German officer of the SS. The picture unfolded in the most gruesome detail and I saw myself hanging upside down from the overhead water pipes that stretched across the dark room. Looking closely at my naked body, I saw that he had used chains around my ankles to hold me captive. For a fleeting moment I wondered why he had not used rope to hoist me up, but as the scene grew more vivid I lost the thought and was drawn back into the horrific detail. I heard him question me about the resistance movement, and when I didn't answer, he took an iron bar and brought the full force of a blow across my left leg at the knee. I heard the grinding crunch as metal bit into flesh, and saw my splintered shin bone pierce the flesh of my leg above the kneecap as my body convulsed under the power of the blow. Blood began to flow in warm rivulets down my thigh. A strong image of the green metal lampshade with its bare bulb swinging above me filled my mind as I swung limply back and forth like a rag doll.

In a hypnotic state, I was totally immersed in the scene. I began to feel the pain of the torture and the angry intention of the Nazi officer; cold and calculating with his questioning, brutal in his delivery of the beating. Then I witnessed a flash of sight from a scene happening in the inner courtyard that the building surrounded. Twenty or so raggedy children aged between about six and nine were huddled together in a group, and it seemed as if no-one knew what to do with them. Frozen into utter silence, tears washed lines down their strained faces. An officer appeared, passing by on his way to some rendezvous. He surveyed the crowd, and with a wave of his hand calmly gave the order to shoot them immediately. They were roughly pushed together and a command came for them to face the wall. At random, a soldier on guard duty was called across from his post to do the job. I witnessed his face tell a story as he raised his gun, lips mouthing a prayer to his God for forgiveness. I knew that he suffered an agony of conscience as he carried out his orders. When it was done, he went to the corner of the building and vomited.

By this time Tom was holding me in his arms whist I sobbed out the story I was witnessing. It was so real. I felt not only the physical pain, but also anguish at the futility of war. Overwhelming sadness and compassion tore at my heart, as I empathised with the desperate fear that emanated from the children. Devastated with grief and emotion, he held me, quietly rocking my body as I cried. He was shocked into immobility at the violence of the reaction I had had. When I eventually recovered enough to return to the moment, we both looked at one another in disbelief. After a while, I was able to tell him the rest of the story over a steaming cup of tea.

During the vision, flashes of related story had been shown to me. Apparently, I was an English woman sent across to France just before war had broken out as an undercover agent. I saw my home in Kent, England, and knew that I had been schooled in Switzerland as a child and was fluent in both French and German. My family owned property in France, and all my childhood holidays had been spent there. With troubled times predominant in England, I had offered my services to the military, and been given work in the war office as both a secretary and a driver. I had been recruited because of my abilities with languages, and my cover was as a governess to two children belonging to a wealthy family living just at the border between France and Belgium.

Just before war broke out, I would regularly send messages via radio. Later, as the war progressed, I joined the French Resistance, and relayed any and all information I could. By an ironic twist of fate, it had been the eldest child in my care who had given me away to the Nazis. Approaching fifteen, he had been intrigued and annoyed by my secrecy, and was determined to know all about me. He discovered my radio set one day, and born out of the irrational jealousy of youth had informed the Germans of my nocturnal activities. I was captured trying to escape with the children as cover, and had been taken into confinement for questioning.

When my husband returned home that night, he couldn't understand what had happened to me. I remained in shock for three days, feeling devastated and unable to stop crying. At first, he blamed Tom and said that he must have done something 'weird' to me. After I had given him detailed explanations he became more sympathetic, and over time, inadvertently gave me clues to his possible part in the whole story.

His first contribution was to tell me that he recognised the building I had seen, and that it was in Lyon, France. He said he had seen it in some book or other, and that it was exactly as I had described it. The second was to shock me into believing that the whole thing had really happened to me, but in some other lifetime. My knowledge of reincarnation was sparse, and as time went on, I began to search for information that could help me to understand.

My husband had a vivid dream one night, telling me that he was a German soldier, and that his home was somewhere in Germany that sounded like 'oranges'. Intrigued, he went to the library to find a map, and came home announcing that he had found the place and it was Oranienburg, a place near Berlin. Then by chance some months later, a book called 'Cyanide in my Shoe' was loaned to me by a friend. It was the true story of a woman who had worked as a spy during the Second World War. I took the book with interest and began to read it. Halfway through, I reached a section that shocked me to the bone. It appeared that there had been a Nazi they called 'The Butcher of Lyon' and he trained his henchmen to interrogate people in his own brutal fashion. His 'speciality' was to torture people by hanging them upside down using chains to bind them.

My eyes could scarcely believe the words on the page. I knew, without a doubt, that I had been tortured by one of the under officers of this butcher. His face was vividly imprinted in my mind, and I began to wonder if it were possible that this man had somehow reincarnated with me again, and had come into my life by cosmic design to teach me an important and necessary lesson. It was only a short time before I found out why this vision had been revealed to me, and when I did discover the reason, it helped me in my understanding that forgiveness was the only pathway for the both of us. I understood why my relationship with my then present husband had been so stormy, and it gave me the wisdom to pour healing salve on the pain that had grown over the years of our being together.

***

Angels are always near

My visions came thick and fast in the months that followed, and I began to learn about myself in depth. Relaxed and in an altered state during a meditation session one day, I saw a vision of a Mongolian horseman. I knew immediately that this was my soul in some other past life, and I began to watch with interest. The scene came swiftly but with unmistakable content. I saw the warrior riding at full gallop across a plain, brandishing an ornate curved sword. He approached his target with deadly accuracy and slid to the side of his horse to take aim. In the ground in front of him a man was buried up to his shoulders in the soil. As the horse galloped by, the horseman took off the man's head with one swift slice of his weapon. In this instant, I recognised that I was the horseman, and the victim in the Earth was my husband now.

One last vision came to me two days afterwards; finally all the pieces fell into place, as the truth of the whole thing hit me. Outside in the garden, I was deeply in thought about it all whilst walking towards the upper lawn to pick some flowers for the table. Suddenly I hesitated as a strange sensation passed through me, and a brilliant light appeared over the flowerbed. In the midst of the light was a vision of an Angel smiling serenely. In front of the Angel stood two souls preparing to incarnate on Earth, and the angel was asking a question to both in turn.

'Whilst you have been in this spiritual world, you have experienced between you the Love that makes us all One. You have agreed in this next lifetime that you will both learn to find forgiveness and compassion. There will be tests and choices that may take you into the realms of hatred and death. Which one of you will be the victim and which will take the task of perpetrator, in order that the other may have the chance to learn?'

I watched the two souls, clearly loving each other, as they agonised over the choice. How much easier to be the victim and feel no guilt; how much harder to agree to cause someone you love pain and suffering. Once an understanding of the whole picture came into view, I began to see the truth. Forgiveness was the key! Revenge is futile, as it teaches us nothing except righteous hatred. Forgiveness dissolves the need to hurt any more. It was as if blinkers had been removed from my eyes, and I began to laugh quietly as the truth of the whole thing hit me.

I realised that the two of us had been perhaps caught in a cycle of negativity towards each other, never learning the lessons at all; possibly exacting pain or even death on each other lifetime after lifetime, in one way or another. Be it for revenge, hate, or jealousy -- it didn't matter any more. What mattered was that I was now conscious of it, and could choose to end the circle of repetition now, in this lifetime.

Called Karma in the East, I knew I could stop it and change the future by learning how to forgive and not hate any more. Equally so, it was needed for him to forgive me all the pain I had ever caused him in this and in past lifetimes. I realised that the primary reason we are all here on Earth is to know ourselves truly. Here was an important lesson for me about righteous indignation and ego, and how it can make us blind to the higher truth. I was not the victim I had thought myself to be, only a player in some vast cosmic play that serves us in our quest to find out who we really are. As I grew in understanding, I learnt more about different dimensions of reality from my guides, and books I found in the town. They taught me that all our beliefs form our personal reality; that each person's reality is different, and that the power to change it is within us. It's only a matter of choice. If the situation you are in causes you pain and suffering, it's because you have chosen it in order to learn something. When the lesson is learnt, then it becomes easy to choose another path. I found the most important thing to know is that you are responsible for yourself and your thoughts, emotions, and actions; and that only *you* have the power to change them if they do not serve you well. I remembered a line from the bible, 'Man, Know Thyself', and it began to make real sense at last.

Changes do not always come overnight, and respite from my problems didn't come all at once. Having the concepts in my head about these things helped, but they are easier said than done and I still lacked the courage to change my situation. Try as I might I could not reconcile my worries about the children and the effect that a divorce might have on them.

Knowing that the constant problems between us had affected Alex very deeply, and that Kate would support me no matter what happened, I still couldn't face my own fears and take the final step. Although I was still caught in my old worries about how my husband might react, it was the old story of better the devil you know, coupled with the fear that I might not survive on my own.

I was out reluctantly one afternoon in August with my husband and son, walking in the fields behind our home. All around us the wild beauty of the lush green hills abounded. Meadow flowers, blooming in unexpected corners decorated the fields here and there with bursts of vibrant colour; and the soft lowing of cattle grazing contentedly, wove gentleness into the hazy heat of the afternoon air.

Too deeply into my problems, I saw none of the miracles around me, only conscious that my mind was awash with anguish and distress. I stopped for a moment, some yards in front of them and raised my eyes to heaven. Addressing God, I whispered, 'If you don't send someone to help me soon, I'm going to kill myself'. With every fibre of my being, I meant it. Over the nine months that we had been at the cottage, life had become emotionally impossible for me. Now I felt I had reached the end of my tether, with nowhere to go and no way out.

***

7

A Different World.........

One week into September, I saw a solicitor and started proceedings for separation. With this news my husband became alternatively sad and then angry, followed by aloof secretiveness. In my distress with it all I failed to notice the unusual amount of time he was spending with Alex. Little did I know that what was coming was more than I had bargained for. The biggest shock came just two weeks before my husband was to leave. Alex, then aged eleven, came to me and said he wanted to go and live with his father. He explained that as Katie was going to be with me, then it wasn't fair that dad should be left on his own.

I agonised over his decision, feeling as if I had somehow been a bad mother, not wanting to upset him further by demanding that he stay, but not wanting him to leave either. My nights were filled with tears and sadness, and the days leading to my husband's departure filled with trauma. His anger at the divorce was evident, and it only served to make the parting more difficult. He called me insane, and blamed the spiritual aspect of my life as the reason I no longer wanted to be with him. It was at this time that I saw another vision that helped me to see the whole thing through.

One afternoon, exhausted from housework, I knew I had just a fifteen minute break before I had to go to pick up the children from school. I decided to sit in the sunshine in the back garden for a short while, and lying in a deckchair, I closed my eyes to the bright sunshine around me. Suddenly, I became aware of the figure of my first husband John, walking down the garden path towards me. I smiled in surprise and sent my welcome, loving him as always from the deepest part of me. Seeing him so clearly was a rare occurrence, and what happened next brought me hope that help was finally on the way.

He walked to my side, and knelt down beside the deckchair. With my eyes closed, I felt a strong tingle go through my fingers and up my arm as he gently took my hand in his.

'I have come to tell you that I am sending someone to save you'.

Tears sprang into my eyes. Momentarily stunned by a strange feeling washing over me, I surrendered totally as his shimmering energy passed right through me. It was as if both of us had melded into one, and in that moment, I felt the power of his love engulfing my entire body. To be held in the stream of his energy was an electrifying experience. It passed, and a wave of calm acceptance left me with the knowledge that this unique experience was a gift to be treasured forever.

I got up, as if in a dream, and fetched the car keys, asking him if he would stay for a while. Getting into the car, I knew his presence was close, and he travelled with me whilst I drove first to fetch Alex, and then Kate. With them both safely in the car, I began to tell my daughter about it as we drove home. Kate was a little confused at first, but knowing me as she did she accepted that this was the truth. When we got home, I asked her to come into the quiet of the living room, and sit still for a moment and close her eyes. I then asked John quietly if he could repeat the feeling of love with Kate in the same way as he had done with me.

The warm oak beamed sitting room was silent except for the ticking of the clock, and I almost held my breath as I waited, eyes focused on Kate. I saw a light envelop her, and watched with love as tears began to trickle down my daughter's cheeks.

With eyes awash with tears, she spoke.

'I can feel him mum, I can feel the love. Is this really my dad?'

I smiled, my own tears flowing freely now.

'Yes, it really is your very own dad, and he loves you so much, he's come to show you.'

As the moment and the energy passed, I knelt down beside the chair and put her arms around her.

'I miss him so much', Kate whispered.

'So do I darling, so do I........

His presence faded and was gone, leaving us with both warmth and sadness. We both knew that help was at hand and I felt a strengthening of spirit and a new resolve to go forward.

So my husband finally left, and life had hardly begun to settle down, when the next blow fell. My beloved Kate, now aged sixteen, came to me one day and said she wanted to leave home to live with a man she had met when she was just fourteen. My daughter had unconsciously been searching for the love and fulfilment she had been missing, and as a consequence had fallen in love with the first boy to come along who said he loved her.

There was nothing I could do. I knew that if I fought this, then my Taurean daughter would leave anyway. Kate even vowed to run away from home and not be seen again, if I didn't give her permission. Headstrong and determined, Kate had presented a 'fait accompli' and I knew I had to let her go with love. My secret hope was that one day when Kate had matured a little, she would come back. Things looked bleak as Kate was giving up college and the possibility of a career to work in a factory in order keep a man who could not even hold a job.

Kate moved into his parent's home for a while, and eventually at eighteen announced she was going to marry him. I cried for two days, and then, having accepted that my daughter's path was one she had to travel in her own way, gave her my blessing. The wedding was certainly different, with the bride in scarlet and black, escorted by a full complement of leather-jacketed bikers. Heavy metal music by Guns 'n' Roses roared out, and the deed was done. They moved into a tiny flat in a tower block that was damp and depressing. Kate did her best to make it homely, filling every corner with plants, but this only served to make the humidity rise and the damp problem worse.

After a while, her new husband became obsessed with the idea that I would somehow influence Kate, and make her leave him. My policy of non-interference meant that nothing could have been further from the truth, but this fear would not leave him, and so he insisted that she was not allowed to visit me without him, and then on rare occasions only. He couldn't see how this was creating the opposite effect, and making Kate feel that she had no freedom at all.

Over the next three years, I hardly saw my daughter or son at all, and held my deep aching sadness in silence. Although separate from my husband, life was not the way I thought it was going to be. I presumed I would be free and happy with my two children by my side, and now I ended up with nothing but an empty heart. With both children gone, my life was staring me straight in the eye, and demanding to know what I was going to do about it.

I constantly worried about everything. Afraid of my husband returning, afraid of what the neighbours would think of me, feeling guilty about my choice to do what I knew in my heart was right. Every time a car went past the house that sounded like my husband's, my heart leapt in fear, and I found myself running to the window to see who it might be. Confused and depressed, this was a watershed in which I was faced with my biggest tests. Where to go from here? All my hopes and grand ideas had taken a back seat and were watching my pain and confusion from a distance, obscure and obsolete now in their importance in my life.

Now I was faced with the emptiness of life without my children. Why had it happened like this? Even my beautiful house that brought me an income from bed and breakfast had to be sold. When life takes you to breaking point, then you either go under or you fight. I fought, but not with words or solicitors. I came back to life by learning yet again to face my fears. Slowly and surely I defeated them one by one. So what did other people think of me? Nothing! How much time did anyone spend thinking and being critical of other people's problems? No longer than a few minutes! Who was there to be afraid of? No-one! So it followed that my fears were just rabbits that skittered about my mind looking for something to grow fat on. Was I a bad mother? My heart overruled my mind and convinced me I was not. Who cared anyway? No one did. I was just another face in the crowd. Believing my actions were justified, I soldiered on with the belief that everything must come to those who wait.

***

A Healing Miracle

In the autumn of that year there was big excitement in town about something called a 'Time Warp'. News had come through the New Age grapevine about there being a special day in which people were gathering together to celebrate and integrate 'new energies' that were being directed towards the planet. It was a sign that the consciousness of the people of planet Earth was changing. I thought about it, and decided that it was time for me to come out of my troubled state and try to do something for the good of others and the planet in general. I wasn't sure what I could do, but thought that maybe an organised meditation and some information on this 'Time Warp' would benefit people and encourage them to deal with the problems in their lives with new insights. I put posters up in the town, and on the appointed night sixty four people turned up to join me in quiet meditation. What a surprise! I was very nervous, but luckily I had written out a guided meditation beforehand, and so was at least prepared in case my nerve failed.

The theme was for people to realise that old thought patterns and negative thinking in general manifests as illness in the body. Everything went exceptionally well, even if I was a little nervous, and spoke a little too fast at times. About half way through I took a mental breather and tried to compose myself a little, when suddenly I felt a strong rush of energy enter my body and engulf me in complete tingles from head to foot. It was just as if someone had plugged me into the electricity! A strong impulse came into my mind to put down the paper I was reading from, and just let go to whatever came through me. I knew in this split second that I could 'channel' some higher energy. Whether it was from within me or from some outside force, I didn't know, but my guess was that it was not from inside me. What to do? Everyone was sat in silence, listening to the words I had carefully written down. What if the things this other force said didn't make sense? Scared for a moment, I decided to let it pass and continue reading. My fear of what people might think of me had won again, and so I missed a possible opportunity to learn. The evening ended and everyone went away happily unaware of what they might have heard, had I been brave enough to let go of control and trust.

To meet my ever-growing need to be of help to others, I joined a weekly meditation and healing group. With this as my focus, I began to practice refining my healing work, and reconnecting with my inner guidance in this peaceful atmosphere. Once a week I spent a day at the healing centre, being on call for whoever needed me. One afternoon a man came in, and as I was the only person free, I took him into the quiet healing room and sat him down for a session of spiritual healing. He was an ordinary man, of middle age, with only one lung functioning and a cancerous growth on his left shoulder. As he began to talk to me, his story was filled with so much heartfelt remorse that I felt the tears welling up in my eyes. He told of how he had lived his life never thinking about other people, and about how he saw the error of his ways and was ready to change. He explained that he had been skiing and had swerved off the slope and fallen onto a marker flag. It had pierced him through the body and punctured his lung from front to back. He told me that he had clinically 'died' on the slopes, and that the rescue helicopter had got him to the hospital in miraculous time, and they had revived him. He spoke about reoccurring cancer of the skin, and the upcoming operation that was needed to remove the growth on his back.

I listened and felt his remorse and pain; it was as if he was quietly asking God to forgive him and allow him a second chance to prove himself. He had touched death once, and now cancer was knocking on the door of his life, telling him he would not come back this time. I placed my hands upon his shoulders and began to send healing and love, calling upon the energy of Jesus to help me. Such an overwhelming compassion for him came over me that when the session was over and he had gone, I broke down in tears, crying for him with love at the brave changes he vowed to make.

An arrangement was made for him to come a second time before the surgery was due, and once again I gave all that I could for the twenty-minute session. This was in May, and after the second session, I did not see him again. In June, three weeks later, I received a letter from him:

Dear Elaine,

You were kind enough to give me Spiritual Healing on two Wednesday afternoons at the end of May-I asked for healing on a cancer growth on my left shoulder-I hope you can recall me.

I am writing to tell you that a few days ago I noticed that the growth was shrinking and the associated 'itching' had gone. Last night I reached over my shoulder to explore with my fingertips and the growth had gone! Terrific! There is now just a small red patch of skin left, and I look forward to that healing in due course. I am delighted to be able to cancel my appointment at the hospital for surgery, as it is no longer needed. I am most grateful to you and to those in spirit for this evidence of God's Love.

Thank you.

I felt both humility and joy, and on an inner level I was smiling with every part of me. I glowed with the knowledge that all things are possible. I remembered that the bible records that Jesus had once said to his disciples; 'All these things that I do, you can do also', and I knew it was true.

I knew that only the combination of his readiness to let go of old ways and change, and my heartfelt compassion for him had made it possible for him to be miraculously healed in this way. I also realised that all those who are not healed, are on some level not ready to change their emotional patterns or their thoughts, or take responsibility for themselves.

I was at the healing and meditation group one night when a strange thing happened. A man who was new in town had arrived for his second visit. All the chairs in the healing group had been filled that night, except for mine. He sat down to receive healing, and accepting him, I closed my eyes to prepare myself. After a short prayer to both Jesus and my guides and helpers, I placed my hands on his shoulders and began. I had an unspoken rule never to mix healing and clairvoyance, but as I stood there, pictures in my mind came so strongly they could not be ignored. Scenes from ancient times flashed past, and I saw myself and this man standing together in a barren red desert landscape, lit and shadowed by two fiery suns. This could surely not be planet Earth? I became wary of any interfering energy, and trying to clear my mind, I moved around to the front of the chair, and placed my hands over his to complete the healing. As our hands touched I had an overpowering feeling that I had known this man forever, and that every cell in my body held some kind of timeless love for him. I blushed. This was ridiculous! How on earth could there be emotions like this for a man I didn't even know?

The session finished, and as it was the custom for some of the group to congregate in the pub across the road afterwards, we both went. I began to tell him of the things I had seen, and introducing himself as Patrick, he began to tell me excitedly about words he had heard in his head whilst I had been working on him. Backtracking to tell me about himself, I learned he had lived in the town before, and some eight months previously had met an American woman and fallen in love. They planned to return to her hometown and get married. After six months they had saved enough for the flight, but once they got there, things had not worked out well at all. They parted, and with most of his money gone, the only option left was to hitchhike across America before he could fly home. With only a few dollars and his return ticket in his pocket, he set out to cross the desert. His first lift dropped him in the middle of nowhere.

Feeling devastated over the failure of the relationship, he ended up sitting on his suitcase by the side of the desert road. Night was falling, and as the stars came out he was in tears, praying for guidance to help him begin again. Suddenly a voice boomed inside his head telling him to go back to his old home immediately, and to make sure he went to a Wednesday night Meditation group he would find. He was told he would meet a woman, and this would be 'the one'.

As I was giving him healing, these words had rung clearly in his mind. 'This is the one. This is the woman you came home for.' The two of us sat in the pub, embarrassed and incredulous that this could be happening. This was like a fairytale, or a scene from the movies! I thought of John, and with trembling heart wondered if this was the 'saviour' John had spoken about.

Our compatibility for each other was instant, and we met again and again. Gradually he became the one who brought me out of my turmoil by loving me and teaching me more about my spiritual self.

After a while, he encouraged me to go 'public' with my talent as a clairvoyant, and so I began to advertise in the town. What an exciting and scary adventure! The experiences I had spanned the spectrum from hilarious through to pathetic and taught me volumes about people and they way they function. I learnt that when you have the gift of knowing, the way you wield it counts the most. I attracted lessons to teach me about the true meaning of personal power; how to say no, how to choose what feels right and true, and how to discern between intuition and desires of the personality. I was tested one day when a woman came wanting to know the outcome for several books she was writing. Would they be successful? Would she earn lots of money? Someone was suing her, and she had to know who would win. The more questions she asked in this vein, the more uncomfortable I became. The woman had a very domineering personality, and was aggressive to the point of being obnoxious. The final straw came when she questioned me about the man accompanying her, who was sitting in the other room.

'His wife has left him, and he's with me for the weekend. Yesterday she phoned, and now he's all upset. What I want to know is, will he be ok for sex tonight?' I can laugh about it now, but then,

I was astounded by such a question, and found it difficult to believe my ears. How could someone expect spiritual guides to even bother with a request like that? What was this woman thinking about? She didn't appear to be aware of who it was that I was talking to; did she think that it was just some casual fortune telling that she was paying for?

So the test landed fairly and squarely in my lap. I returned from my deeply altered state, opened my eyes, and told the woman that I was not willing to put questions like that to my guides. I was there to help people along their pathway in life with spiritual guidance, and if she wanted to find out about the likelihood of sex with someone, then the best person to ask was the man himself. The woman was taken aback and with a disgruntled air she begrudgingly agreed. With this test passed and under my belt, I thankfully did not attract that kind of person again!

What happened next was that I found my abilities advancing to a higher level. Reading the client's energy field gave me information on all aspects of their personal life, including wants and desires, and access to relatives who had died. Now I found myself able to go to a higher source, discovering an optimum pathway for the future for my clients. During one session I found myself telling someone in a novel way about the options they had; a picture formed in my mind of a hand holding balloons - every string was a pathway, and each balloon represented an end result. Some could be let go of because they were smaller than the rest; some were bigger and had stronger strings. I saw that there was always an optimum future for everyone, providing they made the right choices, and 'let go' of the right balloons. I could translate this and see into real life situations, advising people of events that might occur, and what signs to look out for. In this way, they would know when they were on the right path, or 'hanging on to the right balloon'.

My guides began to change too. New ones came to speak, and input from the original two became less and less. One that I called 'The Light Being' arrived, and she was named so because I could not see her face, only the image of her figure held in blinding white light. I 'knew' all my guides by feel, sensing when the personality that represented the being was powerful or peaceful, wise or fun loving.

But it was not with my guides that the next two startling events were to happen.

***

8
First Contact........

The Christmas after my husband left was a quiet and sad time. I would make tea, sit by the crackling log fire and gaze into the dancing flames thinking of my children. Gone were the times when the children were sent out to gather fallen branches, with a promise of buttery toasted teacakes by the fire as a reward. No more happy feet, clattering around the house, and noisy mealtimes. No more good night kisses and loving words, just the ticking of the clock and my memories.

I longed to see my son. He lived not far away with his father, so I was able to visit him, but he existed in a world that had no understanding of the true meaning of what was going on. As a result, our meetings were strained and painful for both of us. Alex had extreme difficulty with his emotions, and was not able to express himself, and was faltering and embarrassed. I always left his house with a lump in my throat and pain in my heart, often breaking down once I was out of sight. There was so much anger, sorrow and sad feelings from my husband, that it drove a wedge between me and my son, making Alex afraid to show his love for fear of disapproval from his father. My only hope was that as he got older, time would heal the problem for all of us. Maybe he would see the situation with clearer vision, and come back to me someday. I lived in hope that this would be, and kept faith that all things were perfect for my learning, even if they are unbelievably painful at the time.

The Christmas festivities came and went without much celebration for me. I hoped that as time went on, I would find once more the sweet joy that had been missing from my life for so long.

The New Year was coming in a few days, and there had been a buzzing of news in the town about a world-wide meditation that was due to happen at midnight on New Year's Eve. Organised by a man named Jose Argüelles, the plan was for groups of people to mentally send Earth greetings into outer space. The purpose being to welcome any Extra Terrestrial life forms to planet Earth. I couldn't help but feel a frizz of excitement at the prospect of doing this, and wondered if anything amazing might happen, like lights in the sky or perhaps the sighting of a ship.

In a light-hearted frame of mind, I approached the whole thing with a spirit of fun. The night was full of eerie expectation when it came, and was typically bitterly cold and blowing a gale. Only the hardiest people were out that night, standing on the top of the hill. We all held hands, and formed a circle to send our nocturnal greetings; the sky was cloudy and dark with no moon to light the way and the wind cut through my heavy topcoat like a knife. My friend Patrick was with me, and together, we repeated the given meditation with the rest of the crowd gathered there. Over and over the chant rang out, but after twenty minutes, still nothing had happened. After almost an hour we were numb with cold and chilled to the bone. We were still merrily into the spirit of the event, but finally decided to give it up and go home to the comfort and warmth of the log fire. By the time we reached my home, it was about ten past one in the morning. I was feeling exhilarated after the walk in the freezing night air, and we struck up a conversation about the whole concept of calling the Extra Terrestrials. The inspiration came to me that even though it was past the appointed time, we could try one more time from the comfort of the fireside. Agreeing, we settled into the cosy armchairs and closed our eyes, searching for the clear space needed to send out mental communication. Warmed by the fire, I went immediately into a deep state of peace, and closed my mind to all thoughts. I repeated the invocation slowly.

'From the Earth to my body, from my body to my heart, from my heart into space I send greetings. To all beings not of this Earth, I bid you welcome with love'.

Twice, three times I said it in my mind, and then in a flash, it was as if a television in my head had been turned on.

Up came a grey screen, and on it appeared a silvery three-dimensional diagram of a space ship. Like a computer graph line drawing, the inner workings were all visible. It was revolving slowly, showing me all angles, first top and bottom, then the sides. I saw three metallic legs extend from underneath, shaped like jointed spiders legs but with no visible joins. On the end of each was a large droplet shaped metal foot. As the ship touched the imaginary floor, each foot spread out like a water-filled ball to cushion the weight, enabling the craft to land on any terrain, uneven or smooth.

Then the top of the ship came off, showing me the inner workings. The spaceship seemed to be like two discs sandwiched together; looking at it from above, you could see that when taken apart, the lower half was fashioned and divided like the sections of a halved orange. My vision zoomed in, and I could see in each of the triangular sections, thousands of squares of crystal, all standing at an angle to the base. I was shown the underside of the top half of the ship, and this too had the same configuration of crystals, only leaning the other way. Apparently, the top and bottom halves of this middle section of the ship rotated in different directions, and the electrical field created by the crystals passing over one another gave the ship some kind of power. Then the underneath central section of the ship began to telescope out and down, like upside down layers of a wedding cake. The internal camera of my mind zoomed underneath the ship and I saw a set of metal doors that were designed to slide open, but closed with a fit so tight that they seemed sealed without any joins.

The scene changed, and I found myself inside the ship at a control panel. Two round metallic spheres were at my fingertips, and a large video screen rose up in front of me.

Quickly a question formed in my mind.

'What are you doing here?'

'Making maps' came the telepathic reply.

'Why can't you just photograph or record from the sky as we do?'

'Our maps are different. We use them in a different way. Watch.'

I stared intently at the screen, and a landscape appeared. It was in three dimensional computer graphic form with the images appearing as line drawn models.

The trees and hills that formed were detailed in every way. Millions of blades of grass jumped out at me, and every inflection, bump and blemish on tree and flower was being scrutinised microscopically.

'We make our maps with something similar to your sonar. We measure in detail in order that the intelligence system of the ship has accurate co-ordinates to go to. When we think of a place we would like to be, we do not use names. We visualise the place in our mind. The system recognises every tree, flower and blade of grass from within us, and by a simple process, we are taken there.'

The being that had spoken to me placed his hands on the twin orbs in front of the screen.

'By thought transference the intelligence system of the ship sees the place, and matches it with an internal map. This is a basic function and all we need to travel'.

He signalled that he would demonstrate, and my eyes grew wide as I saw the landscape begin to move. It gave the illusion of coming towards me like a racetrack in an arcade game. I felt I was flying through the air, piloting some invisible ship over vast areas of computerised terrain. It came faster and faster at me until I actually began to feel queasy in my stomach. My head jerked up and away from the screen as I took a deep breath.

Like an explosion inside my head, the vision in all its detail vanished. Coming back to the reality of the warm room, with only the soft crackle of the embers glowing in the fire grate, I saw that half an hour had passed. Whilst lost under the spell of the vision, Patrick had got up and crept silently out to the kitchen to make tea. He peered around the doorway and smiled. Two steaming cups preceded him as he pushed open the oak door with his foot, and asked me what had happened. Amazed at what I had witnessed, I started to babble my story like a brook tumbling over a waterfall. Excitement filled me and overflowed contagiously whilst he listened, nodding and smiling at the content of my story and the enthusiasm with which it was delivered. He said little, except to encourage and agree, and that quiet nature of acceptance was what I needed more than anything.

***

Amazing people

Life went on, with its ever-flowing contingent of guests for bed and breakfast. They arrived in the little town having travelled from all over the world. It was famous world wide, and attracted pilgrims and spiritual seekers of every persuasion and denomination. Looking after them was both a funny and an interesting job, and one that kept me permanently on my toes. It allowed me not only to meet unique people, but also to make lifelong friends in the process. Some were 'weird and wonderful'; others gave as much to me in the way of spiritual guidance as I gave to them.

I had always had a secret yearning to be a trance medium. I had seen trance mediums at work, and knew that they let their own spirit 'move over' to allow control of their actions and voice to the spirit entity that would come through. I thought that if I was totally in a trance then there was absolutely no chance of my own mind coming into the readings that I gave and influencing them from my own biases or judgements. Basically this was insecurity on my part, as I was still in the process of really trusting my accuracy when it came to giving people guidance.

One day in spring, when the early sun shone its encouraging rays on the first crocuses, I invited Patrick to come for a cup of coffee. He arrived, finding me almost waist deep in the weekend washing quota of sheets, pillowcases and towels. It had been extra busy with guests- the last of them had just left and now came the clearing up process. The dishwasher and washing machine hummed in the background as we sat at the breakfast bar sipping rich dark coffee. Gossip about some of the funny behaviour and strange requests of the guests flowed around the room, interspersed with gales of laughter at how I had coped with some of them. One guest, who must have been completely mad, had run around the lounge saying he could hear a strange ringing in the air. Lurching to a halt, he grabbed a bunch of dried lavender from a flower vase in the window, held it up to his ear, and with total seriousness had told me that somebody wanted me on the phone. Yet another had arrived with seven black suitcases trailing behind her. Cloaked in black from head to foot and wearing a large hat with a veil, she entered bearing an armful of red roses. She disappeared mysteriously upstairs and was not seen again until she came down for breakfast and asked for a glass of cold water and a banana. When I went into the bedroom to make the bed, I found the whole room decked out from wardrobe to floor with black material like a tent from an Arabian night's tale. The woman popped out from under the swathes of draped cloth, and announced brightly that it was ok and not to worry, as she was just reliving an Arabian past life and it wouldn't take long!

***

The Galactic Federation

We poured more fragrant coffee and grinned at the humour of life. We were still laughing when I heard myself saying that today I would go into a trance and do some channelling at seven o'clock. My jaw dropped because I realised that I had no idea where that notion had come from and it had slipped out of my mouth without any conscious thought from me.

The heard the washing machine finish its cycle, and I promptly forgot that I had said it as the call of housework pulled me back into the present moment. All day long I worked around the house, cleaning, polishing, washing and cooking, and in between the chores trooping in and out to hang the sheets out to dry.

It was a glorious day. The air smelt of fresh clean washing, the birds sang for me and high in my cottage on the hilltop, everything was in harmony. Seven o'clock came and went as the pile of ironing grew bigger and bigger, and still I worked on, determined to get everything done by the end of the day. At almost nine in the evening I was walking through the kitchen with a basket full of the never-ending sheets, when a strange feeling overcame me, and I felt compelled to sit down. I recognised it at once; sometimes, when I promised to sit and talk with my guides, and forgot, I would suddenly feel a huge change in my energy which forced me to stop whatever I was doing. Somehow they could influence my energy field so that I couldn't think straight or continue with whatever job I was doing. This was one such occasion, and so I knew someone wanted to talk to me urgently.

I ran into the bedroom, muttering, 'All right, all right, I'm coming', grabbed my hand held tape recorder and jumped into bed, fully clothed. Sitting with my back up against the headboard, duvet pulled snugly around me, I turned on the tape, and closed my eyes.

Within seconds of preparing myself with my usual prayer, I heard a strong voice in my inner mind. I knew it was not one of my guides, and with ears pricked, I listened eagerly to find out if I was going to go into trance, or perhaps something else would happen?

'We come from realms you do not know of, and we bring greetings. I come to tell you of your future. You will have a house of Light, high on a hill, and there you will create a place where people will come to be healed'. The voice, deeper and more resonant than a church bell, continued on and on, leaving pauses between the words, so I could repeat them into the tape recorder.

'We are from The Galactic Federation, and we are sent here to help mankind.

I am Commander of an Intergalactic Task Force, present around planet Earth to be of assistance to humanity. You are not the only one we speak to. There are many all around the world who will hear us, and there will be other places such as yours'.

At this point, it was hard for me to believe what I was hearing, but as an unwritten rule, I removed all judgement and listened on. The message lasted for almost forty-five minutes, and finished in a spectacular way. The being must have known that I was couldn't believe he was from some other planet, so he paused, and I felt a strong tingle start in the crown of my head, and ripple down my body. Then I began to spin. My body was still, but internally, it was as if I was spinning at high speed on a children's merry-go-round, or in the vortex of a tornado. I began to feel disorientated and nauseous. Instantaneously and as if by magic, the sensations stopped abruptly.

'I am sorry I had to do that. I understand how your body feels. I superimposed my energy field over yours, in order that you understand **absolutely** that I am real, and this is not an illusion. It was necessary for you to feel my energy pattern, and know that I am not of this planet Earth'.

I felt as if my jaw had dropped to the floor, and even felt embarrassed at the thought of telling anyone. Who would believe me? I had never even heard of this 'Galactic Federation'. Was it some big joke, or a test from my guides? I spent hours wondering about it, and yet it was a clear and tangible sensation that I felt, and the message was absolute and unmistakable. Where was this house on the hill? It was obviously not on the hill where I lived now. Could it be the house I had seen in my original vision?

It could, and it was.

***

A woman lived in the town who was a sort of 'grandmother figure' to everyone. She owned many properties here and there, and acted as benefactress to many people trying to promote spiritual awareness. Two events then manifested in my life, and slid together like an avalanche coming down a mountain, colliding like fate and destiny in a big snowheap of potential. The first was a chance meeting with this lady and the man who now played an important part in my life. She stopped

Patrick on the street one day, and asked him if he thought he could run a guesthouse, and was he interested in doing so? Then she wanted to know if he knew me, and as she had heard I had to move house, did he think I would help out?

Well. You can guess the rest. The guesthouse was the one on the hill I had seen in my vision, and this opportunity would allow Patrick and I to be together running a business I was now very familiar with. The house was let as a rental, and so there was no need for a mortgage, or any kind of big financial commitment. Apparently, the old couple who had been in the place had fallen ill. The place was now run down, and in need of loving care and attention. The couple were asking to leave, and someone was needed to take over, redecorate, and begin again. What an opportunity! Between running my own business and trying to sell my house, I managed to put in many hours of painting and decorating. All my friends rallied round to tackle the huge amount of work to be done in the new house, and within three months we held a grand re-opening party. The whole street was invited; local guesthouse and shop owners came, offering a spirit of camaraderie that brought a warm glow to my heart.

Spring swept into summer like a fragrant sea breeze along the prom, and at first, there was no sign of a sale for my house. I became increasingly impatient to join my friend Patrick. I would double between the two houses, putting in as much work as I could by dividing myself and my time into what felt like ten people with forty-eight hours in every day. The house was certainly impressive. With six bedrooms, it sat on the top of a windswept hill, with a fairy filled terraced garden sloping away to the sunny south side, overlooked by a balcony with a view to set your heart racing. The breakfast room was a little glass conservatory to the side, where the early mornings were embroidered with enticing smells of creamy yellow scrambled eggs sprinkled with chives, nestling side by side on an artist's palette of steaming brown mushrooms and juicy tomatoes. The canvas was complete when the sun broke across the peat moors, hit the hanging crystal droplets in the windows, reflected rainbow lights on every person in the room.

I set about creating a haven for people in need; travellers and pilgrims, those who wanted healing and guidance; they all came through the door as promised. By early December I felt I could wait no longer, and deciding that action was needed, I began to pack all my belongings and transport them to the new house. Some of them were already there, and so I began to sew up the final seams to join the garment of my life into a whole. Finally, a couple turned up who were interested but reluctant to buy my old house, so I rented it to them, and made my move.

9

A Greater Learning.......

The days at this new house were long and full. I was on call from early morning to late at night, making sure the guests were settled and all was in order. I thought a lot about the couple who had left, and how ill they had become, leaving the place to fall into quiet times. We finally began to realise just how much hard work was needed to run a business of this sort. As time went on, we poured all our energy and attention into the house and its magical garden. It was heavy work with a lot of sweat and toil, but the surroundings were so beautiful that the job was a pleasure, and the rewards of sitting by a blazing bonfire at the end of a long hot day in the garden were more than adequate compensation.

Word of mouth was our only advertisement, and pretty soon people began to flock to our door from all around the world.

There were many myths and legends about the town, and I had a large library of books and videos covering all the wildly different aspects of this special place. There was sacred geometry, Ley lines, the Arthurian legend, Crop Circles, UFO's and much more, and was always a talking point at the breakfast table. Life for me was fascinating, exciting, and at times unbelievable.

All the while, my heart was still pining for my son. By now, my daughter had married and was leading her own life in her own way, but my son continued to be a painful wound that would not heal. On his way home from school, he passed by my house almost every day. I was always eagerly watching out for him, and you could always find me standing in the doorway at four o'clock, trying to catch a glimpse of him as he walked home. I knew he deliberately avoided coming that way on many occasions, and time after time, I waited in vain. My son Alex was uncomfortable and uneasy when he did come in. No matter what I told him, or how much I tried to explain, he was afraid to listen. He made his excuses, only staying for a quick cup of tea, and no more. My heart felt as if it was breaking on so many occasions, I lost count.

By now, my ex husband was renting a house where the landlady lived in, and he had struck up a friendship with her. This added to Alex's problems, as she was a little strict and sometimes intolerant of him. He was growing fast, and at thirteen, he needed the kindness of a woman's touch. In truth, he needed his mother. My break came when his father organised a holiday with a friend. Alex had been abroad with them before, and had felt both out of place and awkward. I saw my opportunity and grabbed it with both hands. I offered that instead of going on the holiday for Christmas, Alex come and stay for the two weeks with me. There was some reluctance from his father, but as Alex was getting older and beginning to speak his mind, he made it clear that he didn't want to go, and the only option was to come and stay with me.

Glory Be! My heart sang at the prospect of having him with me for the first time in three years. I could barely contain my excitement. All the love I had stored away was bursting at the gates of my heart, just waiting to flood out.

He arrived, and at first he was shy and pink faced as he cautiously familiarised himself with the big house. He had never ventured further than the kitchen before. Whether he was afraid of what he might find, or just confused, I didn't know. But I did know that in the past his head had been filled full of misguided untruths, which didn't help at all. I left him alone to find his feet and waited downstairs as he wandered from room to room. I had given him a bedroom with the most spectacular view, and decided to turn down any bookings from outsiders. I wanted every uninterrupted second of these two weeks to last forever. Slowly the expression on his face turned from worried concern to a grin of wide delight, as he voyaged around the house and found that behind all the many doors, things were absolutely normal!

***

<u>The best Christmas present ever</u>

I began preparing all the things we had ever done in Christmases past; I took him to the local forest to choose a Christmas tree, and as the joy on his face grew, so the pain in my heart receded. We put on our wellingtons and collected ivy and fallen branches to decorate the living room, staying up late to pin shining bells and tinsel to the ceiling. I found thick ivory candles to grace the mantle over the fire, and made a holly wreath arrayed with red ribbons for the front door. We decorated the Christmas tree together, and when it was finished, we turned out the lights and sat by the crackling fire, watching the dancing lights shimmering around the room. We found a piece of heaven there together, and as the hours ticked away, sorrows of the past were chased away, and the hurt we both shared began to heal.

He didn't speak much about his father, still unwilling to breach any loyalty to him, but he did begin to talk about his life in general, and from this I began to realise that he was far from happy. I offered that if he chose, he could come to live with me, but I made it clear that the decision had to be his. He said he didn't feel able to ask to his father, and so I didn't pursue it. I didn't want to lose any further opportunities to see him by appearing as if I was trying to take him away. Those two weeks were just the *best* time for the two of us, and at the end we parted with a new understanding of one another. On the day he left, I could see he was nervous and I read the question in his eyes. How will it be when I get home? My inner mind reminded me to let it go and trust that all things come right in the end, and so I did.

Patrick was usually ready to support me in new ideas. He was interested in the guides I saw for other people, and out of the blue one day, he innocently suggested that as I could paint portraits, and saw so many intriguing guides in my readings, why didn't I draw them? Another string to my bow was born, and before long, I was inundated with requests for guide pictures. My dear friend and fellow healer from Europe told all of her clients about me, and in the twinkling of an eye, my mailbox overflowed. I just needed a small picture of the person, and using psychometry, I could see their guide. Then I would sketch, and use watercolour, airbrush or pastels to finish the painting. I always wrote down any messages the guides gave me, as all kinds of guides from different levels came forward, including Guardian Angels, and to my amazement, Extra-Terrestrials! One a picture I got was of a man who was a bank manager, and when I tuned in to his photo, I was alarmed to see an alien figure standing there next to his guide. The ET stepped forward and said he would not move until I had drawn his picture. I asked what he was doing there, and this is what he said.

'There are many people from my planet who have come to observe the ways of humans. We want to take incarnation here, and it is our job to learn and report back to our high council. We are following the life of this man as one example of how you live your lives'.

I was shocked. How could I tell a bank manager that he was being watched by an alien? I summoned up my courage and did; I drew his guide as well, and he ended up with two pictures for the price of one. He was delighted! In all the dozens of pictures I painted for people then, five Extra-Terrestrials showed themselves, proving to me that there was far more 'out there' than I had ever realised.

I began to be in great demand, and was asked to go to Europe to give clairvoyant readings. It seemed as if the Universe gave me every opportunity to get what I wanted, providing I worked hard.

And, boy, did I ever work hard!

Amongst the many people that passed my way, one amongst them stood out like a shining beacon. A woman arrived at my door one day, asking for bed and breakfast. There was instant rapport between us and I felt like she could have been my sister. We were in the kitchen talking over a cup of tea, when she put forward an odd request. She was from America, presenting a slide show on Dolphins at a conference in town. Due to some unfortunate miscalculation she was short of money, and asked me if she could stay without charge. A bit taken aback, I thought for a moment, and to my surprise, found myself agreeing. I heard the words come out of my mouth, and just knew that it was ok. Once we had agreed, the woman then told me that she lived in Hawaii, and that she was a dolphin researcher.

'Come and stay with me anytime' she said. 'I would be happy to take care of you, and you can swim with the dolphins'.

Wow! What a thought. I dreamed about it, and decided that of all the choices I could have, this would be top of the list for incredible experiences. But how could I afford it? I couldn't! Determination began to burn inside me. Here was an experience not to be missed, and all I had to find was the airfare and money for food. My dogged desire to go grew stronger day by day, and I knew come rain or shine, I was going! I scraped together the money and before I knew it, I was on a flight to Los Angeles, my case bulging with newly acquired snorkel, mask and fins.

My old fears about the deep sea flittered in to haunt me, but I blew them away, too excited to care.

***

Entering another reality

The island was all I could have imagined. The heat was intense, and rainbows of tropical flowers showered down on me from around every corner. Joan's house was at the bottom of a steep hill, tucked inside the arms of a wondrous lagoon. The peace and tranquillity was overwhelming, and I had never before felt quite like this. Here was a kindred spirit who was like a sister to me, and to my surprise and delight, Joan had also had experiences with Extra-Terrestrials too. It was as if we were meant to come together, and all the hand of fate had to do was give us a nudge.

At the edge of the water, the house dipped its palm fringed toes into the lagoon and at six in the morning in came the dolphins, leaping and calling to us to come and play. This was another world! To get out into the bay, I had to follow Joan, swimming through a narrow passage in the volcanic rocks and out into the ocean. The first time I was so scared, they almost left me behind. I stood at the edge of the water with snorkel, fins and mask on, desperately trying to keep my balance as the waves swept in, turning up the ends of my fins with every movement. It was hysterically funny and frightening at the same time. Finally I took the plunge, and discovered to my delight that the water was so warm, it was like getting into the bath. Exhilaration coursed through my veins like liquid fire as I powered my way through the water, following Joan. The fins gave me so much speed it was easy to keep up, and before I knew it, I was half a mile out into the lagoon. The first five hundred yards had been an astounding revelation. Tropical fish of all description were everywhere. Yellow and blue, sporting stripes and spots, they swam underneath my body, nibbling at the coral and playing hide and seek with each other. Prickly puffer fish bobbed about with their tiny fins waggling around, making me laugh and shriek into the tube of my snorkel. I felt like a child again, swamped with the delight of all things new. I was so busy following my friend, I hardly noticed how deep the water was, and how far out we had gone. A mile out into the bay, I stood up on my fins, and treading water, took my first good look around.

Suddenly, there they were, carving sleekly through the blue right in front of me. Eyes down in the water again, I heard the calls and chirrups they made to one another in the back of my head. It seemed as if my ears were bypassed, with the sound registering straight into my brain. Whooping with excitement, a new reserve of energy filled me, giving the endless strength needed to follow them.

They were everywhere. There must have been at least sixty dolphins in the pod, cruising around, leaping with joy, passing under and all around me. Then a moment of magic was made. Three large dolphins swam straight at me, passed by my face, and looking directly at me. It was an unforgettable experience. The huge mammals seemed to speak to me with their eyes, asking me with curious gaze who I was. A flood of simple knowing came over me, and it was as if I had been privileged to look into someone's soul.

In the distance I could hear Joan singing to them, dueting with the songs they made. Daring to bare my soul, I joined in the aria as they pirouetted around me, nodding and singing in unison. I watched them play the leaf game, catching a palm frond on a fin or a tail, diving, and letting it go for Joan to retrieve. Unable to dive with her, I watched in awe at the intelligence of these beautiful creatures, unable to believe my eyes. They were actually playing games! Diving deep they blew rings of air into the water, coming up from underneath when the circle was big enough, and passing through it like hoops in a circus. They nibbled at the bubbles, nodding and laughing at the patterns it made. Baby dolphins put on shows of bravado, practising squiggly leaps and frantic dives, all the while their mothers close at hand. Herds of larger teenagers flew into the air in unison, showing off their prowess at jumps and spins. All around me I could see a parallel to humans with the same hierarchy at work within this pod. They were more than human; they were super intelligent with an undeniable consciousness, and above all they knew how to have fun!

What an experience!

We were in the water for over three hours, and it passed so quickly I didn't realise how tired and hungry I was. It was only when the dolphins disappeared as quickly as they had come that I came back to reality with a jolt. I began the long swim home, spying on the way a large speckled stingray. It was basking on the seabed as I swam past. Noticing my splashes, it began to head upwards through the water towards me. I knew that it carried a pretty hefty sting in its tail, and as a novice mermaid, I didn't know whether it was intent on attack or was just curious. I froze momentarily and held my breath. Lying motionless on the surface of the water, I waited, watching it as it came ever closer. What to do?

I was so relieved when it levelled off ten feet below me in the crystal clear water, and headed away. Now I really *was* eager to get back to shore, and swam on with adrenaline pumping my muscles into action. The entire holiday with Joan was more than I ever dreamed of. I found in Joan not only a new 'sister', but someone who understood the visions of ET's that I had seen. She confirmed to me that others around the world were seeing them too. We talked about Sirius, Andromeda, and Arcturus over cups of coffee at breakfast, and I learned that the gift I had that enabled me to see these wonderful Star Beings was precious indeed. During extraordinary meditations, beings from these places made contact with us, and I began to draw them. Always aware of my imagination and ego, I was testing in my contact, and asked for proof time after time. One moonless night, they gave me proof in a spectacular way.

We all went to bed early, as everyone got up at five thirty to swim with the dolphins. This night, I was in bed by nine, exhilaratingly exhausted after another day swimming in the lagoon. At five minutes to three, I awoke suddenly, checking the time on my bedside clock. There was a brilliant light outside. Only twenty feet away from me, I could see that this light had sharply defined edges, like a searchlight beaming down from above into the middle section of the garden. It stayed on for ten seconds, and then went out. A minute later, it came on again, repeated for ten seconds once more, and went out. The third time, the light stayed on for two minutes, before it went off altogether. I lay back in bed, wondering what it could have been. Was it a spaceship?

Suddenly, my bed began to vibrate gently. I felt waves of energy begin at the top of my head, gently sweep down the whole length of my body, and then back up again. Backwards and forwards it went in gentle rhythm, making my whole body tingle.

'I'm being scanned!' I thought, and smiling to myself, I knew somehow in my mind that it was safe. The whole thing was done in absolute silence. After a while it stopped, and looking at the bedside clock, I saw that it was three fifteen exactly.

The whole process, whatever it had been, had taken fifteen minutes. Sleep then overcame me, and I knew nothing more until the next day. When I woke the next morning, the final proof that it had not been a dream was there. My bed in the downstairs room was wedged up against an old doorway that was bolted from the inside. As I sat up to get out of bed, I saw that the bed was now six inches away from the wall, and the door was open! The vibrations must have shaken loose the bolt, and moved the bed as well. What other explanation could there have been? I felt honoured and incredulous that someone as ordinary as me could be here right now, experiencing these things.

Joan was excited when I told my story at breakfast. Being upstairs, she had slept through the night and not seen or heard a thing, but she wasn't surprised at all! Although I didn't know it then, Joan was to emerge as the major catalyst in the biggest events in my life.

10

A Dream Come True......

I have always been keen to use my gift of healing to help others. I worked part time for three years with 'hands on' healing for the NFSH (The National Federation of Spiritual Healers). One night during this period I had a remarkable dream that I remembered in detail, which was very unusual for me. I woke one morning with my head filled with information about how sound could heal people, and had the thought that if I could just find the right musical notes, I could make tapes for people, and they would be healed just by listening. It was frustrating because I didn't know how to go about it. There was never much time, and I hadn't a clue about the right electrical equipment to use for making tapes either. There was nothing I could do about it, so my dream was shelved in the recesses of my mind, waiting for the right time some other day.

Joan knew I was interested in energy healing and sound, and it followed that whilst I was in Hawaii she asked me if I would like to see a video about Sound and its uses for healing. I was intrigued, so I sat down in the lounge and turned on the videotape. What a revelation! On the tape was a woman talking about the very things I had dreamed of, and to make it even better, she was advertising that anyone could learn how to do this. She talked of miracle cures, and made claims of healing that were almost unbelievable. On the video were people testifying that they had been brought back from the jaws of death and had been helped with Sound when surgeons and doctors said they could do no more.

I leapt up from the chair and rushed into the kitchen, calling to Joan that this was the most incredible thing I had ever seen. Joan just smiled and then laughed with joy at my child-like enthusiasm.

I'm going to find out about this', I yelled at the top of my voice, 'I knew there was a way, and either this is the biggest con trick I have ever seen, or it's the most amazing thing since sliced bread!' We fell about laughing with one another, but the seed had been planted now, and its growth was to be one of the most major events in my life so far.

The various flights to get me home took over twenty hours, and all through the long journey my mind was on overdrive, turning over all the events that had happened in the space of those amazing three weeks. Encounters with Dolphins and Extra-Terrestrials, Healing with Sound, being 'scanned' and more besides. What was I to do with it all when I got home? I made up my mind to write to the woman on the video tape in America, and find out all I could about this therapy. The course to learn about it turned out to be very expensive, and the equipment I needed added even more to the cost. But I was determined, and I began asking friends and relatives to sponsor me, telling them that I would give them free treatment when I got home. This was just one of the ways I raised the extra money to get to America. Finally, after much hard work and an exhausting two-week period in Europe doing readings, I had almost all of the money. Trusting in the Universe, I had already booked my flight, even though the final total of money needed was far from there.

Then divine intervention came to my aid once again.

My closest girl friend Susan had promised to donate some money. No-one knew that I was still one thousand and twenty-six dollars away from my target, and I was beginning to worry that I would never find enough in time. Maybe Susan will sponsor me for a hundred pounds, I thought, but I knew that I would be grateful for anything! She phoned to invite me over for tea, and so I finished my chores and off I went, eager to talk about my upcoming adventure. We sat around a roaring log fire, drank tea and ate sandwiches. Susan then produced a letter from deep in her pocket, and asked me to open it. Inside the letter was a cheque for *One Thousand and Twenty Six US dollars*. How could Susan have known how much I needed, down to the exact dollar? Short answer.....She didn't!

With my jaw dropping at such a large gift, I asked how could this be? Susan smiled knowingly, and began to tell me an extraordinary story. Susan was a professional singer, and one year before had been on tour in America. There had been a mix up on one of the coaches, and one of her bags containing a lot of expensive clothes had been mislaid. She filed an insurance claim at the time, but had gone on with the tour and forgotten all about it. This cheque, which had arrived only two days ago, was the insurance payout from one year before! She explained that she had never expected to get it, and as it was in dollars, she wanted me to have it with love. We were both staggered that the cheque amount and the money that I needed were exactly the same. How can you explain something like that? It just had to be Divine Providence at work, and of course, the loving generosity of my very best friend.

I was absolutely sure now that this was a 'meant to be' trip. What I found there when I was training both amazed me and brought me to tears at times. I saw people responding to Sound Therapy within a matter of moments, often after years of pain and disability. I learned about sound as it relates to colour, voice analysis, spectrographs and waveforms, chemistry, biology, and diseases. My mind exploded with new knowledge that enthralled me beyond anything I had ever known before. I came home with a new career, and a new vision that was to take me far into the realms of healing and beyond.

My beginnings were wobbly, taking me *six hours* to work with my first practice clients from start to finish. Those who had sponsored me came first, and all of them generously allowed for the fact that they were acting as guinea pigs. My teacher had said that only when I could complete a session in an hour could I call myself proficient.

***

Everything changes

What came next brought me the most difficult learning years of my life. This was the biggest left-brain learning curve I had ever undertaken. For someone who dealt mostly with feelings and not logic, I found it slow going to grasp the basics of computer skills, and even harder to fit in all the necessary requirements that were needed for me to become fully qualified, such as learning about anatomy, chemistry, physics and more. I needed to build a 'Sound Studio' and this meant the sacrifice of two of the single bedrooms that were part of my business. I had to submit case studies to qualify for the second part of my training, and although I had plenty of people wanting to try the therapy out, it took up lots of my precious time, and there was still nowhere that was soundproofed that I could practice in.

All the while, Patrick was becoming less and less interested in the running of the place, needing to find his own niche in something other than making beds and cooking breakfasts. It was true that he enjoyed the extraordinary variety of people that came, but he was a quietly spiritual man, searching for his own path in life in his own way. His life had been full of trials and hardships, and he had at one time taken refuge in the quietude of life as a monk. He had spent four years before he met me tucked away in prayer and devotion, looking for his inner worth and seeking his own power. He was the saviour John had talked about, coming into my life and giving me strength to follow through with the divorce, and peaceful space to be myself. He had brought me heaven in stark contrast to the continual arguments that had epitomised my life before. But now he had begun to turn his thoughts elsewhere. We still had a loving relationship, but his restless need to be out in the world pursuing his own path surfaced time and time again. So it began that every year with unfailing regularity, he packed a rucksack and left to go travelling.

At first, he had said that he didn't know if he was ever coming back, and I was heart broken at the prospect of losing him. We talked about his leaving for days and weeks, making the pain even more chronic by his need to be understood. I knew his views on personal freedom, but it was a bitter pill for me to swallow. It seemed as if all my hopes for the teamwork he had promised me and the success of my dream would be dashed to the ground.

I suffered all of this in fearful silence, as I didn't want to face the prospect of being on my own. There was love between us, but he had taught me that to love someone meant letting them go if the need arises. He taught me that possessiveness and jealousy are born out of fear of loss, and I knew he was right, because in this life we must all face our fears, or they will come back again and again.

His plans that year were to head for Morocco, and when the fateful day came I watched him walk away over the hill with just one backward glance. Never knowing if I would see him again, I turned back into the house, and broke down completely. Only my closest friends knew about the situation. My girlfriend Susan stayed with me, wiping my tears and supporting me as only good friends can.

Two weeks later, I had a phone call from Southampton. There he was, telling me that he had encountered so much trouble that he just couldn't make it. He had spent all of his money, and he asked me if I would drive to the port and fetch him. I was shocked, overjoyed, and disbelieving all at the same time. We had little to say to each other during the journey home, and the uneasy silence was finally broken when he started to reveal all the difficult and outrageously testing situations he had placed himself in. I began to see that this was his innate way of learning, intrinsic to his very nature. He was seeking his own power, and the only way he knew how, was to test himself to the limit with reckless and dangerous adventures. Time after time, year after year, it took him nowhere. He taught me that all the answers are within the self and not 'out there', but couldn't see it for himself. For the first two days, I felt compassion for him. On the third day, I erupted with an anger born of the intense pain and heartache I had been put through. How could he do this to me? To tell me he was leaving, maybe forever, and then calmly turn up just two weeks later.

Before he left, he knew my heart was breaking, and he had still stood firm in his resolution to go. But his nature towards me became so soft and loving, and his story spilled out so full of hardship, that I couldn't help but listen and forgive. At that point, I had no idea that this was to become an agonising pattern that was to repeat itself year after year. I hoped one day to own the Guesthouse, and as things fell into place with my new found career in Sound Therapy, the possibility began to come closer. Unflinchingly sure of my need for this, I knew that now my old house was sold, I had enough money to put down a good deposit on the new one. With the help of a mortgage, I could maybe even expand a little. At the time, the property market had slumped, and the gap between the value of the house and the price I could afford inched closer. I put in an offer, and because the place now needed extensive repairs, it was accepted.

At first Patrick had been keen to support me in this, but when the crunch came for signing the mortgage, he could not bring himself to do it. He did not have the same commitment as I did, and at the last minute, backed out. He was still deeply unsure of where his destiny lay, and would not become involved in anything that could tie him down. As the business was flourishing I took this disappointment on the chin, and took the gamble of signing the papers in my sole name. With hindsight, I realised that this was actually a good thing, and taught me that I could make it in this world without the need to lean on anyone. I bravely decided to call in an architect and see what plans could be made to expand the building. If I was to have a workroom for my Sound Therapy and still be able to accommodate lots of people, I needed more space. Little did I realise that what started out to be a small extension would turn out to be a massive undertaking. The alterations yielded a wonderful result, but with disastrous consequences. The architect, who was full of grand ideas, proposed that as the flat roof leaked, it should be replaced with a new tiled roof, adding a top floor flat with a balcony. The old conservatory that had born witness to so many glorious breakfast times was to be demolished and a whole new corner added to the building. Then the car park had to be completely remade, and this started a ball of events rolling that never seemed to end. Being on the top of a steep hill, the house needed far more construction work than I had ever dreamed. The reinforcement of the car park alone involved hundreds of tons of earth being moved. In the end the builders had to make a reinforced concrete wall, twenty five by three feet thick and fifteen feet deep just to hold the side of the hill up! Whilst all this was happening, I had my 'Sound Room' built, and attempted to see my first 'real' clients. The continuous barrage of noise from the building works was deafening and made my first faltering steps with my new therapy very hard and somewhat embarrassing. So with a lot of the rooms out of action, my income dropped rapidly and I found I was struggling to make ends meet. A pressing tide of bills started to roll in; unpredicted extras to finish the house multiplied like rabbits, and I found myself in dire straits financially. It meant yet another trip to the bank manager, using my enormous enthusiasm and powers of persuasion to ensure I could borrow more money. When the final tile was laid and the last window installed the original cost of the improvements had doubled from forty five thousand to ninety.

It was all or nothing now and I set about working with a vengeance. The completed house looked wonderful, and the crowning glory was the light filled apartment on the new roof with its patio doors and spacious balcony. My house was the tallest building on the hill, and up there almost in the clouds, it felt like I could touch the sky from on top of a mountain. The panorama of sky was vast from up there, and day and night, called to me incessantly. Early mornings I would wake to the rising sun in the east, and hurry to the balcony with my camera to catch the beauty and glory I saw there. Like some sumptuous ice-cream, the heavens were rippled with raspberry and apricot hues, cocktailed together with the ice blue of the morning sky. Sometimes breathtaking mists enshrouded the entire landscape, weaving their ancient magic and leaving the lonely church tower on the nearby hill as the only visible marker.

Ah, but the nights captivated me the most. Wrapped up warmly with an unending supply of hot tea, I would set up my tripod and binoculars. Hour after hour I scanned the star-strewn skies hoping that some miraculous event would occur. In all the long cold hours I spent hoping for UFO's, satellites and shooting stars were my only companions. Lights in the sky were many, but I could never be really sure that they were who I hoped they would be.

***

Joy comes home at last

In August of that year, I flew again to America to finish the final part of the Sound Therapy course. The tuition wasn't difficult for me, but applying anything you have learned to *real* people is another matter. I was a bit better equipped now, and with many clients on my waiting list, I felt more confident in my ability to deal with people and their many problems. Armed with even more complex computer programs and trailing an extra suitcase to carry all the heavy manuals, I arrived home from the final training tired but elated. Patrick was there to greet me with his quiet manner and soft welcome, but as I began to recall my adventures, I could feel that his heart was always somewhere else.

The next day was busy and full, and still jet lagged from the flight, it was hard to tolerate the incessant ringing of the phone. Bookings for bed and breakfast overflowed, and the multitude of trivial requests I usually dealt with grated on my nerves. This month was one of multiple festivals and events, and thousands of visitors drifted around the town, floating in and out of the shops like wind blown blossoms on a pool. At teatime that day, there came a loud knock at the door. Tetchy and tired, I left the pile of ironing I was doing to answer the door. My transformation was immediate as I opened it wide to find my son Alex sitting sheepishly on an old battered suitcase. Heart leaping into my mouth, I grabbed him up and hugged him tightly; almost afraid he would disappear like an illusion. At first I was speechless, and I hung on to him, shedding tears of joy that he was actually there. Then came a torrent of questions as to what had happened, and over a cup of tea, he told me his story. During the months between our Christmas together and now, he had been desperately planning and worrying about his situation. His father often came home from work late, which meant that Alex fended for himself a lot of the time, getting his own meals and sometimes spending hours wandering around the town with his friends. Still not able to cope well with his father's relationship, he had gotten more and more stressed as time went on. He began to smoke secretly, and been caught out once or twice, and this had naturally caused a lot of rows between the two of them. Unable to stand the situation any more, he had finally plucked up the courage to ask his father if he could leave. Surprisingly, he had not met much resistance. His dad had said if that was what he wanted, then he could go. I was overjoyed and a bit taken aback with the suddenness of his arrival, and to top the situation, there was no room in the house for him to sleep, let alone have a room of his own. The whole of August was fully booked. Where was I going to put him?

Determined not to ruffle his already distressed soul by sending him back, I made a makeshift bed in my sound room, and he spent his first night there. All through that month, he was shifted from room to room, grabbing bed space as it became available. Space was made either from cancelled bookings or by juggling the sleeping arrangements around. I sweated over his welfare, and prayed that he would not feel out of place, or regret his decision to be with me.

Thus began a new stage in my life. My beloved son had come full circle and returned to me, but I was now faced with a set of different problems. The first became apparent when I saw how Patrick reacted to his presence in the house. Patrick was a kind man, and didn't make a fuss, but from the way he quietly withdrew, anyone could see that he was not happy with Alex around. In a way, it was as if he resented the attention I gave to my son, feeling somehow left out. His response was to go quietly to another room in the house and read, or sleep. Still happily taken up with the newness of Alex living there, it took me some time before the implication of this began to sink in.

At first, I was happy to have my son to myself, and didn't notice that Patrick was always missing. But then nowadays he usually was missing when the mundane chores were calling to be done. This had developed as part of his need to be somewhere else, and the new situation only served to strengthen it. For me, it was like being between a rock and a hard place. The four years I had been with Patrick had had its share of ups and downs, and now he was presenting me with a veiled choice between him and my son. He suffered too, as he loved me and didn't want to hurt me. He spoke of this many times, but as the time wore on, we realised that we were hurting each other with the very nature of the ties that bound us together. He knew that the business was too much for me to run alone, and felt duty bound to stay. On the other hand, he desperately wanted his freedom. He now barely tolerated the guesthouse duties and took every opportunity to opt out of responsibility. Entangled and confused about knowing the right thing to do, we spent the next four years dancing around this situation before either of us found enough courage to end the partnership.

When it finally happened, everything went with it.

Despite all my personal problems, my work as a Sound Therapist went from strength to strength. I wrote to a popular New Age magazine, sending them a video of the work along with an invitation to come and try it out. The editor was so taken with the idea, it wasn't long before he phoned me and a day was set for him to come. The meeting went so well that he stayed for ten hours.

I gave him a personal analysis, and by the time I delivered his sounds to him, he was as totally convinced as I was about the revolutionary potential of the work. He interviewed me in depth, and we talked on excitedly for so long over endless cups of tea that we became ravenously hungry and had to send out for fish and chips! It was fortunate for me that the article he wrote took some months before it was published, giving me time to get the building work finished and the house straight. It was a brilliant article, well crafted and delivered, and when the magazine was printed, the response was astounding. I was deluged with an avalanche of people wanting to try the therapy out. The mail arrived in sackfulls, and the phone never stopped ringing. Before a week was out, I was looking for a secretary. It was time for yet another big reorganisation!

11
Close Encounters.........

Then a wonderful woman came into my life and became not only my secretary, but a close and supportive friend. Synchronicity once again flowed for me, bringing us together in the street one day. I remembered Ann as a guest that had written to me some years previously from Australia, saying that she was coming to live in England and wanting somewhere to stay whilst she looked for a new house. Due to problems with timing, her stay never materialised, and she had come later, finding a new home in the same town as me. We knew each other in a casual way, but now this chance meeting had revealed the fact that Ann was in need of a job, and as secretarial work was her forte, we agreed to work together. Ann took the reins of the job with ease, and brought smooth organisation into my life. It was a truly exciting time, with its fair share of both difficulties and joys. The popularity of my work was so great that I was fully booked with appointments for seven months in advance, and still the phone kept ringing!

Life overflowed with both stressful and busy times, but was full of learning and plenty of humour. Ann was a marvel, helping me in my new role as a therapist to many different kinds of people. They came from all over England, and some even flew in from other countries to experience this amazing Sound Healing treatment.

I found out that Ann was also a healer, who gave massage and healing sessions in her spare time and counselling sessions to those in need. So began a new partnership that gave me the strength and support I needed to work the long hours that both the guesthouse and the Sound Therapy called for.

During a well-earned break one day, we were chatting over a cup of coffee and Ann told me that her ex husband had been a trance medium. Ann told me stories of the channelling sessions they had held, and I was intrigued that her life experiences had run almost parallel to mine. She talked about her own spiritual experiences, and out of this was born an idea that opened up a door to new and amazing knowledge for both of us. We spoke about the need to write down our experiences, but we both lacked the time and the discipline to do it. I told Ann about a message from the Extra-Terrestrials that I had had three years previously, in which they had asked me to write down their communications as a book. So the idea was born to meet once a week at Ann's house, sitting in meditation to communicate with the ET's.

The first date was set, and I arrived at Ann's house with a feeling of excitement and trepidation. I didn't know what was going to come, and in a way, I prepared myself for it to be a big non-event, realising that if my expectations were too high, I may well be very disappointed.

Ann had a lovely little house close to the Abbey. It was cosy and welcoming, with an open fire and ever ready pot of tea to be shared. There was a special room on the side of her house where she held her meditations. Going in, I was enveloped with the calm and peaceful atmosphere of the little room. There were crystals on the shelves, and comfy seats around a little table in the centre of the room that held a perfect red rose from the garden in a vase. The energy and aura of the room was perfect for the task that lay ahead.

On that first session, we sat quietly for a while with closed eyes, asking for our Spiritual Guides to be present. I felt myself going deeply into the altered state I was now so familiar with, and with a prayer from Ann, we began. It was decided that whoever felt first contact would be the one to begin. It turned out that I was the first to see the Extra-Terrestrial beings, and smiling, I realised that they must have known that *at last* their messages had a place in which to be delivered. I gave my greetings to them, and began to listen.

I told Ann I was talking to four beings I saw gathering around me. She turned on the tape recorder we had at the ready, and I began to speak. I recognised one of the Beings immediately, and he told me that he was from the Arcturus system. I had seen this ET before in Hawaii when I was visiting Joan, taking blissful time out to go swimming with the dolphins. Then, seeing him from a distance, I had drawn a picture of him. He reminded me that he was neither a 'he' nor 'she', but I used the term 'he' for convenience sake.

Mentally, I asked all of them all to come forward: the others said they represented Andromeda, Sirius, and Arcturus. There was also another being who was a little in the background. I couldn't see him clearly as he was standing in a bright light. The Arcturan came forward first to speak, and his tone of voice was friendly but very matter of fact. He felt to me as if he had a very concise 'no frills attached' type of personality, and he began to talk very quickly, as if he were dictating.

Arcturan: This world you live on is by far the greenest planet in this galaxy. The osmosis by which *we* live is similar to the chlorophyll absorption of your plants. We want to tell you that we are more 'sentient' beings than beings of five senses as you know them. The energy fields that surround us extend over vast distances, and we absorb our life sustenance from the energy in the air and the light given by the suns that our planet orbits around.

Then the Sirian came forward and said:

Sirian: We have a similar process, but there are times when we take a kind of food via the mouth. It consists of nutrients that are easily absorbed into our bodies. There is very little end product that could be thought of as unusable, and this is secreted through our skin. I am trying to give you concise and brief information about the difference between our physical make up and yours. This is because I understand the work you do, Elaine, and we know you are extremely interested in the physical make-up of your own humanoid form. We sometimes stand in fields of what you call 'cosmic rays'. We absorb these energy rays very easily; this is because particles of the light carrying frequencies of electrons, the electro-magnetic force, and tachyon energy lie within them. This revitalises our physical forms or any different bodies we 'adopt' at times. Even though we exist in a different dimension, we can still take on a kind of physicality for recognition and communication with one another.

It pleases us to be able to sit amongst the trees in bodily form, surrounded by sweet grass, flowers, and water; and to be able to communicate with one another in a pleasant way.

Ann: Can you change into different forms whenever you wish?

Sirian: Yes, we can change our energy forms at will. To put it in your terms, we can disappear into thin air, or change the shape of our form into anything we like. This could be a rock or flower, tree, or person. We take delight in doing this when we want to travel anywhere over long distances as a group. This ability also allows us to create our travelling ships around us, using the power this energy affords. We manipulate the energy forming a cohesive skin around us, and in this way our inner group energy is contained. We can then use the 'ship' as a vessel or container, which represents us as a whole. As a group consciousness we can direct the ship to wherever we want to go. Imagine dividing your mind or brain into sections. As a group, we form and come together within the ship like individual parts of one mind. One of us will become the directing force, one the sensing force, detecting what we pass through and the time/space we are in; others will regulate the energy of the magnetic fields. We all have an individual part to play, but come together to work as one complete unit. An easy example is this; imagine eating a meal. You do not think about all the tasks you perform such as chewing, swallowing, sitting in a chair or lifting a fork. It happens automatically as one combined action. This is how we work together as one. We can also take on whichever body form you think you wish to see us as. The way you see us now pleases us the most for the time being.

I took a breather for a moment, told Ann that I had seen these Sirian beings before, and said that all the beings that came from their particular planetary region were extremely tall. I described them as maybe 14ft (4 metres plus) tall, with a very light white, ethereal appearance. They all had large heads with the skull dipping in the centre from back to front; their eyes, radiating clarity and kindness, looked like human eyes although deeper set, and their foreheads were full and rounded out. They were wearing long light coloured robes, very wide at the shoulder, falling in pleats to the ground.

I was prompted to listen again as there was more to be said.

Sirian: We like to adopt this type of body form when we return to our own planet. Our energy fields can change to suit various dimensional levels - for example, seventh, sixth, and fifth. Some races living on our planet have a very humanoid form, and use physically solid craft in which they travel. They don't 'travel' the universe as you on Earth understand it; they time warp from one place to another by thought conduction. Your concepts on Earth of time and space are not totally correct.

I was intrigued by all of this, and I decided to ask him what would happen now they had come here to Earth. Why were they making their presence known, not just to me and Ann, but also to others around the world?

The Sirian spoke again, and reminded me that they had connected with me before. This happened on one occasion in 1992, when I was at my first guesthouse. That first time, he had come to give me teachings in story form and told me that they would be helpful as a teaching for humanity in general. I had written the stories down, but had not put them into any order. With the events of my life moving so rapidly, they had been forgotten until now. I felt a bit embarrassed at this reminder, but let it pass as the Sirian spoke again.

Sirian: We are extremely pleased that you and Ann have decided to come together. Our wish is that you put the messages we will give you together as a book. We want that the people of your world get to know who we are, and have an opportunity to learn about us. The representative from Arcturus is here on a somewhat different mission than ours; we have agreed on different agendas. His purpose here contains much more curiosity concerning the people of planet Earth, and he has a much wider spectrum of interest in the flora and fauna of the planet, including your wonderful dolphins. His group is spending more time with physical things, and are concerned with planet Earth and its condition, including the land and the atmosphere.

We from Sirius are more attracted to the soul aspect of human beings here, and we are here to try to help you learn about yourselves. We hope we can teach you about transmuting from one dimension to another. We can point the way, giving you instructions as to what you can do for yourselves in the future to make the way forward easy, but in truth, you must do it alone when the time comes. There have been times in the past when our friends from the Andromedan Galaxy have visited you Elaine, when you were much younger. Their primary interest is the brainpower and creativity of mankind, and they want to study the emotional concepts and feelings that everyone experiences on this planet.

The Andromedans say that studying Earth people is like being presented with 60 billion computers all working at different speeds and rates. Their interest is to find how you are expanding emotionally; to what extent your awareness and knowledge is growing within the physical and emotional cycle from birth to death. The Andromedans include reincarnation and the development of emotional purification in this, which is highlighted by the universal need to refine the emotions so none is lost, all are perfected.

Elaine: My attention was drawn now to the female in the group, and

I asked if this was the Andromedan woman that I had first encountered when I was three.

Sirian: Yes, the female you see before you now is the same being you saw as a child. She will speak to you later on the nature of emotions, and the capacity of the brain in both its physical and energy forms.

Momentarily stunned, I took a good look at the beautiful female standing in front of me. Here was the Lady in Blue that had given me the golden light of courage. Had she been watching me all my life in some way or other? Had she known how my life was going to turn out? Had they all been watching my life unfold like a book? Could the Andromedan have interfered in some way? There were a million questions I wanted to ask, and now I had the chance ask them all. As my mind took in the magnitude of the situation, the voice of the Sirian gently caught my attention again.

Sirian: I explained to you before about the nature of our bodies, and a little on how they function. Concerning osmosis, I must tell you that not all bodies function in this way. Some races that exist on other levels need nothing but light and energy to sustain their form, and on other levels they do not need to sustain a form at all. Only consciousness is present, and if they wish, they can take on any given shape or form at any time. We who encompass the seventh through to the fourth dimensions on our planet can choose (when interacting with other beings) which physical shape to take. We tell you that you too, as a race, will eventually be able to take more nourishment from energy rather than your normal food; beginning with solar rays, and the electro-magnetic fields that surround your planet, and eventually using a form of osmosis.

There are people on your planet now who are working towards this end. They eat only fruit, and some take no food at all. We understand that those people who live with only this kind of nourishment are finding it increasingly difficult to sustain themselves normally and still be part of the everyday life on this planet. A dimensional or consciousness energy shift of the body and mind is needed whilst doing this refining of the body. You cannot survive well in the density of third dimensional matter on fresh air alone, as you would put it. It is a very difficult thing to do, but as you make this shift and lose your density, you 'lighten up' in every respect, mentally and physically. You will find that you need less and less food, but you must ensure that you are selective in the quality and quantity of what you do eat. You will find that simply taking a walk by the sea, or being out in the sunshine, will nourish you almost as much as a full meal. This is something that we will teach you. There is much more energy inside, outside and around you than you could possibly see with your third dimensional eyes.

We hope that we can teach you how to begin to see things from a fourth dimensional point of view. Those of you who have developed the ability to see 'clairvoyantly', and are developing their spiritual knowledge to a higher degree are now beginning to see the edges of the fourth dimension as auras and energy fields, and also some of the things that occupy the fourth dimension.

Sight in physical terms is not the only sense that can go forward into the next dimension. You must learn to feel and expand your awareness much more than you do now. You exercise your intuition or inner knowing, and start to sense much more around you. Your sense of touch must be developed. Noticing energy fields and allowing your sensitivity to become more refined will start to develop a parallel existence for you. When you begin to develop these higher unused senses, you will become much more aware of the forces of energy around you. These energy fields exist everywhere, and just by walking along a road you will sense and know that you have possibly passed through a fourth dimensional building; or you may enter a green field and will sense that you are walking in fourth dimensional water. It is there but you don't see it as yet. Learn to feel it!

These extra senses are not limited to anyone with clairvoyant vision. They can be felt by everyone and can be completely adapted to encompass your whole being. Every single cell in your body knows when it hits an electrical field or an energy change. We know you have verbal expressions, such as 'my hair is standing on end', or you feel 'goose bumps' on the skin when you feel a change in the atmosphere. If you learn to extend all your senses as you walk along, you will encounter much more than you ever realised was there. This is another step forward into the fourth dimension. Once you realise that something *is* there that has not been perceived before, you can then begin to visualise it with your mind's eye. This will help bring it closer to you in a reality form.

I will now talk to you about what we call the 'eggshell of time'. Imagine a hen's egg, make it empty in your mind, and then expand it to the size of your planet Earth. See it as translucent, and I will try to give you a concept of time and space. On Earth, you are totally encapsulated in what we call an eggshell of time; it surrounds and protects the planet. It has been totally created by you for good purpose. As third dimensional beings it serves you well to have regulated time; it fits the complete pattern of what you have created for your own learning. Outside this 'eggshell of time', time and space is only relative to where anyone is standing in any given moment. Hold the image of this eggshell of time that you are in, and I will try to explain why people of Earth believe they have a past, present and future. This also includes past lives and future lives, and why time has been set up to function in this manner.

It is because of the nature of emotions, especially the two extremes of love and fear. I include hate with the word fear, as fear usually produces a reaction of hatred or violence of some sort. Love and fear are like two ends of a pole. These are emotions with massive energy and potential; in order that they are not radiated out all over the galaxy unchecked, causing ripples in the time/space continuum, you yourselves created this shell as a safeguard. Eons ago a higher source of knowledge was used to do this, and so no indiscriminate effects could be let loose to harm those planets around you.

This eggshell of time around your planet acts as a constraint for the more violent aspects of the emotional fields you generate, and which you are immersed in. This was set in place as a safety precaution, and we thank you for it. Without it, multiple repercussions would be felt throughout your solar system and galaxy. Yours is a very powerful planet which generates an incredible amount of energy, and so this shell acts as a buffer zone. It helps and protects you, and also serves to shield all other beings and life forms in other places. However, to live on Earth is very desirable as the emotions held within the energy fields teach us many things.

It is essential for all dimensional life forms throughout the known galaxies to have experienced the nature of planet Earth at least once. Because of its rawness, beauty, and sometimes extreme danger, all beings can experience multiple emotions found in the symphony of an Earth life existence; we must all gather every emotion for ourselves as an experience, then we are able to recognise and understand your feelings when we speak with you. If we had not had this experience, we could not relate to you adequately.

Some of us have spent many lifetimes here simply because of the joy we experienced; many extremes of emotion can be gleaned from spending time on your beautiful planet. When we talk about our experiences, we refer not just to those with western man, but also to those with indigenous people who inhabit the natural environment. I speak of Pygmies, Aborigines, Red Indians; indeed, all native people who feel their connection to the Earth deeply.

As people living close to the Earth, they are genetically more familiar with the type of sentience that we have. In their need to grow, western men and women have clothed themselves with many layers of problems; for example the monetary system and the pressing need to grow ever bigger and better. Civilisation in its race for technology, functions using external computers and machinery to communicate. Indigenous people use their senses to a greater extent and there is an innate wisdom within their communications. Half of you have technology but those with awareness who live closer to the Earth hold the wisdom. You cannot have one without the other, which is why it is important for you to recognise each others value.

Beings from other solar systems sometimes choose to be close to, or to incarnate within, the bodies of these native people. They spend entire lifetimes in jungles or on desert plains close to the Earth, seeking and finding the intense emotional joy that can be felt there. The knowledge of both the planet and personal awareness that can be gained this way is a wonderful experience.

We have also occupied many other bodies within different cultures. This is to try and understand the logic you find in war, why you need to revere money as a God, and what you are actually doing to release yourselves from this situation.

We can see - which is why we are here - that you now want to learn how to change from these patterns of thinking. Many of you have asked why we are here. We have come to teach, illuminate and assist. Not to hold your hand and pull you through to the next dimension, but maybe just to turn a light on in the 'darkness', so that you can see clearly what you need to do, and where you need to go.

I felt now that the Arcturan was impatient to talk, but I didn't know if the Sirian had finished talking. I could also see the Being that was enveloped in a bright light, and I felt I recognised him, but didn't know from where or when. Suddenly, the urgency of the Arcturan vanished, and this 'light being' stepped forward to speak to me. He was a tall thin willowy being with a large head and glittering almond shaped eyes that shone as black as the night. They radiated a presence filled with love and compassion, and reminded me of the beings from the film 'Close Encounters of the Third Kind'. He wore a long robe that glowed with a bright luminescent light, and as I looked at him, I began to feel very strange. His telepathic thoughts penetrated deeply into my mind, creating an incredible wave of peace and calm within me.

Light Being: We first came to you when you were two Earth years old. We did not wish to harm you, and so did not place any device in you to track your movements. We have, however, monitored you with common consent since that time.

I come now to speak of this, as now it is coming-of-age time, when the reasons for our presence will be made known to you. We were on a craft high in the distance, watching your contact with one of our beings, when you were 12 years old. The flower that was given to you was a token of our gratitude that you had undertaken to assist us in this manner.

Elaine: My mind was filled with fondness as I remembered the little being I had encountered in my beloved forest. The memory of that hot sunny afternoon lying on the stone by the river flooded into my mind, and a wave of love enveloped me, thinking that at last they had returned as promised.

Light Being: We have studied your biochemical system, and have all the information on how your particular body functions. We know your blood type, your chromosome patterns and your DNA; we are interested in your potential to assist us as a human being. Our repayment to you is that you will be enabled to assist your fellow humans in this world. By your actions, you can choose to make a waveform that will ripple out and touch as many people as you need to touch. We have promised you some technological information, and in due course, step by step, we will reveal to you all that you need to know.

Elaine: A bubble of excitement grew inside me now, as I realised that this information could be to do with my work with sound. What if I could find some miracle cure? What if I was given the technology to help millions of sick people? The thoughts began to race away within my mind, and I quickly calmed myself in order hear the rest of his message.

Light Being: All things, as you have realised, are synchronistic. There are no happenings by chance. But not all events that have happened in your life were pre-destined. Allowing for fluctuations in your emotional field, most things that you have accomplished so far and most emotional states of being you have experienced have been previously agreed on. You are due to return to us shortly, although you will not be conscious of this. The purpose will be for integrating new experiences and opening your memory. New sections of the knowledge that we gave you earlier in your life will be released.

I know you remember the Andromedan you saw when you were three years old. But what is not in your conscious memory is that we were the first ones to make a 'contract' with you. The Andromedan beings were interested in what we were doing, and joined us in our project. We agreed on a partnership, and as a group we have shared an interest in your progression, as well as our other projects involving the Planet Earth.

The spiritual guides that have been with you over the years are fourth dimensional beings, who have spent many lifetimes incarnating within the eggshell of time enclosing your Earth. Over the last three years the two guides most known to you have been merely holographic representations, and not physical entities. It was enough for you to have only the images, and I know you felt they were not as tangible as they were in earlier years. I will conclude by saying that as a group, we *all* have information to give to you. One by one we will come and give our thought forms and energy to you; write it down and give it to others for learning. Information for your personal work and research will come. This is the technology that we promised to give you when we first encountered you. This is the exchange we give to you for allowing us to study you in depth.

With these words, his energy began to flicker and grow misty, and I saw them all fade into nothingness in my mind. It took a moment or two before I could open my eyes and focus on the room. This was just the beginning of the most detailed encounters I had experienced so far, and I couldn't wait to meet them all again. I wondered how they would take me to visit them. Was this possible? How I wanted to know about it and remember! It made me feel as if I had to be alert every minute of the day, just in case I missed something! But of course, I began to realise that out of the ordinary things can happen in the twinkling of an eye, and in a busy life, can go entirely unnoticed.

Ann and I breathed deeply in unison, acknowledging the vast output of energy the Extra Terrestrials had used in making this amazing contact. Then we burst into giggles and words of amazement as we realised what we had just heard. We got up and left the room, heading straight for the kitchen and a nice hot cup of tea. We were both incredulous at the content of the contact, and Ann promised to type up the whole hour so that we could read again what had been said. It was time for serious thinking here. We both knew that this was important information, and the thought that there could be much more where this came from excited us both so much, we were in fits of laughter and hugging each other for joy.

I drove the short distance home and began to wonder at my life. How had all these things come about in a life as ordinary as mine? It was true that I was not quite the same as many other ordinary people, having had the gift of clairvoyance most of my life, but still, I had followed the same route as most, been married, had children, cleaned house, worked for a living. How was it that I was getting these messages from beings that said they came from another world? I had heard plenty of stories about close encounters, had seen the films and read the books. But here was the real thing, presented to me like dinner on a plate, and I knew it was so real and not in any way imagined.

Over the years, life has given me a down-to-earth grounding in the ordinary and everyday things that we all experience. There is nothing unusual about that, but this? Who would believe me? Would Ann and I be labelled as just another couple of cranks with their heads full of imaginings? If I turned it all into a book, how would these things be received? Only time would tell, so I decided to put my trust in myself and plough on regardless; maybe there would be some information that could help me to help other people. If this were true, then I would go on until I found it.

***

Life raced on, with the unending round of guests sprinkled with my popular trips into the Wiltshire countryside to see the Crop Circles. Now *there* was a phenomenon that was amazing to see! People from all over the world came to see them and I really enjoyed any excuse to take a day off and visit the beautiful messages in the grain. Everyone wanted to know how they were made and whether or not they were hoaxed. I believe that some are made by hoaxers, but most of them defy imagination, and studies done on them gave me reason to believe that they were made by some unknown force. I knew in my heart that it was the Extra Terrestrials who were doing them, but at that time, no-one knew for sure. Patrick sometimes did the trips himself, and drove the space cruiser car that I owned. He went to Stonehenge and the surrounding vales with the famous white horses carved into the hillsides and had good days and bad days. Sometimes if the group was noisy and full of fun, he would arrive home harassed and worn out. He got on better with quieter more spiritual people and enjoyed being with them, helping them with quiet meditations to feel the energy generated by the ancient stone monuments and the shining circles. He was keen UFO fan, and took an interest in the nuts and bolts of physical sightings to an extent that he became the one to talk to when someone wanted to see a UFO video from my extensive collection.

There were some good films made on the history and legends of the surrounding area, and this was part of the attraction of the centre for many who visited over and over again. I began to reap the rewards of my hard work with the Sound Therapy, as more and more people reported back to me that they were becoming well again. I dealt with many tough cases, especially those with serious problems such as being confined to a wheelchair, or being unable to live a normal life because of their illness. Ann was always stalwart throughout, and kept the wheels running smoothly despite the stressful situations that always seemed to be standing on every corner.

The highlight of the week for me now became the meetings at Ann's house, and the second meeting brought us to a closer understanding of why this was happening, and what the messages were all about.

The Andromedan Female as I first saw her.

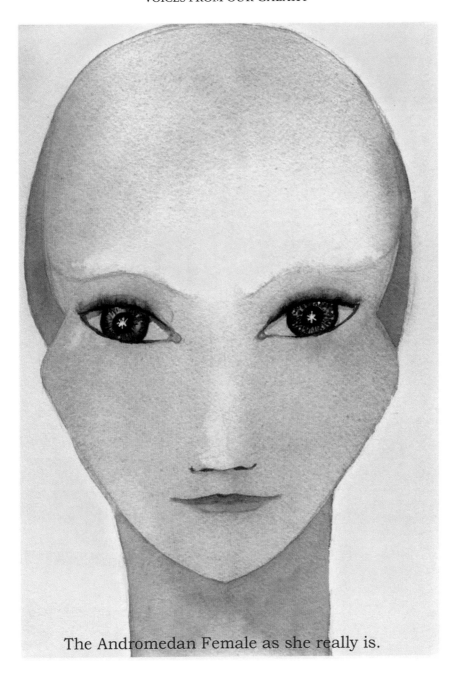

The Andromedan Female as she really is.

The Andromedan Female as she really is.

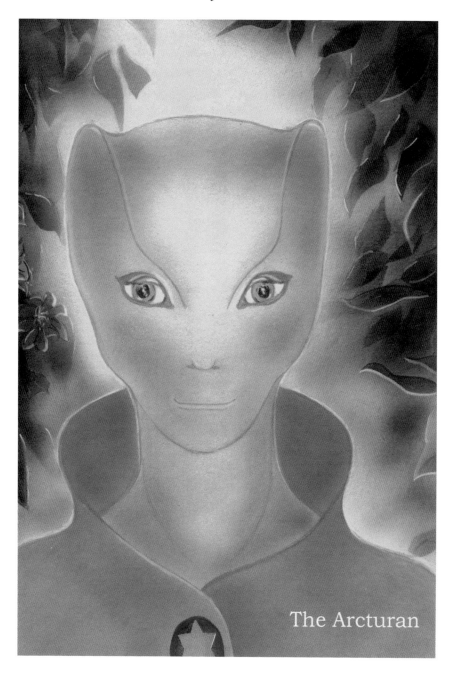

The Arcturan

The Arcturian Botanist

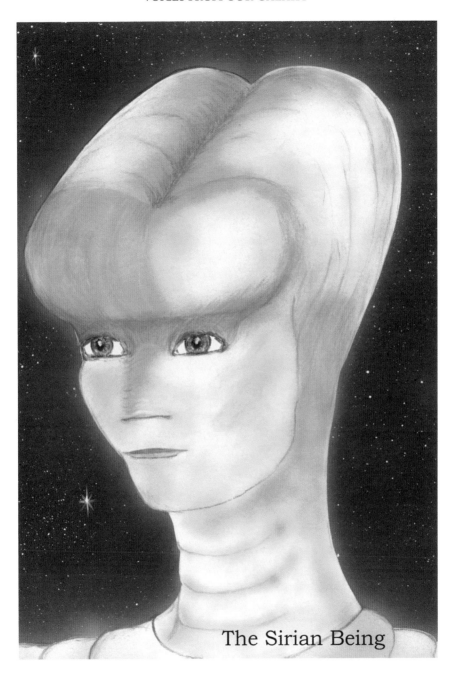

The Sirian Being

The wise Sirian teacher.

The Aquatic Being

The powerful Aquatic Being.

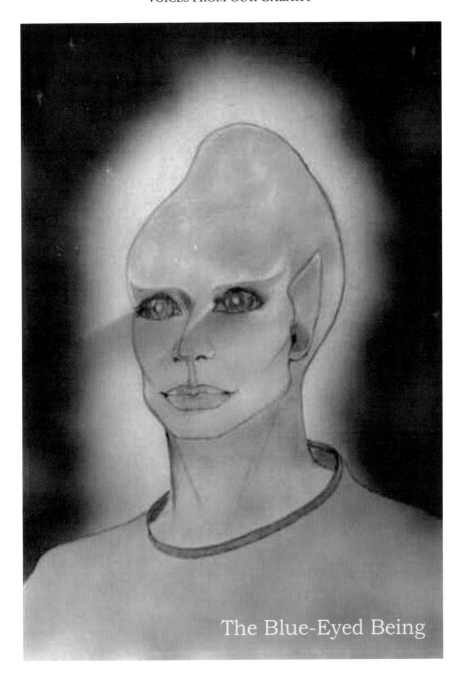

The Blue-Eyed Being

The creator of multi-sensory experiences with music.

The Reptoid Being

The Galatic Explorer.

Home City of The Reptoid Being

Home city of the Reptoid beings.

PART TWO

The Transmissions.

This is the collected work of the transmissions received by me over a period of eight months, together with my good friend Ann. It is given as received in weekly chapters, and ends with 'A trip to Sirius', which was written in 1992.

12
The Next Meeting.......

A t eight-thirty on the second Wednesday evening, I found myself preparing for whatever communication might come. In a way, I half expected it to fizzle out at this point, and I had had worrying thoughts that maybe there would be nothing to be received. To our joy, the contact was once again as strong.

Sirian: Tonight, we will speak about the Andromedan Council. The reason will be made apparent as we go on; we want to make it really clear that there is a place where the Andromedan Council regularly hold their meetings.

At the moment, there are one hundred and thirty six representatives from all parts of the galaxy who meet to sit around the Council Table. It is presided over by a being we call the Elder, who maintains the energy of prevailing peace in the Council Room. On either side of him sit seven other members of great standing; they hold the qualities and key attributes of wisdom and great experience, and help the Elder mediate over both the problems and joys that are brought to the Andromedan Council Table.

There has been a great deal of concern and debate over planet Earth for some considerable time now. The issue has been about the vibrational emanations you have been sending out into your atmosphere. We understand that you do not realise the extent of damage that is being created; the most destructive vibrations being from nuclear detonations, and also from discordant frequencies that are being emitted from your people - the consciousness. Some of this conscious energy is positive and some negative, and therefore not in harmony. This makes a hubbub of distressing unbalanced vibrations from the planet that spread across the galaxy.

Please understand that vibrations once created and given form, do not simply disappear, but go on for a great deal of time and can eventually touch other systems. This can be shown by comparing the huge influence that the other planets in your solar system have on planet Earth. These planetary vibrations are finally absorbed or used by other levels of being. For example, when a sound hits a wall that is permeable, the vibration passes into, and is absorbed by the wall. It may pass through the other side, but the essence of the vibration is read and understood within the wall. So we have been reading and understanding the thoughts and frequencies emanating from your planet, and seeing very clearly that you are dividing into levels of consciousness. Some of you are beginning to understand the beauty and grace there is in positive thinking. Some also understand the different dimensions and realities of life, but there are a large number of you who do not.

It was decided some period of years ago in Earth time that we should come closer to your planet; many representatives of the Andromedan Council have been to Earth in their individual ships from their own home planets, making personal observations. Individual and group reports have been made, as to what has been seen. I see what springs into your mind. You are picturing the analogy of an elephant surrounded by five blind men; each touching the elephant in a different place, and none finding the same thing! I understand your concern. We have heard many different reports about the nature of the planet, including the kind of reception that the various emissaries received, and the observations they made.

I must also include here that there are some races from outside the Andromedan Council that have also been visiting Earth for other reasons. We have come to the conclusion that if a big enough percentage of you on this planet want to make positive changes to your way of living, and are mentally asking for some assistance to make this change, then we must help.

We know very well that many of you now recognise, although not always clearly, that we are here. The impact of actually accepting our presence and experiencing us in the flesh is vastly different to just believing that there is 'life out there' in the universe. Mental communication is very different to a face-to-face meeting. Although we have not totally made our designs known to you, you must understand that we will try to be of as much assistance as we can.

I speak now in the capacity of general spokesperson for the majority of the members of the Andromedan Council. Not all of us agree; some members feel that a stronger more direct approach towards people is necessary, and other members feel that the actual planet should take priority, and that the population should be left to their own devices without interference. This has presented a problem to some, as there are those of us who see with love only the souls who are here, and some do not recognise this as the first priority. We see your souls as kindred spirits who are all part of the same universal energy that pervades all galaxies, and we believe your inner mental call for help is of paramount importance.

Under the according laws that we work by, we must come to your aid, and indeed, we are very glad to do so. I will add, however, that for the most part it is not an easy task to give assistance in an intelligent and comprehensive way to beings that actually exist in a different dimension. The whole plan must be approached with exceeding delicacy, which is why most of our communication has been telepathic. We have selected to bring our messages to those who are capable and who choose to do this job. We understand that these messages do not reach the whole of the planet, only a small percentage, and so as a result there is a division in consciousness and sometimes misconceptions as to who and what we are exactly.

There are different stages of realisation occurring and an almost parallel reality is being formed. If this division continues to grow, the third dimension will continue with certainty, but the fourth dimension, which has been closed to you as a population in previous times, will then be more accessible. I do not mean easily accessible, but *more* accessible than it has ever been in your entire history; and by this I mean the history of this present civilisation and not previous civilisations that have inhabited this planet.

This will mean various things; there will be difficulty for you in trying to change the nature of your reality. For example, I select from your mind the story of Moses parting the water. If you want to create a channel into the next dimension or reality, you need to part the waters of the reality you exist in now, and walk forward into the new. Whilst you walk this pathway towards a new reality, the existing reality continues on all around you. We ask you to trust that it is this way, and that with our assistance you may begin to utilise other areas of your brain and recognise the signals as they come in. Use them and your other senses to detect the changes happening around you.

There are many cultures represented in the Andromedan Council, and the Pleiadeans wish urgently to say they are well represented, with more than twenty members from different parts of their solar system. They are as many and as varied in their solar system as you have races upon the Earth.

Elaine: And now the Light Being wishes to speak for a moment. He is the tall, willowy Extra-Terrestrial that has been with me before, and I believe we can call him a Lyran.

Lyran: I come to you bringing only love, so please be assured and comforted in your heart. Strange things may occur in the future, and to some people they will be frightening, and their fears will be brought to the surface. *I speak for all of us*: Please know that we come only with love for this planet and its inhabitants.

We send love and concern that there will be no more death, no more war, and that raising of consciousness occurs worldwide. This is so you can really know and understand that the Great Creator, who is the Source of us all, is within and without every one of you and every one of us. In this way we are all the same flesh, even though we appear in different forms. If you will allow us, we will counsel you along the way; we will give written material to help people understand that the path forward can be easy. In your terms we will light the way, and we hope in your future, as you call it (for us it is all one time), that we will interact with you on many levels.

As the time approaches (in your time), you will see that instead of the fearful abduction scenario that has been created by certain factions, we can and will begin to demonstrate that we can indeed speak to you face-to-face. Remembering that we can speak best in the telepathic form where there are no hidden agendas, and no lies. You will feel and know rather than hear what our intentions are. We would like to select from all around the globe those who would come to us to be taught that they may be your leaders. Not to dominate, but for them to teach you in your own language what they know and what they have felt and understood from us.

We are trying in as many ways as possible, via your right-brained perceptions, to access your understanding, so we can let you know what our message is. We have all taken part in the formation of the pictorial circles (viz. crop circles), and in them are given messages on many, many levels. We are purposely (because we understand the nature of your consciousness) not writing in the crops, 'hello we are here!' We are trying to present information in a right-brained, feeling way. So you must allow your emotional feelings and intuition to understand these messages. Were you to try and understand them logically, the meaning and the breadth and depth of what we represent would be lost.

When we sat around the Andromedan Council Table we all discussed amongst ourselves what part we could individually play in introducing ourselves to your various cultures and peoples without unnecessary fear; the primary reason for this being that we look different and perhaps strange to you. We would like, and I repeat, without unnecessary fear, to introduce all the different species and races that fill the many universes to you.

Humanoids on planet Earth all have two arms, two legs and similar features, albeit your colours are different. Our forms from across the universe, (and this is only one universe of many), have taken on many different shapes and sizes. We adjust our bodies to suit our environment and some of us can change and take on any form we require.

So my message is one of gentleness and love. Deep love and respect for the whole of humanity, because we uphold your planet as a wondrous creation, full of beauty and diversity, and something that must be cherished.

Elaine: And now the being from Sirius speaks again.

Sirian: We are concerned with your education. We will bring you teaching and knowledge of the different levels of reality that there are. Some of your concepts are very restrictive. Your ideas about time and space once you are outside of your planet's atmosphere are indeed not applicable. If you wish to travel the galaxies with space flight you need to understand the laws that govern the physics of the universe. Some of your scientists will be astounded when out of the mouths of absolute 'laymen' come the answers many of them have been searching for, for hundreds of years.

It is not always the best way to present things, but as my friend previously said, it is extremely difficult to approach anyone telepathically unless you access the right brain, and your scientists tend to function mainly from logic. However, some of your greatest stars, the geniuses amongst you, function from a central brain in which they allow streams of information to flow in, and use both hemispheres to solve problems.

Our teaching will come pictorially and telepathically. I hope to give you some pictorial examples which will illustrate the nature of the different dimensions; the nature of cause and effect and the creative powers of the mind. Included will be the nature of realities, and I say in plural because every second, and every breath is a reality in its own right. Every person on your planet has a million realities every day. They all tend to follow in a certain stream, and I understand even now that you are beginning to discover the larger concept of what differing realities means for yourself.

Elaine: Is there anything else that needs to be said this evening?

Ann asks a question to the Lyran. He is so beautiful and really surrounded by light.

Ann: It would be interesting to find out if there are several different types of 'greys'.

Lyran: Yes, there are, and these are our children. They are alive and they are real, but they have been genetically constructed. Not (I feel as you ask) as a slave race, but to help us with those things that need to be done with more manual dexterity than we can achieve. We, as the Elders, function much more from a 'feeling' perspective, and they as our children are the 'doers'. They do things for us and we love them for that. We appreciate them - that is more the correct word - and there are various types.

There are those who you call 'grey', and there are those with a lighter coloured skin, almost the same shade as your human skin. These we imbued with more feeling, more conscious awareness of love and compassion. There are also taller beings. The 'grey' ones we speak of are the ones who in your measurements are three to three and a half feet tall. We have amongst us a group of taller beings. Some may be four feet six inches, going towards five feet tall, and their faces are a little bit more humanoid than the little 'greys' that you are familiar with. They do not have the capacity to be violent; they only follow our instructions and do what is necessary.

Ann: I remember seeing once, on a ship, a tall being who was wearing a dark coloured robe - purple or blue - who seemed to be in charge of these smaller grey beings. Do you know of these? These ships were said to be abducting humans.

Lyran: The taller robed-being is like a parent. They come with their instructions, and no harm is ever intended, but some of the things we do are necessary. If you could see the probable future of your planet, with the possibility of sterile people and the end of your race, you would understand why we need to collect eggs and sperm from your males and females. We store them in banks, and also use them for our own genetic experiments. We are trying to produce a more humanoid being than the little greys, and what is more important, is that one day you will see that these banks will save the continuation of the genetics for your species on this planet.

The destructive forces that are happening here on your planet are only noticeable in a minor way now. During your experiments with chemicals and technological constructions, there are bound to be things that you spoil along the way. Things that are of no use, things that you would have wished you had not created. We too, have been through this stage of creating things that were non- functional or deficient in some way.

With your use of chemicals, additives, pesticides and other things that you feed yourself with, you are changing yourselves and your biological structure. You do not see the genetic damage you are doing to yourselves; so to those of you who *do* realise that everything has a greater purpose, you can see that we do what we do from love; but many still see it as threatening.

We have debated strongly in the Andromedan Council over this method of obtaining samples for the reproduction your species, and it was argued that it was interference and should not be allowed. We put to the vote that as a species in third density, you are worth saving. Forgive me for this term, I do not speak in a belittling manner, but we needed to do this for your sakes. We see that sometimes when you teach your own children, you hold them tightly and they struggle and scream when they would perhaps run across a road. When you know that there is danger, you do things that sometimes the child does not always like, for its own good. If you can see, please, our point of view, you will understand that this is why we do what we are doing.

This is only one aspect of the big plan to aid your planet, as some of you will not need physical bodies in later years. Some of you will end your journey in the fourth dimension before you go on to other things, but there will be those who will stay third dimensional. For them, life could be difficult without our assistance. There could be much disease and sickness, and eventually the cessation of the humanoid form as you know it, and this unfortunately was not part of the original plan. Earth has its unique place in the third dimension. You experience so many wonderful feelings, to lose the physical body and its genetic inheritance, would be a great waste. The uniqueness of this vehicle into which a soul can enter to learn is so precious to all of us that we are attempting to provide a fail-safe for future generations.

Elaine: I am now being taken back to the Andromedan Council room. The being that sat at the head of the council table was from a planet that was very ancient in its history. They tell me that there are only five of them left now, but as a race in times past, they concentrated their energy inwards to such a degree, that their whole consciousness and form was melded together. They had almost disappeared as a race, and they uniformly created these five beings that hold the entire energy of all of them. They are extremely wise, vastly knowledgeable and ultimately peaceful beings, one of which presides over the Council and leads the debate. This is necessary because not all around the table can agree; and all members have differing opinions coming from their own angles and perspectives.

Members come from different planets and different solar systems, and I saw that there were about twenty Pleiadeans represented there, who all look very different, representing different factions of their solar system, like a United Nations. They all have an interest, and they all wish to preserve planet Earth, but they all have different agendas.

To summarise: The Arcturans are more interested in the biology of our planet. In that context, they would not feel they were doing anything wrong to come here and 'take' anything of a biological nature for their own needs. They take great interest in 'seeding' other planets with flora and different life forms. The Lyrans are interested in the quality of the soul; their essence towards us is more parental. The Sirians come for educational reasons, as they wish to teach us as much as we are willing to learn.

13
Our World is a Garden.......

To begin our session tonight, we mentally welcome all guides and Extra-Terrestrials, and asked them to come and speak with us.

The being from Arcturus arrives, and tells me he wants to speak about the biology of planet Earth. He mentions the flora and fauna, weather systems and clouds, and the unusual weather patterns that we have been experiencing all over the world over the last few years.

Arcturan: Our interest focuses mainly on the nature of living things; biological entities, (people and animals) trees and flowers, and the very substance of the Earth itself. We find this fascinating because of the enormous variety that proliferates here. On some other planets there are equal amounts of plants, flowers etc, but they are of a different dimensional state. There is not, (to the same extent), the diversity of animals, insects, or reptiles that you have here. Similar planets are plentiful in the universe, but here on Earth in this wonderful 'garden', there is so much material for us to study.

We have rescued many species of animal and plants, and have been doing so since the time of the dinosaur. This includes many familiar species, and some you have never seen. Other worlds need to be populated; other worlds are like your original concept of the 'Garden of Eden'. They have yet to become full of life. Did you never wonder why, suddenly, the Earth was abounding with dinosaurs; huge mammals of gigantic proportions, and suddenly birds that flew in the air? We are partly responsible for helping to populate the Earth with those various creatures.

We did not do this in the same way as you place animals in a 'zoo' habitation; we utilised planet Earth as a free roaming space in which these animals could develop and grow. The same applied to the plants and flowers. During our travels we gather and plant; we take from one system, and carefully introduce into another. We are like botanical alchemists and we love to see things blossom and grow in harmony and balance under universal law.

I will approach a subject that may raise controversy amongst you. Many aeons ago, we were partially involved in the genetic engineering of human biological forms. This was when humanoids were initially seeded upon the Earth. We did not have an entirely free hand, as there were other races with more technological advancements in genetics than we have taking the prime directive. But nevertheless, we did assist to a certain degree. We are here now, and have been here periodically throughout 'time' (as you know it), to see the results of our labours; and also to observe how, ecologically, which genetic tendencies have survived and which have not.

We are observing the mutations that have come from our 'seedings'. It is extremely interesting to us to watch how things grow and develop, especially amongst the human element on the planet. We have watched how your mental, emotional and spiritual capabilities have developed over the centuries, and in the time we are reaching now, we are fulfilled to see that there is a 'blossoming' in the consciousness of the human race. This work is the continuation of an ongoing project that began as a seed our ancestors once planted, and has taken many thousands of years to bloom. We are happy to be here at last to witness this time. Now is truly the beginning of the blooming of consciousness on the planet. Not all are developing at equal speed, however. As in a field of randomly sown flowers, some develop into prize blooms, and others do not do so well. Metaphorically speaking, personal development depends on the 'soil' of circumstance you choose to be planted in, and the 'nutrients' of learning and choice you receive.

For example, I illustrate again with the human entities here on Earth. As you realise, you are both physical body and energetic soul. If a genetic line has received enough good 'nutrients' over time to the generations of bodies that carried it; if emotional lessons are learned well by the souls inhabiting those bodies to promote soul growth, then you will indeed be blooming in expanded conscious awareness, as you should.

I also would like to speak about other intelligent species that dwell on the planet, in the oceans. These mammals are of course, the dolphins and the whales. This is a civilisation that has been inherent to your planet for many (past thousands) of your years. They have always had telepathic ability to connect both with themselves and with us. This means that they not only communicate with each other underwater but also into the different dimensions to reach beings such as those gathered here tonight.

They are more closely related to the Sirian beings than to us (from the Arcturan system). Nevertheless we have been allowed full access to observe and talk to them, and to study their behavioural patterns. We communicate telepathically with them so we can understand and participate in their joy for living, and their complex family units. Through them we have been able to see and understand the flora and the fauna underneath the oceans. Through them we have been able to study and understand the habits and lifestyles of many of the underwater creatures. So they have been, and still are, our allies and friends.

As far as the whales are concerned, you should realise that they are complex beings that have great knowledge. Whales have been present throughout history since the time of the dinosaurs. These special mammals have the capacity to feel through vibration, what happens both on the planet's surface and within the underwater terrain. They, in their dialogue with us, have confirmed our deepest feelings. We can see what happens on the surface of things. For example, we can see if a flower blooms or does not bloom. Whales are very much more deeply in touch with the rhythm of Earth, and especially the vibrations from the 'inner' Earth. They are in contact with the very 'rocks', as well as all the waters covering your planet, both inside and out. They have given us great depth of insight from their own particular level. This is a level we could attain if we wished, but one needs to be of a certain vibration in order to 'flow free' with this. So they have been of great assistance to us. They tell us that in the last six or seven decades there are strange vibrations coming from within the planet. This is partially caused by reverberation from the nuclear devices and atomic bombs that you have detonated; also from all the other forms of frequency such as is used in human communication. This encompasses radio and television broadcast waves, sonar, radar, and the microwaves that you use for various means. The consequences of some of these frequencies are not so pleasant. The whales are very much aware of this mass of discordant frequencies that passes not just over the surface of the Earth, but through the Earth as well.

We know that humans do not fully realise that these waveforms pass through the Earth as well as around it. When you apply audible and inaudible frequencies to a body of matter, it alters the vibrations within that matter, and things change! Things begin to happen; when you pass a specific audible frequency through humans for example, emotions will come up. If the Earth could be said to have emotions, they would be shown as Earthquakes, volcanoes, seismic activity, and tidal waves. These things are what the Earth is experiencing as a planet. This has been triggered by the amount of noise, frequency and vibration that you as a race of people have put into the air and into the ground.

We have been making attempts to harmonise and neutralise some of these sounds. We use, for want of a better term, what could be called 'acupuncture', at specific grid reference points on the Earth. You may be familiar with what are called 'Ley lines'; the electromagnetic grid that is around the Earth. We can use points within this grid to 'inject' harmonious frequencies; frequencies that will balance some of the unstable vibrations that are reverberating around inside of your planet right now. We do this in order to help preserve the body of the Earth. If we did not, there would be much more disruption and disharmony with volcanic eruptions and the shifting of the Earth's crust. It would be as it was in the beginning when the Earth was forming; when mountain ranges appeared from low lying planes and landmasses sank into the sea.

We are calculating frequencies to apply as rapidly as we can, in order to compensate for the vibrations that are being generated by you as a collective race. We know that you do not understand the possible damage that could occur. When we have full and open communication with you as a people, we will explain this in greater depth. If you wish, we can re-educate and give you technology that gives you all the things you need, if you want them, without causing so much disruptive damage.

Now, to come to the subject of the weather; there are certain areas of the Earth that are giving out unprecedented levels of heat. This in turn is causing massive cloud formations, precipitation and unusual weather formations. As I explained before, when something vibrates, or is subject to friction, there is internal movement and heat is created. The heat must be dispelled somewhere, so it is rising to the surface of the planet, and it is one part of the cause of the anomalous weather patterns that you have experienced around the planet. There are some things that we are finding very difficult to stop, such as the multiple volcanic eruptions, because they tend to follow a pattern, or chain reaction.

For example, if you had an unnatural frequency inside your body, it might manifest as a disease or tumour; things would be disturbed on the innermost level, and they would possibly erupt on the surface of your skin. Following the same concept, these eruptions on Earth are inevitable. However, we are trying to help you avoid destruction of human beings. When and where possible, we are salvaging flora, fauna and anything else deemed necessary before the eruption of a volcano, or any other natural disaster.

I see that you are thinking about electrical storms. These have always been a life creating natural phenomenon on your planet. Any increase in the intensity or size of storms is due to the temperature fluctuations that are happening in isolated areas. Whether it is beneath the ocean or on the land, the whole thing is intrinsically linked. When you experience periods of very hot sunshine and then suddenly a freezing hailstorm, this is the end result of the internal shifting, vibrations and friction happening inside the Earth. I will pause there for a moment, as I know there is a question from your friend.

Ann: I am interested in the way the weather is changing, with regard to internal vibrations of the Earth actually affecting what happens externally. As I understand so far, the Earth is being upset with our man-made vibrations, and affected by other sorts of energy that we have created in the atmosphere, which is passing through the Earth. So it is all interrelated; is it cause and effect?

Arcturan: Absolutely.

Ann: How can we put that right? I know that you are doing things to help. Is there anything that we can do as a race?

Arcturan: There is a way to have all your technology, and for it be harmless; the answer lies within the spectrum of frequencies. If you wish, we can teach you how to use other wavebands. In the wavelength spectrum you use only one section; we can show you how to shift to a different higher section. This will give you clearer and easier communication with no ensuing damage to the planet.

I must tell you that there are people who are not the same as you, but similar, who live within the planet. In the recent past, they have suffered very much as their internal world has been collapsing. Their living areas and structures have been destroyed with internal earthquakes. Many of their souls have left their bodies, and those left behind have retreated further into the earth in order to avoid these unstable areas. It has become increasingly dangerous even to be there, and we are waiting for their request as a civilisation so that we can remove them from where they are, into the safety of our care. There will be a time in the future when they will have a choice to either migrate to another planet with our help, or be integrated back into your world. But I must remind you that they are very different from you humans.

Ann: Are they are physically different because they live below ground? In what way have they adapted to their environment?

Arcturan: They have a humanoid body type; however their senses are very different. They have extremely sensitive hearing, a very acute sense of touch, and strong sentient feeling ability; however their eyesight is not so good. They are very pale in colour, with yellowy–white hair. They have a different internal body system, and use osmosis as one way of taking in nutrients. Although they do eat some things as you do, they have adapted over the millennia to a life underground, and the requirements that that entails. There is phosphorescent light, water, and many other things underground such as plants; but they operate very differently as a race. They have a very strong telepathic ability, and each one senses and knows where the others are at any given time. There is a great deal of fear amongst them at the moment, as their internal world as we just said, is collapsing in parts.

Ann: Do they have a good relationship with people like yourselves, and other races from space?

Arcturan: They are unaware of us as a race. They cannot see us but they do know of people from space. They know of what they call 'The Ancient Brothers'. They know that they descended from us in the beginning; not directly from 'we' the Arcturans, but from beings from space, and they know that a day will come when they will be returned to the stars.

Ann: Did they come from another planet originally?

Arcturan: Yes. Their planet became no longer habitable, and so they were brought here to Earth by others with the technology to do so. They were fearful of the wildness on the surface of the planet, especially the dangerous animals that were here then. So they retreated into a life of quiet thoughtfulness and safety underground. They have lived there for many generations, but they have not forgotten their heritage. When we do come to take them, they will go with us gladly. Even though there may be a little fear initially, they will come.

Ann: Thank you.

Elaine: And now, the Arcturan is going to stand aside for a moment, and at last, the female from Andromeda is going to speak. She is very tall, slender and graceful, with humanoid-like features. She has a very long nose, almond shaped eyes, and she appears to have long dark hair. I know she shows herself like this for my benefit, because it is familiar. I believe that in her natural state she does not have hair at all. She is maybe six feet six, or seven feet in height, and has an aura around her of love and respect. She extends her hand to me in a very warm and heartfelt greeting, like an old friend.

Andromedan: I have come back into your life to say thank you for all the times we have been together before. I come also to remind you, with love, that all the information we have given to you in the past that was agreed upon, is to begin to be allowed to surface from within the depths of your mind. You can now see before you a model with colour coded wires, circuit boards, and diagrams.

Elaine: I can see the inside of a machine of some sort.

Andromedan: I am going to try to explain to you how the human brain works using this image as a model.

Elaine to Ann: The Andromedan says she will explain the workings of the brain to me; levels of consciousness and how they and the emotional bodies interact with one another. She tells me I need to write this information down, so that people will understand exactly how they can alter the energy field of their bodies in the future. She speaks as a representative of the Andromedan people, but she reminds me that there are many thousands of races within the Andromedan Galaxy.

Andromedan: I represent just one tiny section of the Andromedan Peoples. We are represented at the Council that we talked of earlier, and we have volunteered to come forward and help the people on Earth to understand the nature of their being. When you have understood this, it will enable you to elevate your consciousness, and be at liberty to separate the physical from what you call the spiritual. You will then be naturally inter-dimensional. The physical bodies of humanoids are going through both a poisoning and a purification process at the same time. You are finding now that the toxins you ingest, and that are put upon you from the atmosphere, are altering the structure of your bodies. Whilst your bodies are working hard to eliminate the overdose of these toxins, there still remains a residue. This residue is altering your cellular and genetic structure. There will come a time in the future, when you will find that your 'energy body' will feel most uncomfortable within the physical body. You will spend more and more time wishing to be 'out' of your body, but in full consciousness. This does not mean being *unconscious*, as a lot of you are when sleeping and in the dream state. This is when your energy body returns into the physical body after sleep, and you remember nothing.

We will teach you about the transition, and once you understand the entire spectrum of your abilities, you will be left with a feeling of liberty. There are some of you who spend many hours in the company of we the Andromedans, and with lots of the other races besides. You come in your sleep state, and on an energy level, you have all the knowledge already. We have talked to you, and we have helped to imprint the vibrations of all the answers to all the questions on your energy fields.

The difficulty comes with crossing the barrier of consciousness. When you leave the dream state and come into your waking conscious state, a mental 'safety gate' comes into action, and for the time being, rightly so. We understand that dealing with two realities simultaneously is a very difficult thing for humans to maintain. It could feel like a psychosis or madness; as if you were feeling like two different people at the same time. One part of you, knowing how to be free and liberated, and the other part having to eat, work, clean, and do all the physical things that you do every day, and interact with the rest of the world.

Within the first part, on that other level of consciousness, you can be totally free. You can fly, or converse telepathically; there is nothing in its elementary stage that you cannot do. We find that many of you are prepared on the mental level, but you have no access to it whilst in a waking state. Part of what I will give you to write down will be given so you can trigger other people to remember. We will activate this memory within your mind for you to remember also.

These are just the early stages, and at some point when the other Extra-Terrestrials races begin to interact with you on Earth to a greater degree, we too will come forward. But our race tends to be, how shall we say, more silent? We observe quietly and we will always be found 'at the back of the crowd' rather than at the front. The Arcturans are very open and demonstrative in what they do. They have been familiar with all aspects of your planet for many thousands of years. The Sirians too have been involved with emotional behaviour and politics, and they understand better the working of the minds of individuals. But we Andromedans are quieter, we come silently and on invitation, and we slip in relatively unnoticed. As a comparison, (I feel from your mind) we are more like the angelic race that humans talk about. We only come when needed, and we do not come forward, or push ourselves to the front, unless specifically asked. Nevertheless, we do bring immense compassion and love for you, and you have only to ask for our services, and we will willingly give you all that we have. Do I sense a question?

Ann: Are there any beings on the Earth at present that are Andromedan? Have any of your people come down here and physically incarnated into human form?

Andromedan: There are several species that live on our particular planet, and we do not all look the same. Some of us can take human form very easily. Personally, I would not be accepted as humanoid, because I look so very different. My skin is somewhat blue.

We do, as do the Sirians, have some on our planet who look very humanoid, with fair hair, and humanoid features. These people have been seeded from other races in the galaxy, and we live together in harmony. As a race, they usually work with us and for us. They are our willing 'servants'. I understand the connotations you place upon this word. They serve us willingly; we treat them as equals, and they come with us when we travel, because they are sometimes sent for specific purposes to Earth.

Ann: Would they take a whole incarnation, or would they come in as a 'walk in', as we call it?

Andromedan: No, they come as they are. They appear, do what they must, and then disappear.

Ann: Thank you.

Andromedan: On the planet where my esteemed friend comes from in the Sirian constellation, there is a dimensional level where they too have 'physical' craft, and physical humanoid bodies. They resemble the Venusians very much.

Ann: I was just going to ask you about the Venusians! I did read somewhere recently that Venusians don't necessarily look humanoid, but they take humanoid form when they come to Earth, so that we can accept them. I always think of them as having humanoid form.

Andromedan: Yes, there are many races in the universe that can adapt their shape and form so that they appear pleasing to humans. In a way, it is an illusion. You see them as you want to see them. They can project an illusion to you that can be very acceptable. They do it with kindness in mind, so as not to frighten anybody.

Ann: Thank you. Can I ask another question?

Andromedan: Yes.

Ann: Do you know if there are going to be more contact from Extra-Terrestrials? If so, will it be telepathic, as in the form that we have tonight, or in a more direct physical way with people on the Earth?

Andromedan: Are you asking if there will be more telepathic communication?

Ann: Yes, as well as visitations.

Andromedan: We are finding with the help of our scanners, that more people are developing telepathic skills than were previously found. Therefore more people are open to receive our telepathic messages than before. There still need to be a few steps taken by us to evaluate more of the population for telepathic reception. Naturally, so many people are inherently focused upon their own lives, it's extremely difficult to get past the day-to-day things that people go through and reach them telepathically. We as a race (the Andromedans) do not usually attempt to do that; we only come when we are called. However, other races do 'call out' with telepathy, to see if people will notice.

I want to mention here the children being born into this generation and also those from the previous twenty or more years. Having been born into a time of changing energies on Earth, they are finding their capacity for telepathy much easier; such as receiving thoughts from 'Extra Terrestrials' and spirit guides as you call it. Of course, as people become more accustomed to the fact that we are here, they will venture out with their minds of their own accord.

For example, there is a curve in telepathic ability growth. Once you have one hundred telepathic people, they soon become a thousand, then a million, and very soon there will be enough of these young ones to make an enormous shift in the mental communication that we have with you on the planet. I speak not just about communication with our race specifically, but with all the other races that are more actively involved in telepathic communication.

The Sirians for example are imparting a great deal of knowledge and guidance to people on Earth. They come and successfully connect with many people. The Arcturans do also, but perhaps on a lesser scale. I must tell you that there are many dozens of races who are all trying to bring you holistic or all encompassing knowledge, with as much variety as possible.

Can you remember we talked of the Andromedan council, and the one hundred and thirty six members? They all have a different approach. They all have a different observation to make, and a different knowledge to give. So you will hear many stories of received information, and see books being written about what the Extra-Terrestrials say. The Pleiadeans have done a great deal of work with this, and they are closer to your humanoid form than probably any of us. They relate in somewhat of a parallel manner to Earth beings. They have a much closer understanding of your 'humanness'.

Ann: Are they our closest non-Earth relatives?

Andromedan: No, there are others that are more closely related to you genetically. Serving as a mirror image to your evolution, the Pleiadeans have followed a similar path, but have advanced further forward. So they understand to a certain degree the struggles that you go through, and can help on a more personal level.

I will help in bringing this book together with images of some of the races of beings, their various backgrounds and motives, and their different vibrations. They all have different points of view that are at the forefront of their reason to be here. We come as a group, and are mostly members of the Andromedan Council, but there are other races here that are not within the Federation. We meet them from time to time, to discuss their reasons for being here and to bring about harmony in our actions together.

We realise that some races, thinking that they will help the world with for example, plan X, can enter unknowingly into conflicting situations if some other groups want to help the world with plan Y. Then they do not work in harmony. They know of each other to a certain degree, because there is telepathic communication. They understand what our intentions are, and so we must still spend time around the council table with these other representatives. The Federation directives are that we all work together in unity towards helping planet Earth, and that there not be too many factions participating in different actions. This would bring about confusion with Earth people and their governments. We all wish to help you in our different ways, but there must be unity.

Now I feel I have talked enough, and I will come at another date to explain the functions of the model I showed you earlier. This will include the workings of the human brain, and how you can better understand some of the functions that are available to you, ones that you do not use as yet.

Elaine: The Sirian comes forward now, and says this is enough for this evening unless there are any questions. We say no, thank you, and so wish goodbye and goodnight to all.

14

Our eyes are opened.......

As usual, I am with Ann in her meditation room ready to receive information by telepathy. I've 'tuned in', and invited the group of Extra-Terrestrials we usually work with to come through.

All is well, but tonight there is a stranger amongst them. Along with all the others, this new Extra-Terrestrial is seated at a table. Something feels a little odd about him, but I'm going to continue to communicate and go with what I can see for the moment, because there will surely be something to be learnt from this.

It feels odd that they are presenting themselves as being sat around a table and this in itself doesn't feel quite right. I can see a being who, in my perception, 'whooshed' in from the left-hand side, whilst I was greeting all the others.

He has a most strange appearance. Imagine what a man/being could look like, with very bumpy reptile-like skin. The closest thing you could compare him with would be an animal, but he's definitely *not* an animal. I can see pieces of clothing, or what appears to be clothing. The front part of his face has the kind of jaw that would allow him the ability to speak. The back of his head has bony protuberances, and he has reptile-like skin. It's the kind of Extra-Terrestrial you might expect to see on a Star Trek programme! When he speaks it sounds as though his voice is coming from underneath the ocean somewhere, in very slow, round, echo-like tones. (I hear it telepathically.)

I have asked the being from Sirius to make sure we are totally safe here, and he has said to me, 'We must let him speak'. I also asked how it was possible for a being such as this one to be present with the others. They say what I see is just a holographic image, and that his telepathic power is exceptionally strong. He has projected the image of himself sitting at the table because I have something important to learn here. He tells me he is a semi-aquatic being. He has joined us in our conversation, explaining that at one point in the history of our Earth, his race lived on our planet, both in the sea and on the land. I can now see various images of dinosaur 'type' creatures, and I would imagine that his race were here millions of years ago, when the planet was water, rock and jungle, and that's about all.

Ann: Do they still live like that, on their planet?

Elaine: Yes, he tells me that with the advent of the more civilised land dwellers here on Earth they were removed as a race, and placed on a planet where no other humanoids were. This was a place of their own, which was one of jungle and virgin land.

Ann: Do they live life according to their animal nature, or have they evolved into a different form over time? Are they gradually coming out of the animal nature, or do they not see that as important?

Aquatic Being: We as a species have an entirely different lifestyle to any that you have encountered before. We can, at will, walk upright on the land if we choose. We do not have an 'animal nature'.

Elaine: He is showing me now that they have some kind of power that comes from their eyes. I can see it as mental 'energy beams'. They have a highly developed brain, and yet lead a very simplistic life. If they wish to cut down a tree, for example, they can beam a thought to the branch, and make it drop off the tree. This process is actually altering the molecular structure of the branch at a certain point. You could compare it to cutting a tree with laser power to bring a branch down for fuel. He says however, that they do not use fire as such, because of their nature. They are cold-blooded aquatic beings. They are more likely to use tree branches for construction.

He is telling me now that they are beginning to have a preference for air, rather than being under the water a lot of the time. They can and do breathe under the water. He is turning his head, and showing me that they have a gill system down the side of the neck.

Ann: They are amphibians?

Elaine: Yes, amphibian. They occupy banks and shore lines or whatever watery area that suits them. Usually, it is much like a Florida swamp, being very warm and humid. I can see where they live, with water dripping from overhead, and everything is damp and wet. This is the type of climate that suits them. They like the conditions to be damp, steamy and warm, but are equally happy under the water. I am asking the other Extra-Terrestrials why they have allowed this person to show himself as he is, and to explain this to me.

Arcturan: One of the things that we wish to do is to introduce to you, without any fear, some of the diversity of life that exists, and so help you to discover the intelligence that you will find in the most unlikely looking places. This being looks (to you humans) almost like a man-reptile or an animal. Yet you must realise when you look into his eyes, this being thinks, feels, constructs, and lives according to his own nature, on his own planet. His is the highest life form, although not the only life form, on his planet. The mind-power that this being has is something that you humans would dearly love to have. They use it in a very simple manner, for gathering food. They can create shelter if they need it, or just to acquire things for themselves. The entire source of their greatness is in their mental power. They can see out into the universe, and can project their minds out there at will, like your best and most accomplished telepaths or shamans. They are incredibly knowledgeable, yet lead a simple and uncluttered life.

Ann: Do they play a role in the scheme of things? Are they seeking to evolve, not necessarily into a different type of creature or being, but mentally? Are they following a path that may be of service in some way?

Elaine: The reply from this Being to all of your questions is: 'We just Are'.

Arcturan: They are aware and in touch with 'All That Is'. You might compare this to a shamanic or even Zen way of life, and their choice is to live almost unchanged. I say almost, because they tell me that at one point they lived most of their lives underwater. They have been choosing now for some thousands of years to spend more time daily on the land.

Sirian: Their evolutionary progression will be like this.

Imagine please, the other reptilian beings we have shown you. They pilot ships, construct and live within buildings and are outwardly developed, interacting with the rest of the galaxy. These beings originally developed from a similar type of creature, but without the wonderful brainpower that this being has. The other beings developed an 'outer technology' type brainpower, whereas this race of beings has a greater command of different areas. They have great mental power. They can think things into existence; alter the structure of anything they wish, and yet even with this ability, they choose to live and conduct themselves very simply. When they decide eventually to go out into the universe 'physically', they will indeed be seen as a wondrous race of people. This is because of their deep inner choice of simplicity for so many millennia.

Over the years they have learnt that there is great wisdom in simplicity. It may be that they *never* choose to build spacecraft; they may prefer to go out as the shaman journeys, just with their minds, and stay on the planet in their physical form.

Elaine: It's quite extraordinary, because to look upon this being, it might possibly make you uneasy. (It worried me initially, and I wondered what this was all about). I feel his energy aura as one of noble simplicity. It's very Zen; I feel the sentiment 'this is the way it is', and it's very curious.

Now it is gone!

Arcturan: Now you have the essence of it. Now that you have felt the purpose of this being, we have achieved what we aimed for. The aim tonight was to show you just one out of the great diversity of beings there are out there, and that you should understand that some do not always look as you might expect them to. Some beings may not look 'fair' in your eyes, or they may look similar to your concept of an animal. Do not judge by appearances; I want you to understand fully how vast the power of this aquatic being's mind is, and that they have purposely chosen to be modest in the way that they live.

Elaine: Now they have brought someone new to me. Do you remember the wonderful extra-terrestrial with the blue eyes? He has arrived!

Ann: Can you ask him where he comes from?

Elaine: He is from......................

Oh boy, this is difficult; there are no real words that will describe it, only feelings. He is showing me pictures of musical notes, and piano keys, in fact all kinds of things to do with music. He has previously told me that he comes from a race of people whose interest in music exceeds almost every other interest that they have. They obviously do other things, but this person in particular has a fascination with all the ways that you can produce sound. This means from any given thing, such as stringed or metal instruments; any and all that we would know of on Earth, plus many more! I hear electronically produced sounds; and now he is showing me a Theremin.(This is an instrument that produces sounds via electromagnetic energy as played by the Beach Boys in 'Good Vibrations', and in the original Dr Who series)

Blue-Eyed E.T: There are multitudes of ways to produce electronic music. We can also produce magnetic music from out of the air.

Elaine: I wonder what magnetic music is, and what it sounds like? He is now talking about some of the things you (Ann) have said before, such as the ability of people in the spiritual realms of Earth to produce colour from musical sounds and frequencies.

Ann: Do they produce these musical colours in the same way?

Blue-Eyed E.T: In order to hear the kind of music that produces colour, we have to have special hearing devices, because the sounds are way above our normal hearing range.

Ann: So colour would be there, but to hear the sound that makes it, you must have these special hearing devices?

Blue-Eyed E.T: Yes, simply because the frequencies are extremely high. My people can be compared to solid third-dimensional people, as you are on Earth, but the frequency of my world is more like the Earth's 'Spirit World' i.e. like a fourth dimensional existence.

Ann: Can you come down into our third dimension?

Blue-Eyed E.T: Yes, we have no problem with this. Taking on third dimensional physicality is easy. As a race of people we can manipulate vibration with ease. As fourth dimensional beings, we are exceedingly interested in any type of creative work. We love to be involved with the craft of music, and to experiment with all the different things you can do with sound.

Ann: Do you do this just for your own pleasure?

Blue-Eyed E.T: Yes, but also we provide music for whoever asks for it. To call it music as you know it is not quite correct, because it is not by any means the same. We have music to raise and expand the consciousness; music that will create pictorial art - and this we use in combination with light. We can produce colours with music, but we are also a technological race, and we still use 'machinery' (he hesitated with this word). You on your planet would call it machinery, but it's almost like living or organic machinery.

Imagine the difference between a metallic 'robot' and a human style android (an android that, to all intents and purposes looks real, and has been built with really fine technology). Our musical instruments and machinery, and your machinery and technology, are like a comparison between the two. Our technology is almost organic, and because of this, we can achieve a whole multi-sensory experience when we experience the music. It ranges through visual, tactile, and includes the sense of smell; in fact our music is a whole experience within the body.

Ann: Are some of our musicians influenced or impressed by beings from your system?

Blue-Eyed E.T: Yes.

Elaine: He reminds me now of the first time I saw him. He had contacted a friend of mine, who happened to be a musician, and was giving him inspiration on an intuitive level. The E.T. told me at the time that there was an underlying reason why he was there with my friend. He said that it was because my friend had originated from his home planet, and had now chosen to incarnate here on Earth.

There is an intrinsic link with members of their planet that go 'out' to incarnate somewhere else. There is always a bond; always support and curiosity too! (I have come across this many times, with other races of E.T's, who are watching and inspiring particular people closely for various reasons.)

Blue-Eyed E.T: The fire and passion that you have in your music here on Earth comes from your emotional experiences. We want to have that whole range within our music. We have all that is spiritual, all that is beautiful, and all that is technological. We wish to create sounds that give the same feeling as, for example, a volcano exploding, or a firework display. We need to know how it feels, and yet we don't experience it in the same way.

Ann: Whereas we do?

Blue-Eyed E.T: Once someone has had the experience, they can feel the height and depth of emotion contained in it, and it leads to an expansion of energy awareness.

Elaine: I am going to ask him now why it is that they have such extraordinarily beautiful eyes. (They are the most amazing shade of blue all over). I have often wondered about that in the past. Their eyes are truly amazing. When I saw him first, he was wearing a kind of thin metallic wrap around visor over his eyes.

Blue-Eyed E.T: Partly, it has to do with the nature of our sun, and the solar radiation that comes down onto the planet. But also, indigenous to the planet, there is a mineral similar to your gypsum (a kind of flaky mineral). On Planet Earth, there is abundant calcium, and a form of calcium makes up a large part of your bodies, i.e. in the bones etc. In the same way, we have a powdery blue mineral present in large quantities on our planet.

Elaine: He is smiling and says, 'Think of your pink flamingos that get their colour from the food they eat!'

Blue-Eyed E.T: We, as a race of people, radiate the colour blue from the gypsum. It's in our bodies.

Ann: Do you eat it?

Blue-Eyed E.T: It soaks into our skin, and it's in the water, so not only do we have blue eyes, but we have a blue sheen to our skin as well.

Elaine: Do you eat and drink in the same way as we do?

Blue-Eyed E.T: Yes, we do. In fact, a lot of the habits that you humans have, we also have. We eat, we drink, and we have families and children. Our reproductive methods (he smiles) are somewhat different, perhaps more refined than yours. However, we seek to learn about this from you also, as an interesting addition to our range of emotions. For example, the passion that you experience here on Earth, in all its forms, is not found in many other places.

Elaine: I am asking him now, 'How did you evolve? If you never had those kinds of emotional experiences from the start, how did you evolve? Have you always been the same?'

Blue-Eyed E.T: As far back as I can remember, we have always been the same. We have no evolutionary history that I can remember.

Elaine: He is taking me back to a time when technology was everything on their planet.

Blue-Eyed E.T: There was once a time on our planet when emotionally, we would become 'heated' with one another, and as you say in your terms 'squabble amongst ourselves'. We didn't have wars as you experience on your planet, but our emotions were unsettled. The technology that we had then was very much like an advanced form of the technology you have now. We had satellites, telephones, televisions and monitors; any and all things technological; ours was very much a logical left-brain type of technology.

In our world we have a council, who preside over the running of affairs on the planet. They give guidance as to how people should be, and it was decreed back then that we should all become more creative in our lives. There was so much dissatisfaction and imbalance in the emotions of the people (this was a long time ago), that it was decided unanimously that we should develop our creative side as a collective whole. Although we were already being very creative, it was in a very external manner. The music came naturally from the internal part of us, and everybody loved it so much, it became a way of life. Just as, for example, the cellular telephones are popular on your world. Everybody wanted to do it, and we all found so much joy in creating music and art in all its forms, that virtually the whole planet changed.

We refined the mechanical technology into this organic creative world that we have now. We have become, over thousands of years, specialists in the creation of music and all that has to do with music and frequency. Music is a poor term to use, because it is much more than music; it's a whole experience.

Elaine: He knows what's in my mind, and as an example he is asking me to imagine a floatation tank; being suspended in music, vibration, colour and light all at the same time. That's what it's like!

Blue-Eyed E.T: We are masters at creating an experience. Our minds are busy and eager because we have kept the technological aspect of ourselves as well as developing the creative. We are continually seeking new experiences. Part of our searching has led us into choosing (for some of us) to leave our bodies behind, and incarnate on your planet. This is to experience the full range of emotions you can find there, and also to sample as many of the sounds that there are to be found.

I will tell you a little about my planet. We do not have, to the same degree, the animal life that you have on your planet. Our planet is like this (and he is showing me the surface of the planet now).

Elaine: I can see that there are many buildings apparently made with glass. They look like our most modern architecture. In fact, he says he is showing me some of the oldest buildings on his planet.

Blue-Eyed E.T: When we were at the peak of our logical technology, we had huge buildings that were technologically brilliant, using steel and glass; buildings that are like your most modern structures on Earth.

Elaine: He is now taking me to another place, and showing me some more recent structures. They are much more 'organic'. They are round, like geodesic domes made of very soft material that blends into the landscape; very 'organic' indeed. He is now showing me the surfaces and the insides of these domes; I can see vegetation and plants, but they're not the same as we are familiar with. He tells me the people live inside these domed cities. Outside on the planet surface, the landscape is all blue gypsum rock. It looks a bit like our moon; it's quite pleasant to be there, and the planet's surface looks like sand. Instead of there being yellow daylight as we have, the quality of the atmosphere is like blue moonlight. It's quite beautiful, and everything sparkles. It's daytime there, but it looks like you would imagine light blue moonlight to be.

Blue-Eyed E.T: We can walk outside if we choose and breathe the air. There are no problems or dangers to us out there, but we need all the other colours besides blue, to balance us. So inside of all our vast cities, which are like rolling geodesic domes all joined together, there are artificial lights. We have all kinds of plants, (and even some of these are blue) and trees. These have been created by my people because they don't survive well or exist naturally much outside.

Ann: Do you eat what is grown inside the domes?

Elaine: That's an interesting question!

Blue-Eyed E.T: Yes, we have something similar to your Earth greenhouses. Row upon row of plants are cultivated there.

Elaine: I can see what looks like fruits and vegetables growing there; there are also huge 'poly-tunnels', but much, much bigger than you would find on Earth. Inside this big complex of domes, it's all agriculture, and I am asking him now if it rains.

Blue-Eyed E.T: Not exactly. We take our water from deep within the planet. We have constructed wells, because there are large quantities of water under the surface. Where we live in this block of cities, the outer terrain is a little hilly, but geographically there is not much variety. Away in the far distance there are mountains, and any precipitation there is gets caught up in these mountains and flows underground. We constructed this city in a direct line with the underground water flow, so that we would always have a constant supply from any rain over the mountains. The actual plain that we live on doesn't get much rain at all.

Elaine: I am asking him now why he has chosen to be here tonight. He is actually very 'human-like' to talk to. I remember the first time I ever spoke to him. It was very difficult, because he tried to communicate to me exactly what his language was like, and it was the weirdest thing I have ever heard. It was indescribable, like musical tones. That was about seven years ago, and since then he has spent a long time close to Earth, listening and observing. The ease with which he communicates now is due to his having been so closely involved with Earth for so long. I now pose the original question, as to why he is here. He shows me a picture of an orchestra, and a conductor.

Blue-Eyed E.T: As well as to give support to the one person I am linked to, I am gathering experiences for myself. By standing in the same energetic space as somebody like the musical conductor you can see, I can soak up the energy of the experience from this person. Not to deplete the person, but to feel and register all the vibrations of the experience of conducting a great orchestra.

Elaine: What a strange but interesting experience!

The Sirian is speaking to me now. He says, 'Now it is enough for this evening.'

Ann and I close down the communication and say thank you to all; it was amazingly interesting and an honour to have met you again.

15
The Pleiadean People......

The following week I am again together with Ann, and have welcomed our group of Extra-Terrestrials. They begin by telling me that they are waiting for someone to arrive.

First of all I see fleeting images of a strange being that looks like nothing I have ever seen before. I asked what it is, and they tell me it is just a passing image, and not the being that they are expecting. Then to my surprise, they welcomed a 'captain' from the Pleiadean system. He has come to sit at their table; he is very humanoid looking, has fair hair, and wears a silver (material unknown) spacesuit or uniform. There is an arrow shaped insignia on his chest. He is sending me telepathic images of a mountain range in a desert area. The hills are sand coloured, like the kind you would see in Turkey, or somewhere similar. He shows me his ship; it's a small spaceship, hovering above the hills, apparently watching what is going on below.

He begins to talk about this desert area, showing concern about the difficulties with people in this area (the fighting and political upheavals). I believe this is Earth, but I am not familiar with the politics as I don't read the newspapers or watch the television much. He tells me that they have been watching people with weapons in the hills.

Pleiadean: Let me explain a little more. The area around Israel and Jordan is a designated landing site for Pleiadeans. We requested that this from the Andromedan council, and they granted our wish. This desert area that you see is just one of our proposed future landing sites.

Elaine: I am now receiving images of a huge explosion. I see a big dust cloud, and it's obvious that it was caused by some sort of bomb, but I don't immediately see devastation or radiation. I now see the foot of the mountains in the original desert area; this is where the bomb lands. When the explosion happens, a crack in the Earth appears like an Earthquake, and snakes off in the direction of a major city. I see the end of the crack stopping half a mile from the edge of the city; there is going to be mass evacuation because this explosion will not only crack the surface of the Earth, it will have repercussions elsewhere.

He tells me it will be internalised inside the Earth, and will act as some kind of trigger. To illustrate, he shows me a big oil field under the ground, and the explosion causes an internal fire. I see this lake of oil under the ground is set alight by the bomb, fissures in the earth open up, and great sheets of flame are coming up from inside the Earth. Huge spouts of flame are suddenly popping up all over the place. I am seeing incredible amounts of black smoke, making the area uninhabitable, as the smoke is acrid and choking. Now he takes me visually to a huge river or canal (it could even be the Suez Canal). I see hundreds of people flocking to the edge of the water, and waiting to get on boats to get away. He tells me that the Pleiadean ships will be monitoring the state of affairs, and that it could be a missile that does this particular damage.

Now he is showing me three space ships in a row, high in the air, positioned to the front of the mountains. They seem to be setting up a 'field' of some sort. It looks as if they are dropping a sheer curtain of shimmering energy from the ships to the ground, to intercept this missile. This sheet of energy reminds me of the skin of a soap bubble. It's like a thin wavering skin of multi coloured air.

They say it won't stop the missile, but it can change the molecular structure of the contents, thus making it less powerful.

Elaine: Maybe it's a nuclear missile, and perhaps they are making it act like an ordinary weapon, and not a nuclear device.

Ann: Can they extract something from it as it goes through the curtain?

Elaine: Yes, but not so much extracting as changing the structure of the chemical makeup of the missile contents. I'm still not clear about why they are telling me all this, or what the outcome will be if they do change it.

Ann: So it's still a bomb, and still capable of destruction?

Elaine: Yes, but instead of possible radioactive fallout, giving sickness and poisoning, it will only affect the Earth with smoke and fire and cause the Earthquake fissure that comes to within a certain distance of the city.

Pleiadean: We are going to take 'certain people' (those who are at war) up into our spaceship and show them this possible future, in an effort to divert an event that could result in a really bad situation. The people who are fighting are playing a waiting game. Like a nervous cat waiting for a mouse to twitch, they are just waiting for one more thing, and when something happens, they will hit the target really hard. This missile will be sent, and it will go off-course, and overshoot the target.

Ann: So this is a possible scenario, but it may not happen?

Elaine: Well, I don't know. He is telling me that it is going to happen. But I'm very nervous about 'predictions'. I am always open to the fact that anything and everything can be changed. Maybe if they were able to do something with key people, i.e. make them see the possible future, things could be changed.

Ann: So they are not going to coerce anyone?

Pleiadean: No, we will just show them a possible future, and they will remember almost like a dream of what might happen.

Elaine: That is all to do with this subject now. I am going to look closely at the Pleiadean. He is a very friendly and smiling kind of person.

Ann: Can you describe him a bit more?

Elaine: Yes. He has long shoulder length yellowish-blond hair. I am looking at his eyes and they are an unusual shade of green, with hints of gold in them. There are multiple shades and colours, with flecks of blue in the iris. He is very pleasing to look at, and his main characteristics are virtually the same as a human being.

Ann: Are they related to us through genetics?

Pleiadean: We are a parallel planetary system, in the fact that all that you have done, we have done. We were genetically engineered too.

Ann: So Elaine, are they saying that they have not sustained their original form; and neither have we? Do you think that we came from the same source race originally?

Elaine: I don't think so, no. Perhaps the same group of Extra-Terrestrials were involved in their genetic engineering as well as ours, but I think they were given a head start!

Ann: An easier time? (laughs)

Pleiadean: It was an experiment. Metaphorically speaking, if you take two plants, put one in a pot and add nutrients to it, and to the other plant you add no nutrients, but you give it extra sunshine, you get differing growth rates. This is a similar scenario to our race and yours. The Pleiadeans were given different things to the Earth people.'

Elaine: What are you doing with regards to Earth?

Pleiadean: 'We keep very busy and active on planet Earth. We monitor and keep a general check on what happens, and where.

Elaine: He is showing me power lines and nuclear power stations. They are watching to see what happens; keeping an eye on things - almost like scout ships out on patrol to keep abreast of what's happening in the world! He tells me that he was a member of the crew serving on the ship I first encountered nine years ago. He was on board with other members of the Galactic Federation.

Ann: Was it as long as nine years ago?

Elaine: Yes. This was when I first encountered the Galactic Federation. The being that spoke to me was incredibly powerful and superimposed his energy field over mine. This was so I could be absolutely sure of his presence. It was such a strong experience that there was no doubt in my mind. Do you know where he is now?

Pleiadean: He is a captain on a larger ship, and is in control of a large project elsewhere.

Pleiadean: On the working scout ships, we very often transfer from one ship to another, in order to do different tasks. This is all the information I can give for the moment.'

Elaine: With that last comment, they all indicate their goodbyes, and the session is over for tonight.

16
Galactic Explorers......

A
nn and I are at her home, and to begin this session I have given my usual greetings to all the guides.

The very tall 'light being' from Sirius has greeted me, and I have asked who will speak tonight. To my surprise (again) they have brought forward a 'Reptoid'. I thought at first that this is what you might call a 'Reptilian being', but the Sirian says, 'No, this is a Reptoid'.

This new Extra-Terrestrial has a humanoid form; he has two arms, two legs, human-like facial features and reptilian-like scaly skin. He has no visible signs of hair, and he appears wearing a uniform. As far as I can see, it's made of a very fine mesh material, some of which is a silvery colour at the front. There is a plum coloured insert piece across the shoulders, and an insignia on the chest area (right hand side, see picture).

I look more closely at the insignia to see what it is. I see a circle, and within this is a thin arrowhead shape with another circle sitting in the centre of it. Within this circle is a representation of a planet like Saturn, with a ring system around it, and a four star configuration a little bit like the handle of the plough (as known in our astronomy).

Ann: Is this uniformed Reptoid Being standing erect like a human being?

Elaine: Yes. I can see that the top half of the uniform stops at the waist and the 'trousers' or leggings come to below the knee. Here there is a join, and then further material continues down the leg, covered by boots up to the knee. He is not saying anything at the moment, but I am receiving the impression that in the past this race of beings were and still are, great explorers.

Their nature is mildly aggressive, (certainly not violent) and very forthright in their approach to situations. They have been travelling out in the galaxy for many thousands of years, visiting other planets. I am shown a little scenario to illustrate this. I see them actually appearing on a planet somewhere that's inhabited by a very primitive race of people.

They usher the people into a particular place and make them sit down. In reality they are teaching them basics, like how to look after themselves better, and how to grow better plants. They are 'pushing evolution' a little with these people, and the inhabitants respond by being in awe of the Reptoid Beings that have arrived from the sky in their ships.

The people on the planet are at first a little frightened, and then very eager to learn.

The Sirian being speaks now and says:

Sirian: There is a modicum of pride involved here. The Reptoid Beings are great achievers and they feel quite happy to push people's progress by 'helping', in the nicest sense of the word. But sometimes the help is not always what we would all agree with. Within the Federation, we believe that people at that stage of evolution should be left to their own devices (with the exceptions of total disaster or destruction of a race), and not to be given too much technology all at once. If this happens, you may end up with a race of technologically advanced people with no spiritual grounding. They will not have learnt, (or they forget very quickly) how to appreciate the things that actually sustain their survival.

The Reptoid is telling me the star system that he comes from. It sounds like Rigel, but there is a word missing that I didn't hear.

Ann: What colour is his skin?

Elaine: His skin is a greenish-brown colour, a little bit like you might expect a reptile to be. It looks a very natural earthy colour. There are no large overlapping scales; the skin has quite a tightly formed texture, so as to make the appearance look fairly usual except for colour and texture. He has a slight ridge in the centre of his head, which goes from the front to the back, and a little bit more of a pronounced mouth with the jaw lines coming forward more. He has a normal sized head, with deep-set eyes and a slightly prominent forehead. His nose is flatter but with slit nostrils, so it isn't a prominent feature. The ears are very small, just a demarcation around a central orifice.

He is showing me his hands now, and he has three large fingers and a thumb. He has very long nails, a little like claws, but not as pronounced as they would be on an animal (not hooked, just a little elongated). I am shown that his hands have great dexterity, and it is natural and easy to manoeuvre things in the same way that humans do. He is now talking about the kind of craft that they fly. The ship I am seeing looks fairly standard, (if you can class any spaceship as being standard!). It is pointed on one end, and the body of the ship is raised up in a dome or egg shape, like a teardrop on its side. The pointed end creates a slim fin that goes around the middle of the ship and gets more slender as it comes to the back.

Inside, I see large monitors like video screens, and I can also see metal spheres. He tells me that when they place their hands on the metal spheres, they can control the movement of the ship by intention or thought impulse through the hands. I also see some very sophisticated control panels, and in the centre of the ship is a tiered circular hollow that drops down like a small amphitheatre. This is where they sit, in reclining couches. There are three seats, and the Reptoids that sit there can see directly up to the monitor in the front. They are scanning the star fields in front of them, looking for magnetic and electrical anomalies. As part of their mission, they enjoy studying different planetary systems. They begin to reveal a scene to me, as if I was watching it on a video screen. I can see them approaching the surface of a planet, looking closely at it. They even take notes and readings on some of the nearby asteroids, as any explorer would.

They explain that the three seats are not always fully occupied; but whoever is there has mental contact with the one who stands controlling the metal spheres that I saw. When they enter the atmosphere of a planet, the sphere is for difficult manoeuvres and for helping to locate things on the surface of the planet at a much slower speed. They use the screen and the spheres to navigate and guide the ship.

When it comes to long distance travel, i.e. out in space, they tell me that it is a totally different matter. They have a different kind of drive that's linked to the star maps in front of them. When they wish to travel they select a target, engage the drive, then as a group unit mentally focus in on the destination, and the ship automatically takes over and takes them there.

I am very curious about the way they live, and I ask, 'What do you eat, and what is your civilisation like?'

He shows me that his people, (the Reptoids) have a liquid diet when they are on board the ship. It looks like a thick viscous liquid and is fluorescent green. I mentally note that it reminds me of our green detergents, but a bit more yellow in colour. It seems to have a layer of something red on the top. Now they are showing me a panel in the wall; when you press a button, the panel slides open and there is the drink. I am told that this is basically all they need whilst they are on board ship.

Now he is mentally taking me to the planet that they come from. I see that they normally eat leaves, fruit and a variety of anything green. He tells me that they don't have teeth as such, but have incredibly hard jawbones (gums)?

I now feel myself actually *on* the planet and it really looks very lovely. There are flat areas of cream coloured stone, like a park with outdoor seats, curved benches and tables. I can see many of them sitting, eating, talking and walking around. There are plenty of trees, and in the distance behind the park, I see very tall buildings that remind me of Russia. They are tall cylindrical towers that have a round bulbous top, finishing with a point. (See illustration). The vision I see is one of extreme grace. The towers are varying heights and all are a translucent cream colour. I find it strange that I can't see any windows.

Elaine: I ask mentally, 'Are there any windows?'

He shows me that on the domes there are rows and rows of windows all the way round that have exterior sliding shutters that come across. Once they are closed, you can't see any joins and it's perfectly smooth. He explains that during the day, the people mostly like to stay in shady places, under the trees etc., because they don't tolerate the bright light of the sun too well. Warmth is something that they need, and the temperature at this time is very balmy and pleasant. It's not too hot, with a slight breeze rustling the leaves on the trees. This is similar for example to the climate in parts of Hawaii; 70 to 80 degrees approximately.

Ann: Is there much water there?

Elaine: It seems as if it is very dry. He is taking me around past the stone area to where the trees are, and I see there is a fountain, so there is running water. But he has something to tell me about the weather on this planet.

Now he indicates that I should look at the sky. It's quite a strange shade of blue-green, similar to duck egg blue, or pale turquoise green. I am amazed to see that there are two suns in the sky. One is further away than the other, but nevertheless, he tells me that they both have a strong impact on the planet.

Reptoid: When these two suns are in a particular position, i.e. when they both appear close at the same time, this is when our orbit will bring us in between them at an equal distance. It is then that we suffer from incredibly intense solar storms, which is why we have the shutters on the windows. Everything closes down at this time. We have a dome system that encloses the trees to protect them from the fierce heat. This compares to the dark shaded windows that you have on your Earth cars, similar to dark tinted glass. The solar storms bring incredibly hot dry winds. When we know they are coming we close everything down, because the temperature is too hot for us to be exposed to.

Elaine: How often does this happen?

Reptoid: These solar storms come once every quarter. Our seasonal year is two hundred and forty seven days compared to your Earth system.'

Elaine: 'I have a question. If it's so hot, where does the water come from? Do you have rainwater in the same way that we do?

Reptoid: This may surprise you, but we create our own rain. We have a reservoir inside the planet, but it is limited. There is only so much, and that's all. We have to recycle the water continually. I will explain more fully. We need to give water to the plants, in the form of rain, and the rain then passes through the Earth that they are in. We have created an artificial system; by this I mean that we have placed our entire colony and gardens on top of rocky plateau. Underneath the soil and plants, we have built a system that catches all the water and filters it back to the reservoir. It is then purified and begins the cycle again.'

Elaine: 'I am asking about any moisture that is lost from the leaves of the trees, because my thinking tells me that if this happened then it would eventually use up all the water.'

He takes me to see the trees more closely, and tells me that the structure of the leaves is a bit like the rubber plant leaves on Earth. These trees don't lose moisture through their leaves, it is contained; and on closer inspection, I see that it's not actually like a rubber plant. The leaves are quite small, similar to rose leaves; and because of the texture, they don't lose water at all. He says that things have developed this way here because of the dry atmosphere; but they do water them from above with the system that he described.

Reptoid: From this we can serve everything. Over many thousands of years we have learned to create and economise with the things that are most precious on the planet.

Elaine: Now he is taking me inside one of the buildings. He is showing me children and adults, and a form of school.

Reptoid: 'All children we raise are taught individually with the aid of what you would class as computer screens or monitors. They see and learn all that they need to know about the outside world and the environment from these. As for inner wisdom, we have elder members of our tribe (his particular pocket of civilisation) that teach wisdom and the laws of nature, as we know them.

Elaine: (Note that he does not say spirituality, he says inner wisdom.) He speaks of a wise teacher, teaching the children. He talks of a creator (not a god) who created all things. The children are taught about the preservation of life, and also learn to always strive to be the best that they can be.

He smiles at me now and says, 'Hence we have a very fierce pride in our achievements. We like to achieve and become better all the time.'

He is now showing me a Space Centre (in my terms), where space ships are constructed and sent out.

Reptoid: Almost two thirds of the population of our planet, (and it is not heavily populated) are explorers. It is an honour in our tradition to be a member of the fleet. It is considered a prime goal to gain enough respect and wisdom to be allowed to take part in the expeditions that we send out. The other third of the population are the maintainers, and of course, there are also the females of our race. The proportions are about one female to every ten males. The females are happy to be as they are. When the time occurs, the females have many children or offspring; there is usually up to twelve at the same birth event, giving rise to the difference in ratio between males and females. We revere the females on our planet, and usually they do not go out with the space exploration crews into the universe.

There are exceptions however, and he is showing me now a female commander. He says she attained that position by virtue of her age and wisdom. She had gone through the time of offspring bearing, and had been a teacher to others, and then graduated with permission to fly out with the other pioneers.

Elaine: I look more closely at the Reptoid being, and I note that he is here in a very 'physical' way. By this, I mean that he is present with the other Extra-Terrestrials physically, not as a holograph, or mental image.

Elaine: 'What is your interest here tonight?'

Reptoid: 'As always, our interest here is in observing the planet and its life forms, trees, and flowers. We are taking a 'back seat' to see how members of the Federation and others are dealing with particular problems on Earth.

We have been on solo expeditions to other planets, where we were the only ones involved in helping a race to better itself. But we see that there are many different races involved with this planet. As we cannot take the 'glory' we are happy to stand back and see how the whole thing is handled, as we may have things to learn. So I confirm simply that we have no involvement, we are just observers.

Ann: Can I ask what your normal life span is?

Reptoid: The equivalent of seven hundred of your years approximately; that is how long we choose to remain in the same physical system.

Ann: So do you have something beyond life, as you know it on your physical planet? Do you have a spirit?

Reptoid: Yes, yes, most definitely. We have realms of spirit or energy that are on a parallel dimension with us, and can be compared with your ancient Nordic myth and traditions of Valhalla. When we eventually shed the body and progress to the next stage of evolution, we do not return, but progress to a higher council. Some souls amalgamate and become one. I tell you this because you must realise with the amount of offspring that our females have, (albeit that there are fewer females than males) the population does keep growing. So our next dimensional space could become crowded! (Elaine....this is given as a kind of a joke). So we do have a system by where souls can join together if they wish.

Elaine: He is showing me something now, which is very interesting. I see a beautiful circular theatre or gathering place, with a huge dome on the top. Along one third of the wall is a massive screen

Reptoid: This is where we go to consult with those who have shed their bodies and passed into what we call our Solar Space. It is equivalent to your next (or spiritual) dimension. This is where we go to live as conscious energy, and take on a lighter body form.

When our people are very much in need, we call upon beings who have gone before us. They will appear on the screen in this building, and act as council to us.

Elaine: He is explaining to me now about the amalgamation of souls. He says this involves personal lineage. I ask for an explanation.

Reptoid: Imagine you have grandfather, father, and son. Bear in mind that one female will always know which brood of offspring is with which male. So the correct lineage is kept with the males, and the whole of the line can amalgamate into the essence of that one family, as one entity, if they choose. (He asks me if I understand.)

They come to assist us when we have problems, for example in dealing with the solar wind or any other survival problems on the planet. It was they who taught us how to conserve the water. We have had periods of extreme difficulty in our history.

Ann: Was your planet originally moister, with more natural rain?

Reptoid: No, this planet was very bare and quite smooth, with almost no recognisable mountains or rocks. The surface had rounded hills and gentle contours. None of us originated from this place. This was a planet that we found on our travels, and it was decided that the whole population should migrate, and that we should create living space here, for ourselves. The simple reason for this choice was that the atmosphere on this planet is absolutely 100% perfect for our bodily needs. Our original home planet developed tremendous volcanic activity and eventually became quite polluted with sulphur and other air born chemicals. The fumes and pollution began to make us all very sick.

Elaine: I ask; 'Why didn't you use your technology to shield yourselves?'

Reptoid: Even though we had fairly advanced technology, the situation became so difficult it was more than we could cope with. It was decided that we migrate. The elders from our higher dimensions advised us on what we should do, and we did it. So we came here, but it was always felt that whilst this place is now home to us, we do not 'belong' here. We are so very free in our exploration of the galaxy that we don't have a soul attachment to the place we live in now. It's a very nice place, and we have created the things we need, but if the time ever came for us to leave and find a better place, the elders would tell us, and we would most certainly go.

Ann: Could I ask you some questions about atmosphere? As you travel widely, do you find that a lot of planets have the same type of atmosphere, allowing you to land and roam the surface freely? Can you breathe the air, or do you need special equipment?

Reptoid: I understand the question. There are extreme variations on some planet surfaces. Some have high nitrogen, helium and even other gases that are not found on your planet. Usually, if we detect a planet that has an atmosphere, but it's truly inhospitable to our skin as well as our lungs, we will observe from a distance. But in some cases, we use an adaptation system, which is a little mouth mask, which can provide us with the correct balance we require for breathing.

As many of the civilisations throughout different galaxies have a carbon or silicon base, they need a good degree of oxygen for them to survive. We find that on most planets, either the inhabitants have artificially created the atmosphere, or it's all right for us to breathe as it is. There are of course some planets that are incredibly polluted, and some civilisations that you personally would not want to meet. We have observed these, and we tend to avoid them if possible. However, we have sent emissaries onto these planets in disguised forms, just to observe for a short while (a matter of days). We wish to experience interaction with these civilisations if possible. But I can tell you that in the past we have not stayed for very long!

Ann: Who are these civilisations, and what is the problem?

Reptoid: I will try to explain. One civilisation in particular I recall has taken its mechanical technology (not organic) to extreme degrees. In doing this, they have polluted their atmosphere with fumes and chemicals; and everything else that makes deadly toxicity is at the very limit. These people tend to live in protected cities, but despite this they are emotionally in a pretty desperate situation. The consciousness of the population is extremely low, and they are very much involved with materialistic gain and power. Their existence is a never ending cycle, and that is part of what drives them to be the way they are. It forces them into desperate measures when things get bad and there are little or no resources left. So what remains is nothing but a polluted situation, where even a glass of water equals the worth of a life.

Ann: Do they get any outside help, or are they resistant to it?

Reptoid: They are extremely resistant to outside help. Their consciousness does not allow the concept of other beings from outside their world, and as they are inwardly turned and are very violent amongst themselves, it is difficult to help.

Ann: So are they a young civilisation?

Reptoid: I am not sure I know in what terms you consider young.

Ann: I mean that perhaps they know no other way, and do not have the experience to realise that what they are doing is not helping themselves.

Reptoid: I agree that they have little experience, but more important, they have no knowledge of the Creator.

Ann: Do they have free will choice?

Reptoid: Yes, they do have free will choice. But it's somewhat like a spiral that is going down as opposed to up. It's self-perpetuating. I have personal experience of a visit to the planet that we speak of. We searched the surface of the planet for anyone who could and would accept our help; anyone who was open to being lifted up mentally and intellectually. There are a few there; we saw people on the outskirts of the city who had chosen to separate themselves from everyone else in the main. They were endeavouring to live a simple life. I encountered one individual in particular as he was looking up at the night sky. I understood telepathically that he was thinking there must be more than this to life, and on that wavelength I was able to come to him. He saw me, and in that moment he understood that there is more, and that there is indeed a creator of all things.

Ann: So perhaps, in a slightly different scenario, it was like that here on Earth. Some of us feel that in the past space beings visited only when people needed help. Would visitors to any planet have to wait for the people to be spiritually conscious?

Reptoid: The one small spark within that person on that planet could be the key to ending the spiral downwards, if it survives. If it doesn't survive, in the end the population will destroy themselves. It would be like a negative emission that cancels itself out. Not all civilisations are successful in the universe; those that have 'defects' (in the fact that they never attain any form of higher consciousness) self-destruct naturally. We never interfere in these cases. When and if this happens, there is a chance for the planet to recover and for another civilisation to come along at some date in the future (as you understand the future). It's true that these planets have time zones encapsulated around them, so that they will have time lines, past and future. This allows for a physical time space in which to recuperate.

Ann: Does this planet that we are discussing possibly have souls who would migrate elsewhere?

Reptoid: They do have souls, but if you could feel the quality and density of energy of their soul makeup, you would understand that it's a density that is almost solidified into the body. There is no lightness of being inside them; I believe you are familiar with the dark realms of your spiritual dimensions. This is where souls appear to be grey, heavy and desolate. These souls are stuck within a cycle of denseness and their incarnation and reincarnation is an unconscious thing. The souls waiting to incarnate are restless souls, who go in search of a body to occupy. When a child is conceived, they choose to reoccupy and condense down again. I believe this is one of the reasons why this particular race of people has never advanced in spiritual awareness. They have never allowed themselves the opportunity to stay in their 'spiritual' realms long enough to walk towards any kind of enlightenment.

Ann: Will they be held in the spiritual realm if the planet is uninhabitable and there is nowhere for them to incarnate?

Reptoid: They will be contained within their own field of energy until someone amongst them recognises that they can go towards the lighter dimensions. They cannot escape that unless it comes from within. They will be contained for however long it takes.

Ann: Yes, I understand this, as I believe that there is no time involved.

Reptoid: Yes, it could be forever in your terms.

Ann: This is so interesting! It seems like there are so many different ways of 'being' in the universe, that we can only guess at a few of them.

Reptoid: Yes.

Elaine: Now I am coming back from the projection of this planet that they have been showing me. I am back with the Reptoid Being and the other ET's. The Reptoid is saying thank you for the opportunity of discussion, and he reminds me that he is close by. His people are just observers of what's happening with the Earth, and that he is happy to be so. He says he is also happy to be present at an Earth event that will be revolutionary and wonderful to behold.

Elaine: I presume he is talking about the shift in consciousness and self-awareness that is happening now on Earth.

The Sirian comes in now and says, 'That will be all for tonight'.
We say our goodbyes and end the session.
What an exciting meeting we had here tonight! Ann and I can hardly contain our pleasure and excitement that so many different beings are coming forward to talk to us!

17
Can You Fly?....

Together again at her house, Ann and I are sitting amongst the flowers and crystals that create the wonderful atmosphere in her meditation room. We begin with an opening prayer, asking that all our guides be there with the beings from other worlds.

Elaine: I see a very powerful gathering tonight. All my guides are here including those from as far back in my life as I can remember. There are even people and relatives here who were close to me on Earth. Perhaps they are here because Ann and I were talking about them earlier.

I can see the Andromedan female, the Sirian, and the Arcturan sitting around a long table. They invite me telepathically to sit at one end of the table. The Andromedan will be the speaker tonight, and she is sitting directly opposite me at the other end of the table.

Andromedan: We come tonight to tell you about things that have happened in your past, and to explain things a little more clearly.

Elaine: I am relaying this word by word, so I have no idea what is coming next.

Andromedan: Earlier tonight you were talking with Ann about the different dimensional levels that earth people inhabit on and around the Earth. I will try to explain a little bit about the dimensional interface between the worlds, and the scope of what can be done and what is allowed. When I say 'allowed', I am talking simply in terms of what is physically possible on different levels or dimensions of your being. I will also discuss with you the nature of the human brain. I spoke about this in an earlier session, and now I will try to explain how these levels are created.

Elaine: Before I begin, I must first say that I can also see a very strong image of a snake. The image is of a cobra with huge black eyes, and it is raised up with its hood extended. It's not some kind of an Extra-Terrestrial; it's just a snake.

Ann: Does it represent anything?

Elaine: Wisdom, I think. There is a deep rich blackness in the eyes, and they are disproportionately bigger in size compared to the body of the snake. I am feeling infinite knowledge and understanding in those eyes, and it's just hovering in complete stillness behind the Andromedan woman. I must concentrate for a moment.

Andromedan: Mankind's duality is represented in the two halves of the brain. In truth, the logical functioning of the brain is necessary only in the lower dimensions. What seems logical is what appears in the reality in front of you, that *you* have created. It is logical that one brick sits on top of the next brick. But if you remove the logic and see only the energy, then you will see no actual separation between the bricks. When you release the need for third dimensional physicality, you release the need for logic. That does not happen automatically, it comes with understanding. When you begin to understand, you will see these things more clearly.

Firstly, you will understand that you can change shape or be somewhere else in an instant; that you can fly, and send and receive telepathy. When this is fully recognised, the left logical side of the brain becomes a little like a dinosaur. It becomes unnecessary, and more of a hindrance than a help if it interferes too much.

You see, for you there is no logic in being able to fly. If I asked you now, 'Can you fly?', you would say 'No, I am too heavy: The force of gravity is too strong. It is an impossible thing.

If you left your physical body then you could astral travel freely, but as you are still within your body and you relate as being that body, then your logical mind dictates that some things are impossible. Your logical mind dictates that you cannot pass your hand through a wall. In reality, with manipulation of molecular frequency, all is possible.

I feel you ask the question about 'whole brain' function.

Elaine: Yes. Why is it that some of us are striving to be integrated or whole-brained on this planet?

Andromedan: The answer to this question is that as a species, you are changing from logical to spatial thinking. Whole-brained thinking is the middle path, not the ultimate goal. I say this because within the right hemisphere of the brain, all your latent abilities are held. To access this fully, it means not trying to logically understand, but knowing, feeling and grasping concepts without words. If you can forsake your logic for just a while, you will begin to realise the many levels and stages of development that there are to be reached within the right brain.

You are a technological society, and for third-dimensional functioning you need (or you have needed in your past), the greater functioning of logic and understanding. You plant a seed, and it grows. This is logical. But these are just basic elementary facts. What you have missed is that when you plant the seed for growing, it is a fact that without the energy of the Creator, (the energy of All That Is that flows through everything), the seed would never grow. You have all been in Earth kindergarten learning the basics, and now its time to graduate into high school.

The basic concept of logic is within you. It can be compared to the sound and frequency work that you do, Elaine. Once you have learnt the basic logical premise that 'this equals this', you then put it to the back of your mind, and allow your intuition and feelings to come into play. You then look at the person you are treating, and you instinctively know what could be wrong with them. I showed you a model once before. I now show you once again.

Elaine: I can see a kind of metallic egg shape. It's longer than an egg, more like an elliptical bullet, but not as pointed. She takes a lid off, and I see two halves of what I would recognise to be a brain with one side dark, and one light. I am describing colour, i.e. one side is a cream colour and the other side is dark brown to black. I see that they sit side by side like a normal brain would, with a division down the middle. I see red, blue and white wires, just you might expect inside any kind of electronic machine that has circuitry inside.

Andromedan: Your best example of a similar shape is one half of a walnut. When you are sufficiently unencumbered by your belief system and you are advanced enough to realise that you can and do create your own reality, the energy form of the left logical side of the brain will start to diminish. It becomes in essence, smaller. The right side of the brain *energy* will fan out and become one whole unit.

Now note all these wires indicating metaphorical connections from the left to the right side. If one side of the energy shrivels up or diminishes, what happens to the connections?

The connecting 'wires' crossing from left to right (neural pathways) then start to link from front to back. The front of the brain above the 'third eye' and all around the area where the pituitary gland is, becomes connected underneath to the back part of the brain. This 'black area' of the brain, the substantia negra, is an area that your doctors and scientists know very little about. Within this dark area of the brain lie the capabilities of molecular change: total restructuring of the body.

(At this point I was so surprised, I interrupted)

Elaine: Hang on a minute, what do you mean by molecular restructuring of the body?

Andromedan: This is the ability to change from one thing into another: To change your cellular structure, along with your energy body.

Elaine: She illustrates this by reminding me of a documented story about a little girl with multiple personality disorder. This child had two distinct personalities. She could change from one to the other within a matter of minutes. One persona was unaware of the other. One suffered from asthma and needed an inhaler; the other suffered from insulin dependant diabetes. When she changed personalities, the diabetic child had absolutely no sign of asthma, and vice versa. This meant that she was changing the whole structure of a disease in minutes, with no medical signs of one when the other was present.

Andromedan: Here within the area at the back of the brain, there are no limits. There is no logic, and without logic you are free because everything is possible. You use the front part of the brain as a command module, i.e. directing your wishes, your will and your wants. Your truth and integrity come from here, because it is from this frontal area that you connect mentally and telepathically with higher wisdom.

Elaine: She's monitoring my mental questions here.

Andromedan: Your source of energy as always, flows in through the centre: through the crown of the head, down through the body. This is not what we are concerned with at the moment. What we are concerned with are the functions of the brain, and the energy patterns stored there. You understand that once you die and leave the physical body behind, the actual physicality of the brain no longer exists. However, the energy patterns are still there. Within them are held all the memories of everything you have ever accomplished.

And so we are talking in these terms. For example, look at the metaphorical wires in the model, and see them as electrical connections or brain impulses. As the energy flows, you see something similar to a flash of lightning or an electrical current pass from one place to another. It's an electrical impulse connecting from the front to the rear of the brain. I am trying to explain to you in terms of how it would be if it were physical, but you must understand that we are dealing with a highly concentrated mass of energy.

Ann: Can I ask a question?

Andromedan: Yes...

Ann: Would the pineal gland still be there, in essence within the energy, if the body died?

Andromedan: Yes. The pineal gland is like a gateway through which all cosmic energy enters and flows through. So even if you died, and did not have a physical pineal gland, the energy formation would still be there like an open flower receiving cosmic energy.

Ann: So is the pineal gland our link with the energy waves that come from spirit, or not? Is it something that's necessary for keeping our connection to the spirit world?

Andromedan: In essence, the pineal gland is in a central position in the brain, and whilst you are in physical form, it functions as a master hormone producer. The energy and frequencies of those hormones affect you emotionally. Nothing physical is needed once you pass into your 'spiritual' realm. Obviously you do not need your physical body, but the patterns of the primary organs, whilst they have disappeared as physical organs, still survive as energy patterns. Are you asking if you need the pineal gland to communicate telepathically?'

Ann: Yes. I understand that our medical science, such as it is here, doesn't seem to fully understand why the pineal gland is there. I feel it has an important function, but it's not an obvious one. Some people feel that it has a more of a spiritual function than a physical one.

Andromedan: Within the two levels that exist for the pineal gland, (the energy level and the physical level), it is important for the physical body to process chemicals through the pineal gland. But on an energy level you are indeed looking at a kind of gateway. It is difficult for me to describe (using Elaine's mind).

Ann: When you say that, something in me wants to go a bit further, because it feels so important to understand this gateway. The pineal seems to me to be part of our spiritual, genetic heritage. Would that be correct? Does it go back in time to when we were first on this Earth? Was it used differently then?

Andromedan: There are two levels. The all-important factor with the pineal gland and its position is the frequency that is held there. Translated into physical terms, those frequencies become hormones, which affect the way you are, i.e. whether you feel good, bad or indifferent.

Ann: So are those hormones different from the ones triggered by the pituitary?

Andromedan: Yes. If we look at a spiritual or energy link, it becomes a focal point. When the energy that you have allowed yourself to receive in the past various decades comes in through the crown chakra (as you call it), it focuses like a laser into the pineal. When you are energetically or spiritually aligned, you feel a certain balance within the body. This is like putting your finger (if your finger could be the cosmic energy) on a doorbell in your mind. When the connection is there, it 'rings' and it brings spiritual balance to the body. This chakra has not been opened in certain sections of your species for a while. In some other cultures it has been used openly and freely. They were then able to understand and see clearly 'visitors from the sky', and beings that came from other planets to visit.

However, I must now come back to the point that I was making about frequencies; when you are not in the physical body and therefore only in possession of your 'energy brain', it takes on a different format. I will describe it to you in layman's terms. (I am trying to make Elaine understand what I am attempting to convey). The brain becomes whole: there is no division in the middle. But remember when I talk of this brain, it is only energy. It is the concentrated energy of the block of frequencies that was your brain when you existed in the physical.

Maybe I can illustrate. If I said your physical hand resonates at 200 hertz and I cut your hand off, and then extracted the energy from it, the physical is no longer necessary. What is contained within that energy of frequency at 200 hertz, are all the genetic configurations, the memories of everything you did with that hand. So I am trying to explain to you the concept of being in an energy world, or being in the fourth dimension; you would look and feel solid, but in actual fact, your energy is much finer, and vibrates faster. The logical side of the brain has diminished, the right side of the brain has become more whole, and the connections from one side to the other now go from the front to the back. This is just one section of what I am trying to explain to you.

In a way, your eyes do not see. Take the logical physical reality which is presented to you; this you can see, this, you can understand; but in using your physically solid flesh and blood eyes, you cannot really see the absolute reality of all that there is to see.

Again, when we talk of the third eye, or Ajna centre in the forehead, as you call it; this is the energy component of your visual eyes. This allows you to see and to know things that are 'unseen'. There is no left-brain function here at all. This is a completely right brain 'feeling and knowing' function.

Part of what I am trying to prepare you for is the fact that to a certain degree, your physicality is a hindrance to you. On the other hand, it has been necessary for the experiment that you have been completing for yourselves and for us on this planet. This sounds a little clinical, but it is, and has been, a willing and joyful experiment on the degrees of energy expansion that we could achieve at one end of the testable spectrum.

I will try to explain in simple terms.

Imagine creation as a long pole, where one end of the pole is the Creator, and there lays the highest form of energy that one can achieve. The other end of the pole is the densest one can achieve. There are creations and existences much denser than you can understand. You may think that the third dimension is as dense as you can go. Not so!

In conjunction with you as souls, we have embarked upon this experiment; it is not just an experiment, but a great achievement! It is pursuing the will of the Creator to explore every facet of the self. This is part of everything that we agreed to. We all agreed to be all that we can be. In pursuit of all that we can be, we experiment and we try things. Time has no meaning, and it does not matter how long the experiment takes.

We have come to remind you that this is not for ever. I heard you today, Elaine, speaking of a wish to leave your body behind and embark upon fourth dimensional existence. For you, it would be gaining a freedom that you have known many times, and you know it very well. It's all there, stored energetically in the memory bank of your brain. But to leave the physical body too soon would be to exit the classroom before the experiment is finished, and what we are trying to achieve here is the dominance of the right brain over the physical body. We are trying to bring the fourth dimensional concepts into the third dimension, so that you can come half way to meet us.

I will rephrase this, as I see in your mind the expression I am looking for. If you wish to have heaven on Earth, then in a way you must discard your logic. Only when you allow anything and everything to be possible, do you diminish the control of the left logical side. This will allow the expansion in energy form of the right 'anything is possible' side. Within your physical body you will still have two lobes to the brain. You can allow one side to diminish its energy output, and the other side to take over, as it were.

This does not mean to say that you will be totally illogical, and unable to function. Not at all!

What it does mean is this. All the things that you cannot see with your eyes or understand with your logical mind; or that you cannot feel because there are too many words in the way, will become apparent to you. This is when and where the beauty of silence arrives. Simply because in silence the only language is telepathy, and telepathy is a feeling language. It's how you feel....its right brained. The energy of telepathy knows no boundaries. Telepathy can span a universe; it can take you from one place to another, so that your whole essence is present in another dimension if you wish. I am coming back to the illustrated model which I showed you, and the various wires which were just an illustration to show you exactly what can happen and why. I will go more deeply into some of the functions.

Situated behind the ears here in line with the mastoid bone, (she visibly demonstrates) is an important point. If you place your fingers just behind the ears, and to the rear of the skull you will find it. This is the area where the energy, which controls your concept of space and time, is held.

Perhaps you may wear metal on your head sometimes. I notice that Elaine wears her metal glasses on top of her head, when she is not using them. In doing so, she makes a partial circuit around her head touching only the two points that I mentioned. This circuit can be completed with a band of some sort, or glasses and a chain. When you connect at those points with a metal circuit, then you can indeed free yourself temporarily from the concept of space and time.

Ann: This is an interesting idea!

Andromedan: There are different words I can use. These points could be called 'aerial' points or 'receivers' that allow 'stretching' of time. These are inadequate words I feel. For example, you may have been occupied with a task for what seems like five minutes, and you realise that two hours have passed. It is because you have been receiving and transmitting energy from these areas of the brain.

We and the Federation have engaged in experimental tracking (with permission), with some human beings on the planet. When we engage a tracking device, it is usually placed in this area of the brain behind the ear, some inch or so inside. This is simply because it has strong polarity. There is an energy balance somewhat similar to your human ear function that allows for the concept of time and space to be accessed best at those points. At the base of the skull in the brain stem, deep in the centre, is another very important point in your system. Remember at all times, I talk not of the physical organ but of the energy frequency that it holds. It has a relationship to what goes on in the body whilst you are still physical, but once you have left the physical body behind, the vibration of what it truly is acts on a different level. These two interface whilst you are alive (in the third dimension), so that the capacity for both is there.

The capacity to produce the necessary frequencies for the body is there, and the energetic capacity to interlink with 'outside', or next dimensional, is also there. These two things are in place whilst you are alive in a physical body. When you die, the energy is all that is left. But this energy is still the same whilst you are alive.

When you are focused in the physical body and very much alive, the physical part dominates over the spiritual counterpart, although they are in tandem there together.

The important part that lies in the mid- centre of the brain stem is as follows. If you will visualise the centre of your throat or neck at the back here (she demonstrates),.... coming down here is a vortex of energy. You humans have not discovered nor have a name for the part that I am describing. It looks somewhat like a cylinder. It is about two inches long, like a circular tube of tissue, but it resonates at quite a different frequency.

It is, on an energy level, another gateway. It's a gateway in and out for the 'essence' of the body; a place where the soul can come in and go out, without disturbing the energy patterns of the brain.

Do you understand this?

If you left your body at night during sleep and used the channel that goes directly in and out of the brain centre or the crown chakra, there would be huge fluctuations in brain wave energy. In this instance, the liability of no 'early warning system' would be great. For example, if something were to happen to the body, some mishap, when there is no consciousness there, it could mean severe shock to the physical as well as your mental self.

This area at the back of the neck, deep in the brain stem is the best 'in and out' point for the energy body. It ensures that a proportion of energy remains there, and so there is always some consciousness left within the physical body to keep everything running as it needs to. So this is a very important point, simply because it is much more important to the physical body than to the spiritual body. However, once you die, or have 'passed over' (as you call it) and left your physical body behind, there is no longer a need to either exit or come back.

This is also a point that can be accessed by 'other' energy. I believe Elaine already understands a little of other fields of energy. Other souls, or bodies of intelligent energy, can enter the body via the back of the neck. The physicality of this cylinder of muscle is very important, because whilst it is in place and healthy, you cannot be 'invaded' by any passing energy form that would occupy your body. If this is damaged, however, then there is severe disruption to the energy system and the design and pattern of the energy body within you. If there were damage there, it would almost be like your entire energy body could be 'scrambled'. You would feel very disjointed, and not 'yourself'. You would feel very sensitive and open to attack; extremely vulnerable to all kinds of fluctuations in energy fields around you, and very vulnerable to lower density energy forms. With this, I am talking about possible interference from souls who have not gone to where they should be; you call them 'ghosts' or 'lost' souls. These souls are sometimes the cause of depression, mental breakdown or schizophrenic conditions in humans. This only happens when the area at the back of the neck is damaged, and the energy of these souls can 'invade'.

There is also another point connected with the brain that I must talk about. To locate it, imagine first that you made an incision through the roof of your mouth, go straight up for a short distance and you would come to another extremely important point in the brain.

Ann: Can you tell us what that is?

Elaine: Yes, she is showing me what it is, but I am feeling it first.

Elaine: It has to do with vision. It has to do with inner vision. She is showing me, and will describe it.

Andromedan: If you can, imagine your two physical eyes and the muscles at the back of the eyes, converging and crossing at a point in the centre of the head, physically. Then imagine there is a physical 'screen receptor', (like a tiny video screen) enabling you to see the images that are captured by your eyes. Just below that supposed physical screen, is the energy screen that your non-physical Ajna centre (third eye) uses, to see non-physical things. It's the screen on which Elaine is now seeing and feeling the things I am trying to impart to her. If you could draw lines on the head, i.e. a straight line through from the bridge of the nose to the back of the head, and stop directly above the roof of the mouth, the point would be there.

I am explaining these things to you so that you will understand that within your physical body now, are all the energy patterns and all the capabilities (and I have described just a few) that you would use if you were a fourth dimensional being without a 'body'. But they are available for you to use now! What you have to do in order to use them more fully, is to allow the dominance of your left logical side to decrease, and allow the prevailing energy from the right side to increase. I understand that this may seem very simplistic to you, and not even relevant.

There are reasons why I have given you this basic understanding and there is a lot more to explain. The difficulty I am having, and the pauses I am making, are because I find it difficult to extract the right 'logical' words, to explain something that is to you, illogical. You can only 'know' and 'feel' it.

Ann: Yes, I suppose you can sense it.

Andromedan: I have heard Elaine speak today about her wish to be free from the daily Earth traumas that she goes through (as you all do at times). I am coming tonight to say that you have more than enough of what you need to make a transition.

All that is needed are the finer teachings that will enable you to bring all the energy fields of these places within your brain system into use more strongly. It works on the same principle as meditation. The more you meditate the more stable and still you become energetically.

Once you become aware of the capacities you all have to do things not thought possible, then you begin to learn or to know how to use them more readily and easily.

For example, if I were to say to you Ann, would you like to be on a beach in the Caribbean in five minutes? To feel the sun, smell the sea and swim, and feel so physical that you would not know that you weren't there?' Well, there is a way to be there in every sense of the word, and enjoy it physically. I say 'physically' but it is not as you understand physicality. We need to find finer definitions of some of the words used tonight.

Ann: So energy wise I would actually experience being on a beach?

Andromedan: Oh, one hundred per cent! It would be a real event happening, an actuality.

Ann: Do I understand correctly? I would be conscious of all the feelings and sensations of being there, but I would not be in my physical body. Is that what you are saying?

Andromedan: Yes, in a sense. Some people on Earth have termed it bi-locating, and some claim to be able to do this, as indeed some of them can. To bi-locate is fine, and there are various stages.

One is imagining that you are there; but the full blown experience of bi-location is the next step. A further step is to totally re-locate: to take your whole self there.

Ann: Would you be able to come back to your physical body?

Andromedan: If you bi-located, yes you could. If you re-locate, you can hop from one place to another. You could be in your kitchen cooking your tea, go to New Guinea, pick a papaya and come back again!

Ann: (Laughs) Yes!

Andromedan: However, your logical mind says, ah-ha! That's not possible!

Ann: Yes, I see that if you get rid of the logic, it actually opens up the possibilities!

Andromedan: Yes. What I say seems very 'clever' and simplistic, and you would perhaps think, 'Oh yes, I really believe that' (with disbelief).

As I explain things in more detail over the time period of the next few weeks, you will begin to see that it's like a puzzle. When you have all the pieces, you will begin to understand how something like that is possible.

Elaine: She is leaving now. I will give my thanks to them all, and say goodbye.

Ann: What an interesting evening with such strange information. I look forward to what comes next!

18
A Mysterious Story.......

Elaine: I will begin. This is not the usual pattern of what happens, but I will follow it.

The Extra-Terrestrials seem to be standing back, waiting for something to come in. Surprisingly enough, I see the claw of an eagle quite close up, and this eagle has taken off into the air. In its claws it is carrying an old book, like an old fashioned bible with yellow pages. The eagle has dropped the book; it's now on the ground, and has fallen open at a page. I can see the writing on the book and it's in old-fashioned script. I will see if I can read it. The text is as follows.

'In the time of the Hebrews there was built a palace, and some called it a temple. Within the walls of this palace there lived a king. The king had the power of the sun as his energy source. He would often look to the distant horizon, over the water, and wonder just what the meaning of life really was. He was a fair king and good to his people, but he was troubled continually by a feeling that came from within, that all was not as it should be.

One day, the king decided to take his telescope and look at the stars. In the heavens he found his answer, because he saw it was marked in the stars 'And All Things Are One'.

He realised that the source of energy from the sun that he felt was the bringer of life, was merely a ball in the hand of God. He took this knowledge, and began to think about it.

He saw the equality of the people with one another, and he saw himself. He thought he would relinquish his place as ruler, and be as they were. When he tried to make himself as one of the people, they threw themselves on the floor and pleaded with him to stay as he was, being their ruler'.

Andromedan: Because the King was wise and fair, they did not want him to abdicate his position and power. They needed a figure to relate to, and in this way some of you people of Earth have come to relate to your God as the giver of all things; as someone with ultimate power over you. I say to you, and what you must realise is this; the king was wise enough to see that he and the people were one and the same, and the energy of 'All That Is' was everything. This must illustrate to you that you and the Creator are the same.

Your energy is the Creator's energy, and instead of looking to the Creator as being separate and someone you serve, realise that the service is within you. By being all that you can be, and by acknowledging the extent of your power, you can raise the entire frequency of the Earth enabling you to become as your 'God' itself. It's very difficult to put into words.

If I say, The Earth is God, and God is the Earth, it's the same as your expression 'The Hand of God'. It's one part, and yet contains the whole, as in the 'genetic whole'. This is part of my explanation to you about the latent abilities and powers that you have. I am sorry I disguised it as a story in the beginning. Every cell of your being is as God, because all is God, all is the Creator.

The Creator and things that are created are one and the same. All that the Creator can do, you can do. What must be learnt are the various stages in which you enable yourself to allow this to happen.

In your historical times, Jesus of Nazareth was a good example of someone who allowed this to be. He acknowledged this, and explained using the words, 'I am a Son of the Father', meaning that the energy of the two were the same. Sometimes words can be very tricky, in the fact that you think on the surface they mean one thing, and yet the depth of meaning is much more, when you consider it carefully.

Now I would like to show you what it's like out into the universe. You see before you the backdrop of the sky, inky black and full of stars, and I will take you to one of those stars. It matters not where or what it is, it's just a small planet on the edge of a system somewhere. What does matter, are the things I will show you there.

Elaine: She has helped me to travel mentally to this new place. It's just like flying!

Andromedan: Now we have come to the planet, and you can see that there are areas of volcanic activity, rocks, and sulphur pools. It's not too inhospitable, but nevertheless there is not much of a green nature here. If you look closely at some of the indentations in the rock, you will see small pools with (what looks to you) green algae in. This example is like the first stage of life, or waiting to be born. This is the beginning of the fusion of chemicals, aided by sunlight that begins primary plant life. If I were to approach these algae, and take a drop of genetic chemical, and merge the two, I could produce a frog. It's not difficult for me to do that. But if I wanted to produce a horse, we are talking in terms of a different matter all together.

As genetic scientists, we have wandered the galaxies, taking samples from whichever planets were interesting, and yielded something new. We always pay the utmost respect to whom or whatever we find there, and do no harm. Our principle is curiosity, interest, and the furthering of 'science' as you call it, but we do no harm to any living creature.

I hear you ask, how do you create a horse? Well, in normal terms, to create a horse, you take the sperm and the egg, and it will happen. But how do you create a horse from nothing?

When we know the energy patterns, and the genetic frequency patterns of your beautiful equine animals, we can fuse them in certain conditions to produce the entire energy patterns of a horse. Although to you it would not be a third dimensional horse, to us, it's a horse.

This brings me to the differences in dimensions that I must try to explain to you. I speak of the vibrational difference between your third density dimension, and the fourth, fifth, sixth, and other dimensions that we occupy. As I mentioned previously, we are like two ends of a pole. The third dimension, although not the densest dimension that there is, is very dense, and within that, you can have a real 'flesh and blood' honest to goodness horse. However, it is one that can be injured if it falls, can fall sick and eventually will die. With this denseness come certain problems.

If you go to a denser stage, you might consider a rock. A rock is very dense, and the consciousness held within that rock is very slow. It's there, but it's very slow.

If you take a hammer to a rock and break it, it's irreparable. It cannot be joined together again to form the same unique rock.

I do hope that I am illustrating this in a way that's understandable! When a horse breaks down internally or externally, falls and damages itself, or becomes sick from within, the living systems break down. When that physical part of it is irreparable, the horse dies, but the spiritual energy continues on as a horse.

Now I will come back to the rock. You cannot glue a rock back together again satisfactorily. With each individual piece of rock that is left once you have split it, there is a consciousness there, but it does not change. The only change that comes from rock is when it is ground into the finest dust, and the denseness of that energy then becomes lighter; there is more 'space' between the molecules. The dust merges with 'mother Earth' as you call it, and becomes one with other elements. *Therefore, it has changed.* It's like a physical body dying, and the lighter energy passes on to become something else.

The point I am trying to make here is that we must consider the degrees of density. Unless there is radical change to the physical body, then you cannot bridge the dimensions and take the physicality with you. That can be partially achieved by simple modification of diet and in the liquids that you drink; but it can only extend to a certain degree. What I am trying to say to you is that there are some things that you must leave behind.

As the rock form leaves behind the dust, and the horse leaves behind its flesh, so as physical third dimensional humans, if you wish to make a sincere and full transition to the fourth or fifth dimensions, then there are things that you must leave behind.

You will see that some of the people, who are here now on Earth, have extremely large solid bodies. Some people are very slender, some are very frail, and some have a greater degree of muscle. They all have different degrees of physical denseness.

Note when an old person is about to die; even in the last years before they leave their physical body, their bodies can become frail. This you can see especially with very old people. When their energy and spirit occupies this frail body, it's very easy to for them to pass in and out of the fourth dimension.

They very often see so-called 'visions'. This is sometimes interpreted by others as the person 'rambling on' about the past and talking about their childhood, when in actual fact, the images played on the screen in their mind are so strong, that the total recall comes to the surface. As their bodies become lighter, due to less food intake sometimes, or less muscle content, the interface between the energy body and the physical body becomes elastic and therefore much easier to stretch.

Now, I need to explain to you how you can have this elasticity and still be in a very fit body. It's nice to have the elasticity, but not so nice to be very frail, so that you cannot move around and do things as you would normally.

Well. This needs a little bit of thought and explanation. I am trying to gather together in Elaine's mind a picture or a feeling of how this works. It's something that you need to allow to become part of your life. To begin with, I will explain that part of the time we hear Elaine say she feels 'spaced out' or 'not there'. She feels somewhere else, other than in her physical body. This is explained by the fact that her energy body is lifting up out of her physical body by a few feet. She feels 'not in line' with herself. This is when the energetic portal of the right brain is much more fully open than the left. I will give an example.

If you come into your kitchen and you start to wash dishes or do physical work, this can be a 'grounding thing' (as I understand the word). But you can still daydream and be 'out of your body' whilst you do mundane chores. It takes something that needs the left logical brain, like a mathematical puzzle, a crossword or a conversation sometimes, to bring your energy body back down into its rightful position within the body.

So how can you function in the here and now, and be somewhere else at the same time? Instead of having this 'spaced out' feeling that you have of not being 'quite there', we need to teach you how to develop an energetic and mental elasticity. So, for example, whilst you are sitting reading a paper, or peeling potatoes, you can at will come out from your physical body and bi-locate. Remember we talked about bi-location?

Ann: It all seems very futuristic.

Andromedan: Yes, it seems that way. But if you wish to have access to the fourth dimension, as many Earth people are predicting that you will, then you do need to realise or 'know' that this is what you are actually doing, and also practise in order to do it easily.

Elaine: She is leaving now, and I must say goodbye until the next time. I am so fascinated by all of this, and yet I still feel there is much more. Perhaps she has given me all I can understand for the time being, and that must be enough to digest in one go. Some things you have to know *absolutely*, before you can possibly contemplate anything further.....

19

Love is Universal........

Once again at Ann's house, the meditation room is peaceful and cosy with flowers, and the light from a candle burning on the small table gives the roses a soft glow. I have tuned in and now I am watching all the extra terrestrials sitting round a table as they have done in the past.

I see the Arcturan and the Sirian, and tonight the Andromedan is in the background. The tall being who says he is a Lyran is standing out quite prominently emitting very strong energy. He is a very light being energetically, with large dark eyes, tall and willowy, with a thin stick-like body and arms.

The Lyran speaks: I wish to speak to you tonight on the nature of Love. I will also talk a little bit about my race of beings, and where we came from. I will explain why we hold Love so dearly and why we speak to you with compassion and concern.

Back in the history of our time, our original root race was similar to what you would call insects. We too have come under the influencing hands of others, therefore our physical and spiritual progression was enhanced by the intervention of genetic alteration. The Andromedans were partly involved in this, but there were also other races. So we have deep understanding of what has happened here in the past on Earth. I will hopefully be able to explain to you why we feel it so necessary to take samples of your genetic line to preserve your species.

Many millennia ago, we were a simple race. Had you seen us then, you would have said we were like giant insects. Our race dominated the planet we inhabited, and we were omnivorous (we ate all things). We were quite an integrated species, in the fact that we occupied all areas of land on our planet. This part of our history is not well documented or remembered, and we have learnt about it from those who engineered our future. Our genetic engineering and levels of advancement have been very carefully monitored. I speak about times long past, because we are now genetic engineers ourselves, and we no longer rely on other races to help us in the same way. We were closely monitored at every stage of our development, and there were beings from other places and other planets that kept us informed of what was happening. As we came to understand more fully the concepts of what we could become, we became eager to change and to learn.

We all felt a strong preference to being free to roam not only the planet, but also the galaxy. This was a better situation than being confined just to our own planet. We were interested to see what other worlds looked like, especially the vegetation and life forms. Like children, we were unaware of 'self', and that we looked so very different to the majority of other species that can be found within the galaxies.

As an insectoid race originally, we tended towards a group consciousness, enabling us all to know telepathically what was happening in our close proximity. If there was a big event, or food to be had, then the common denominator was that we all knew where it was. We also had a queen amongst our species who was mother to us all, if I may use your Earth words.

Our species continued to follow the same kind of patterns but as our brains became more advanced, our consciousness opened up, and we started to become aware of our 'selves' as individuals. To some extent we by-passed an 'industrial age' and the necessity to build things with concrete and steel as you have done on your planet. We progressed very rapidly into the mental realms of creation, and our development has been in most ways, very different from yours. Our one link is that with the aid of others, we have changed, and we feel that we have changed for the better. We are glad that we now recognise ourselves in the mirror that is God (in your terms), the Creator in ours, and we see that all others are One with the Great Creator as we are.

On the planet where we live in this time frame, there is another civilisation that lives within 'thought created' places. We have gathering places where we meet in structures that would look quite real to you, even though they have been constructed by thought. The small grey beings that are familiar to some on this planet are a race that we have fostered in order that we may help them. They are like our children, and are in one sense of the word, manufactured beings. They have a group consciousness, but they are, (using your Earth words), happily within our control. They do some of the more manual things that we are unable to do physically as we lack the dexterity.

Ann: Are they organic?

Lyran: Yes, they are constructed of organic material. I will explain. They are a derivative of many things; they are the result of our experimentation from a long time ago and we feel a close and dear responsibility to them. We have no need to reproduce physically, but at one point we tried to build a reproductive mechanism into their systems, that would ensure the continuing of their species. However, our work with them was not as complete as we would have liked. There were several ultimate flaws that came to the surface after many years. One of which was their inability to reproduce themselves adequately.

What we did can be compared to Earth humans eventually perfecting what we would call androids. To perfect an android, especially one which is organic in nature, and then enable it become a self-sufficient species that reproduces itself, is a great task indeed. Whilst we have attempted this on many occasions, we have not as yet been fully successful.

Our purpose for taking genetic material from the human race is two-fold. The prime objective is the preservation of your species. We have learnt from our past mistakes that we must preserve any life form before it is changed. If any genetic mistakes ensue, we can always go back to the genetic beginning. So preservation of your species as it is now is of utmost importance. Secondly, we have been enlisted by others to maintain a genetic bank; this is because of the high levels of toxicity that are multiplying daily on your planet. All that we do is for the preservation of your species.

It is true that we have used some of our genetic samples, introducing them into the genetic codes of the little beings that you are familiar with. It is our hope that we can produce a hybrid race that will have individual thinking, recognition of self, and the ability to reproduce freely and easily. We believe very strongly that this will be our greatest success. We know that future races will arise from this, and we are glad.

Ann: If they do become reproductive beings, would you be seeking to implant some kind of control mechanism in them, or would you allow them to reproduce and be free as a race?

Lyran: The answer to that question is very simple, and I hope, very loving. The beings we are creating with our genetic experimentation will form a race of beings that will ultimately be on their own. We will be there to assist them, but we will not implant them with any device to follow them. We hope that they will settle in their own allocated space on a planet somewhere. We wish to give them what our genetic engineers gave us, and that is guidance and awareness all the time as to who they are, and what they can achieve. We hope to save them the pain and struggle of the harsher aspects of life, by being always there to support them and give them new teachings. Federation members and various others from around the galaxy have also offered aid, and they all have gifts that they will give. So these people will eventually be free people, and not subject to control.

Ann: Can you tell me if there is any point at which those beings, or even yourself, would receive a soul, and receive that part of divinity as a soul?

Lyran: They all have souls now, as we do! In the newly created beings, their energy form is such that the soul is within. It is not a multifaceted soul, as you understand your souls to be. These are new beings, with just one part of them beginning to develop.

You create things for yourselves with your own hands, like bread, or perhaps televisions. We use the tools that are of the Creator, and within this process of creation, any being automatically takes on and integrates an energy body. That energy body is virgin, and as such without experience, because it is still at the beginning stages of its learning. So you could call it a soul in its first stage of growth. Does that answer your question?

Ann: Yes I understand now. It makes sense. So is it envisaged that there will be an opportunity for these new beings which you are nurturing to find homes on another planet?

Lyran: Absolutely! As a temporary measure, they live with us on our many vast ships. But as a race of beings, we know that they are at some point entitled to the wonder and beauty that we have all shared, in a place they can call home. We would hope that one day, when the genetic codes are perfected and a suitable place is found, they will colonise and start to make an infrastructure for themselves which will enable their consciousness to be raised by self recognition. They already have a kind of self-recognition, but for the moment they take their directive from us. They see us as parents, and so initiative and free thinking is limited.

But please remember that some of the genetic inheritance of Earth humans is being placed within them. Within this is a great strength of spirit which we see with joy will come through, and be the driving force that pushes them towards self-realisation. We are happy to allow this when there are sufficient numbers, and we have found a suitable place. Maybe these beings could integrate in some areas of your Earth if it is ever permitted. Then they may be helped to recognise the diversity and the vastness of the universe that they live in. These new beings have also inherited certain cellular memories from the genetic material introduced into their bodies. This has helped them with a certain degree of emotion, which we watch develop with fondness and gratitude. The original little grey beings you are familiar with (that we helped create) have no sense of varied emotions. They have a group mind, and we (in a sense) control them for the most part. We tell them what they must do, and they do it. They are sometimes extremely disconcerted by strong displays of emotions; they recognise extreme fear and when there is a high degree of love present. In fact, they are very attracted to the energy of love, because it brings an aura and vibration of peace. Within the emotional energy of Love, they become quite still and almost motionless. We have very often to remind them of their tasks when they come up against this energy.

In a way, we would wish for your compassion and sympathy. (I pull this word from Elaine's mind). But sympathy is the wrong word to use. We ask for your understanding of what we have come through and experienced as a species, and how we regard life. To us, life is sacred, and we do not willingly do any harm. But we are curious, and we do wish to keep our rate of improvement and change at a rapid pace. So sometimes we feel compelled to be involved in genetic assistance.

Because we wish to better ourselves......now, I have just found a relevant example in the mind of the person who is talking,(Elaine) and I will use it to illustrate. When a person or race of people want to heal themselves or make their lives better, and they do not have or know the means to do it, then they feel compelled to try to heal or improve others. They continue on until they find the mirror that they need to look in, (i.e. a person or people with the same problems) in order to find themselves. Then understanding occurs, and they no longer have the need to improve or heal others.

This is as we are. We need to go on and on until we find peace within ourselves, until we find exactly where we fit and who we are, because we were changed. Our natural state of being and environment was changed. We were happy with this, but there are feelings within us that we still cannot understand, and we have no way to relate to others exactly what these feelings are. It's difficult to try to convey this great need that is within us.

One thing that is always overwhelming to us, is our love and joy for others. When we see other races and other beings, we look upon it as an opportunity to share ourselves. To talk with them and bring forth our joy, and maybe see once again if this new race holds the mirror that we need to truly see ourselves in. It's a process for us, and the joy that we feel when we meet new people fills us with a wonder that we recognise. Love was never a thing that our root race understood or knew. Only when our brainpower and consciousness expanded did we even begin to touch upon what the nature of higher emotions were. And so we have been endowed with a parental nature. Whilst we, as parents, feel compelled to continue to help others in our own way, essentially at the core of our beings we need to find our own 'inner child', because it seems as if our inner children were never there. In our memories, we cannot understand how we were before, and we need to do this.

Ann: Do you have a cycle of life, death and rebirth?

Lyran: No.

Ann: So are your memories important to you?

Lyran: It seems, when you ask me this question, as if I do not truly know what you mean. But I do understand because I have seen life, death and rebirth within many other species. But it seems as if we have always existed.

Ann: Is there any period of change that you go through (like our death), or are there only structured genetic changes? Do your bodies die, or do you just change in some way?

Lyran: We have a long and vast memory bank concerning the subject of how our lives have changed over time. I think I understand now how I can show you. We enter gladly into our next stages of improvement, and to do this we go to a place where we can be restructured, revitalised, and given a new level of understanding. I suppose you would compare it to your death and rebirth stage. Unlike your species, we are always conscious of what happens. It is like when you go to a shop for a new coat. We know when we are going to change, we choose the time, we are aware of the process, and we remember it when we come through it. So this is our cycle, but the difference between you and us is that we are always alive throughout the process.

Ann: Does that mean then that you have no need for a reproductive cycle?

Lyran: No. We have no reproductive cycle. We are *Always the Same Number* as we have been, since the beginning.

Ann: I believe that there are planets where other beings exist in the same way.

Lyran: Yes there are.

Ann: So, for you this is a continual cycle of improvement?

Lyran: Yes. To reiterate, our physical bodies are rejuvenated if and when we need, but there is never a loss of consciousness. We always choose and are fully aware when we go through the changing process.

Ann: Do you come from a planet that is unique?

Lyran: The beings that are like me are all from one planet. But our one planet is in a constellation of many. There are others of different races that we are involved with, but there are no others who look exactly the same as us.

Ann: So are you unique in your universe?

Lyran: Our species, and from whence it came, is unique. We understand from our teachers that there are races of people who have come from other basic genetic stock similar to us. But they are all slightly different. We only know ourselves as 'we'. We do not feel we have any relatives who are close, except of course our creations. These are our children.

Ann: You have obviously learnt a vast amount, to be able to create other beings.

Lyran: We were given the knowledge. All that we have learned in our stages of development has been given to us by The Higher Beings, who brought us from what we were originally. There is a place where we go (and I have put the image into the mind of Elaine). It is a vast room, where there is All Knowing energy whose powers, as far as we know, are unlimited. We go very rarely to this source, but it is a centre source of power and energy for all of us, and it holds us together like a queen in a hive of 'beings'. That's as close a parallel as I can bring, but it is All Knowing for us, anyway.

Elaine: If I can just take a moment here to describe what the Lyran showed me. I saw a huge room with what looks like a waterfall of energy in it, to one side. This 'waterfall' is like a moving sheet of electric blue energy and it's falling from the ceiling to the floor. Three quarters of the room is full of this energy, and it is conscious. There really is an energy being in there. I get the feeling that you would go in there with absolute reverence, and almost kneel in front of it to address it. This is a new and quite strange thing for me to see. It's like an inner sanctum with an All Knowing 'consciousness' in there. That's as close as I can come to describe it.

The Lyran has finished talking for now, and the Andromedan is going to say something to me. She says that we have almost finished the part of the book that needs to be presented. The task of illustrating is of equal importance, because it's necessary that readers see pictorial representations of the Extra-Terrestrial people.

She is now showing me an inside section of a body from chest to groin. She is talking about how 'other' bodily systems work (other than humans). For example, there are some beings with no intestines; therefore they don't eat in the same way. She tells me there are so many things for us to learn!

Ann: Is she showing you this because Earth people have very complex bodily systems?

Elaine: Yes, she agrees with you, and says the complexity is due to the density of our whole Earthly physical system. In order to process things that are as complex as the food we eat, we require a complex system.

She is leaving now, and says she will tell us more another time. So we say our goodbyes and end the session.

20
The Future is Organic.......

This is an interesting change tonight, because I suddenly see all the Extra-Terrestrial beings; not appearing in their usual format seated around a table, but actually on a spaceship. They are all standing in a room within this ship. I see the Andromedan, the Arcturan, the Sirian and the Lyran. I believe they want to take me on a tour of their ship tonight. This feels very different to the normal flow of things.

I look around, and I am aware that the lighting is very subdued, casting a soft glow around everything. I am asked to look closely at the material on the inside walls of the ship. It has a soft finish like satinised steel, with a very sparkly quality to the metal on some of the walls. I see soft upholstery on some seating areas, and lots of partitioned areas, separated with windows. They appear to be like glass, but they are obviously not glass. The strange thing about them is that they have a peculiar green glow.

This glow looks like the green algae you get on a glass of flower water when you leave it in the sunlight for too long. This green is lighter in colour, and it's very sparkly and clear, with an almost phosphorescent glow. It looks as if there are two sheets of glass, with the green liquid in between the two. I have no idea what that is!

I'll ask what this is.

Andromedan: 'This ship is organic in its nature. The substance with the green glow is similar to organic chlorophyll. It flows in between a membrane system throughout the ship.

Elaine: I can see that this green liquid is very fine. I could barely see that it was a liquid at first; I find it amazing that it's actually flowing around the ship!

Ann: What sort of properties does it have? Does it help in any way to support the ship?

Andromedan: It provides Life force, or life energy, because it is alive.

Elaine: Now that's interesting!

Ann: So it provides energy that sustains the people in the ship?

Andromedan: No, not exactly. I will answer this in a moment. I will show you first the qualities of the 'metal', because it isn't metal as you know it.

Elaine: She is showing me the structure of the metal, and it's something like a weaving, as in the warp and weft in a rug.

Andromedan: It is the interweaving of energy strands that come together cohesively to form the fabric of what looks like metal to you. But it's actually constructed from a complex source. We have an organic 'computer' that can weave energy forms, and create them around and about itself. It uses the energy of the green liquid to do this.

Elaine: She says the green liquid is comprised of life forms like one-celled amoebas, and it looks to me like a kind of green plasma. The computer combines with this, and uses the radiating energy. It utilises auric energy given off, and also the magnetic energy field of this plasma to feed itself, enabling it to hold the woven construction of the ship in place. She gives me an example of how this living 'computer' constructs and holds the ship in its desired form.

Andromedan: If you turned on a machine that produced a laser beam, it would continue to produce the beam as long as the energy source is engaged. As long as the machine is on, the laser beam exists. As long as our organic computer is engaged, the ship exists. This is because it both creates and uses the energy field that's flowing. But if you disengage the organic computer, the ship disappears.

Ann: I am trying to understand. Is this correct? The organic computer is creating the ship around it, and it can create a substance that is hard, looks like metal but has this fluid contained within it?

Andromedan: Yes, the computer is an organism in its own right. It's a conscious organism. We have used the word 'computer' so you will have something familiar to relate to, in the fact that it will do complex tasks when given commands.

Ann: Does it have embodiment in any shape or form?

Andromedan: It is housed in a protective shell. I will show you.

Elaine: She takes me into a circular room, with a large cylindrical structure (like a cake tin). It's about ten or more feet wide, but not very deep. On the top of this is what looks like a clear glass or perhaps Perspex dome. I look into the inside of the dome, and it's so beautiful! I can see a vortex of deep misty colours and energy moving around like swirling fog, with the occasional bright spark of something glittering in there.

Andromedan: This is where our computer, for want of a better word, is housed. It remains in there for protection and containment. Its energy field extends into every part of the ship, because the ship is created by it. So it maintains the ship as an extension of itself, as it were. If any damage is sustained to any part or system, the 'computer' immediately knows that it needs repair, and will attend to it. So it is self-repairing.

Elaine: She is now showing me something amazing. As a visual aid for themselves the whole top of the room we are standing in suddenly becomes like clear glass, enabling us to see the stars outside. It's absolutely wonderful. I have never seen anything so beautiful. I can feel and hear telepathically that they said 'Computer, open to the stars'.

Ann : Will your spoken voice also activate a response?

Andromedan: Yes, if you request.

Ann: Does it usually work by thought or telepathy?

Elaine: Well, I think that's probably how they do it. She confirms that they don't actually need to speak the words. I ask her why they need to see the stars outside. Obviously, with a computer as sophisticated as they have, it must know what's going on outside, concerning navigational matters.

Andromedan: Simply, because it's so beautiful. We use it sometimes as a viewing port when we approach a planet, enabling us to soak in the colours and the wondrous beauty of it. There are an infinite variety of things to be observed in space; gas clouds and comets, different phenomenon and swirling nebulae, and all manner of energy formations of different colours.

Ann: Can you give us some more information about those formations?

Andromedan: There is outstanding beauty and strangeness to be found in space. Some of the energy forms we have encountered would be a little bit beyond your comprehension. There are insufficient words in your language to adequately describe these things. We have dealt with energy forms that stretch even beyond us sometimes.

Ann: We see Star Trek on our televisions here on Earth. Are some of their concepts close to the things you have seen?

Andromedan: Yes, indeed they are, but you have only touched upon a fragment of the beauty and diversity that can be found.

Ann: I presume that you travel for various purposes in your spaceships. Are you expected to travel for long periods of time on your journeys?

Andromedan: Yes, and no. When we embark upon a mission, the ships are created for us to travel in. There is a passage of time within the ship, but the ship actually travels outside of time as you know it, and this is very different. We could travel from where we come from to where you are, and if you measured it in your time, it might take an Earth week. But if you want to travel telepathically, all things are instant. If we decided we would be here now, instantly, we could. To achieve this however, our energy forms and dimensional placing would be different. We usually travel by a means we call 'displacing space'. Simply put, it's when you displace space and enter in to the vacant spot.

Ann: I have heard some theories about this. Does the process you use take place in something called a relative time/space dimension?

Elaine: Yes, she says it is to do with relative time and space, but using different words. The Andromedan wants to carry on with taking me around the ship now. We walk into a central meeting room where the Andromedan crew members get together to talk. Again, it's a circular room with tiered levels that go down into the middle. The centre is not small, and there are just two levels that step down into a flat central space. There is seating there and she shows me little concealed monitors that pop up out of the floor, used for transmissions to other space vehicles. I am told that they can also pick up transmissions from Earth, i.e. frequencies of television and radio channels, and that kind of thing.

So they obviously use some kind of technology. A big screen has now appeared. One minute the wall was blank, the next, a screen materialised on the wall. It's just as if they said, 'Computer, create a screen', and there it is! On that, they can watch things of interest on a much larger scale. The screen comes alive, and she is showing me a picture of an American President. This is strange; it's President Kennedy, for goodness sake! It's a live picture of Kennedy giving a speech in front of microphones, and it's there on the wall, and it's almost like he's three feet away, it's that close! I'm amazed!

Ann: And is it very life like?

Elaine: It's him! It's like a virtual reality camera or even better than that, like a holographic representation. The Andromedans tell me they can select any time frame of our history and view it. I am going to ask her if it needs to be a recorded broadcast for them to view it on screen. I am curious to know if you can pick up past history, maybe the battle of Waterloo for example, because obviously there was no television then!

Andromedan: Yes, it is possible to view different time frames. We have sensory scanners that can take up an event that is happening, or has happened, and relay it back onto the screens. We can go to any time period we wish.

Ann: Even forwards?

Elaine: Good question, Ann!

Andromedan: Yes, even forwards. But when you go forward there are different time lines. Backwards is slightly different.

Elaine: What's a time line?

Andromedan: I will explain. If we go backwards, we can view events in one dimension that have taken place and were physically enacted. When we want to go forwards in time, from a position of now, the procedure is different. If I start at certain place during this year, and I want to view this space in 2060, I follow the time line of this time/space I am in, from now into the future. The third dimensional time line that I follow relates to where I am now. But there are many other time lines. We don't project too far into the future, because the time lines are so multiple that the choice is enormous.

Elaine: I understand what she is showing me now, and it's quite amazing! Imagine a garden rake for clearing grass. The long prongs come out like a large hand. Here at the root or handle of the rake, you stand in the now. You have many time lines as possible futures spreading out like the prongs of the rake.

She says that she can go forward into the future to any one of the 'prongs' or distant futures. Then, she can select the best possible future, follow that time line backwards through the events that will take her to the beginning of that future, and see what actions need to be taken in order to reach that particular future physically!

Ann: Yes, I understand, we always have choices about how we get to anywhere we want to go, and choices in what we do.

Andromedan: If you take the worst possible future scenario, and follow the time line back to now, you can see where the mistakes will happen; the things that went wrong, leading you to that difficult situation in the future.

Elaine: Goodness me! Now I can see how they can justifiably say that something will be in our possible future if we don't do this or that right now.

Ann: But then, they can't force us to do what they think are the 'right' things to do.

Elaine: No, definitely not. That's why there is only a choice for them to intervene. Maybe the Extra-Terrestrials know that the future will be not so good for us if we do certain things now, and if they don't offer intervention, we will never get to where we could go for optimum advancement with maximum harmony and peace. This is interesting! We have gone to another room and she is showing me what she calls a 'refresher chamber'. It's a circular glass tube that they step into like a shower, controlled by the computer. Once inside, you become infused with energy. I can see many different colours in there, like a tube full of rainbows. She says it is a total re-energiser for them whenever they need it.

Andromedan: These re-energisers do not always suit all the different personnel that we have on board this ship. The Arcturan, for instance, does not particularly like the refresher chamber. He has to have something totally different. As it has been designed for us, it suits us very well. The Sirians can also use it well, as their energy form is more compatible with ours. The Arcturans are much more physically solid, as they are of a different dimensional type. The Lyrans also do not fare well in there, because the harmonics within their bodies are different from ours. They resonate to a totally different pattern. The computer can adjust to this however, but the Lyrans are extremely tall. The computer will do some complex calculations to redesign the chamber so that it will suit, if needed.

Elaine: Now she is showing me what the Arcturan does to refresh himself. I can see him lying on a couch. It's like a flat bed with no sides, and it's on a raised plinth. On one wall is clear 'glass' and you can see the stars outside. I see he is in a kind of sleep, lying very still with his arms crossed. He telepathically tells me that he is checking through his body and energy sources with his mind. Like in deep meditation, he is mentally focusing on all areas of his body from his toes to his head. He is mentally communicating to all his cells that they will detect if anything is wrong, out of balance, needs energy or repair.

He is doing it all with his mind! It's a self-regulating and healing mechanism. As long as he is able to put himself into a peaceful meditative state for a while, it works and he can self repair and regenerate.

Now she shows me the Lyran being, and I see that he also uses mental energy but in a different way. He mentally connects to the room with blue energy in it that we spoke of previously. She asks me if I remember it. Oh yes, I certainly do! It is full of exquisite blue energy flowing like a waterfall, which to the Lyran is like an all-powerful 'God', or a Parent being. All that the Lyran needs to do is connect mentally or energetically with this blue room and its energy source within, and he is renewed. It's like an inner sanctum that he can go to. He can do that anywhere, anytime. He just takes a moment to be still, and he is renewed. But I don't think that's all............

She says that there are set periods of time when Lyran beings know they must return to their home planet for rejuvenation. They can function well and keep themselves maintained by connecting to the source when they need it, but only for certain periods of time.

Ann: I think that that might have been mentioned before. I can remember this.

Elaine: Yes. They continue to live as normal until the time draws near to when they must return. Then their energy starts to wane and they know they have to go home.

Now her thought patterns change, and she is attempting to show me the outside of the ship. It reminds me of two bells placed mouth to mouth. The general shape is like a rugby ball, with a big band around the middle. From this central band, it goes up in reducing tiers to the top, and it has a smaller but similar tier shape underneath. Around the centre is a big band of lights, forming a circle. It looks quite complex and the band around the middle reminds me of the rings around Saturn. But I know it's attached to the ship.

Ann: Are they bands of energy, or are they solid like metal?

Andromedan: It's all energy. We choose the organic computers that create these ships. There are different types, and each model creates a different shape for itself. In your terms, it's like choosing if you need a car, or a truck! The particular computer we have with us this time will create this shape you see because that's the shape it's most harmonious with. Another one will create a different shape. We enjoy this shape because (in your words) it has the ability to be upside down, (and to illustrate she is showing me a gyroscope) or downside up, but within it we are still the same way up! So we can turn, navigate, and see in any direction, without difficult manoeuvring or needing to change the gravitational fields.

Elaine: I would imagine that maybe the band around the outside of the ship is an energy field, working something like a gyroscope, and that it creates a force field that the ship moves around in. Maybe she will show me a bit more. She does not tell me if my thoughts on this are correct, but goes on to say that one of these ships has actually landed on the surface of the Earth.

I see a mountain range. Some of the mountains have snow on them, and I think it's in a pretty deserted place. The ship is sitting in a hollow amongst the peaks of the mountains, and it's so deep, it almost looks like a volcanic crater. The ship has descended into it, and is well hidden. It's so huge! When I first saw it, I didn't think it was this large. I can see across the tops of the mountains and its just sitting there. As I get closer, I see that it must be five kilometres across, if not more. Good grief! I am stunned by the enormity of what she is showing me. We zoom in to the area around the ship, and I can now see lots of other people.

Andromedan: There are many different races of people on this ship. They are representatives of other races that joined us on the journey culminating here. They are helping us to aid your planet and its inhabitants. We talked with these others, invited them to join us on the ship, and have now formed a cohesive working group.

Elaine: I can see lots of people working together, so busy doing things! I see greenhouses, and the people there are active with different tasks. I am told that duties include everything from cultivating new strains of grasses like barley, agricultural projects, and calculations on the weather. I see people checking the composition and content of the atmosphere for levels of acidity in rain. They monitor everything, all working on different projects. Some work using telepathic communication, and some use audible language.

Elaine: I have just asked her a question. Are you personally resident on board this ship we can see?

Andromedan: This is the ship I came in on originally, but I am based on a smaller ship now. When I visit the surface of Earth or make personal contact with people, I travel on this small ship as obviously the mother ship is too big to move around for small missions. So we have stationed it out of the way. The reason we brought the mother ship here to the surface is because it's easier for us to operate and take our measurements inside your atmosphere, than outside. We were outside for quite some time, but it was decided that we should come in and be more closely involved on Earth.

Elaine: This is interesting! The shuttle that she operates from is shaped like the dome of a bell on the top, with two levels and a curved piece underneath. So instead of the ship being domed on the top and then flat, the sides curve down, and then there is a curved piece underneath. It's a bit like a jellyfish shape.

Ann: When she talks about the mother ship being here at the moment, do they expect to be here for quite a while, or do they come and go regularly?

Andromedan: The mother ship is here on a permanent basis for the time being.

Elaine: She is showing me dates of at least until 2050 or 2060. The mother ship is not scheduled to go anywhere, and from out of it will come all the smaller ships, as it's their home base.

My mind has immediately gone to our spy satellites, because there is nothing on the surface of the planet that they miss! You could spot something like that from outer space without a problem, and I have asked her about this.

Andromedan: We have taken this into consideration, and we have placed a holographic energy projection above the ship, simulating the tops of mountains. So, to any outside observer, it would appear like an undisturbed mountain range. It functions like an umbrella over the ship.

Ann: So, the whole thing just blends into the landscape?

Andromedan: Yes, it cloaks our ship, like camouflage. We don't need anything else other than that.

Elaine: With that, she tells me she is leaving now. We wish them all goodbye, and all the people present now fade away. I bring my consciousness back to the present moment, open my eyes, and focus into the room. It always feels as if no time has passed at all, even though we have been talking to them for over an hour.

21
Andromedan Children........

It's a cold night tonight, with frost sparkling on the pavements outside. Ann and I are again in her cosy meditation room. I have welcomed all the guides and Extra-Terrestrials; the Sirian doesn't seem to be here, but those who are here include the 'Blue Eyed' Extra-Terrestrial, the Arcturan, the Andromedan and the Lyran.

The Andromedan female opens her arms to welcome me. She embraces me, takes me by the hand, and points the way forward down a corridor. Before I begin my journey with her, I must say that I have also seen images, shown to me by the Arcturan, of a large orange planet. It is huge, but he makes no other reference to it, and so I will continue on. I am now walking down the corridor with the Andromedan. As we walk I see that there are rooms on either side. Some of the doorways are diamond shaped, and some are circular. Several rooms have large viewing windows, and the whole corridor is very softly lit.

The first window I am shown is circular. Looking in, I see there are dolphins swimming in water, and also a very tall thin being. I think it's an Andromedan; I can't see if he is wearing any kind of clothing, but his skin colour is a very pale greyish blue, and he has no hair. I am observing the rather strange shape to his head; he has a very large cranium, and his face tapers thinly towards the chin. Looking through the window is like looking upwards into a tank at an indoor aquarium, allowing me to see the surface of the water from underneath. I see what he is doing; looking beyond the water, the room is perfectly spherical like a ball; and above is a walkway with a handrail all around. It's made of a meshed metal (like a fire escape), so the water can flow up and down through it, and it's positioned about a foot above the water. Inside the room on the surface of the interior walls there are all kinds of monitoring screens, knobs and dials, perhaps 'recording equipment'. This is what it looks like to me, but it's difficult to know exactly. I can only guess by what I know of our own technology on Earth. To describe the rest; the whole top circle of the roof is bright, reminiscent of a ball with the top sliced off and fitted with a wonderfully soft light source. I am going to ask what is happening here.

Andromedan: My colleague is talking to the dolphin. We are imprinting (note she doesn't say recording) this conversation for our data collection. These are not dolphins from your planet; they came from another planetary system.

Elaine: Now I look at them more closely, I can see that their skin is a wonderful shade of green, as opposed to blue. Other than that, they look exactly like our own bottle nose dolphins. We exit and go along the corridor a bit further in order to see another room.

I am amazed at what I see in the next room- a beautiful specimen of a sabre-toothed tiger! It has huge teeth that come right down over its bottom jaw, and in fact, I can see two of them in there. One is walking up and down, and the other one is lying in an extremely relaxed state on an upper level. It's like a jungle in this room, and they both look quite content and happy.

Ann: Is this real, that is, not a hologram?

Elaine: Well, they look real to me. I can see the fur and the teeth in detail, and they have very long tails. But there is a difference; on the ends of their tails they have a hairy tuft. Their paws are huge, like dinner plates.

Ann: Do they seem aggressive?

Elaine: No, they seem quite docile. They are making rumbling noises, like heavy purring. I ask her if this is a zoo or something similar.

Andromedan: No, this is not a zoo, but they are species that we have collected for a reason. They are for redistribution onto other planets.

Elaine: Now she takes me to the other side of the corridor, and there are some primates in this room. As far as I can discern, they are exactly like chimpanzees from our world. It's a very clinical white room, with various levels to it, giving them the room to jump about and do natural things. However, one of them is writing something, and crayoning with colours on the wall. There is another one who is sitting on the top level, just looking at the other one. Now the one who was crayoning on the wall has taken the crayons up to the other one, sitting on the higher level, where there is paper on the floor. He is showing the other one that you can make marks on the paper. He is actually offering the crayons, as if to say, you do it too.

Ann: Can you see a purpose to all this?

Elaine: I don't know at the moment. She tells me this is not the only way they behave. They jump up and down and screech, as they would do in natural surroundings, and I see them doing all the things that a chimpanzee would do normally, i.e. swinging around from different pieces of equipment, eating fruit in a normal way. She tells me that they put very soothing music on in the room. It calms them, and as a result, they become more interested in things around them. She says they are just stimulating their intelligence.

She is taking me further on now, and the corridor is going on in a curving circular direction. I can see all kinds of things. There are crocodiles in one room, giraffes in another. The crocodile room is a steamy watery place with lots of greenery in. All the animals seem very docile, and each one has its own special environment. Some of the settings are unnatural. The only two rooms I saw that were close to looking natural were where the tigers and the crocodiles were. Of course, the water that the dolphins were in is normal, but it was not like the ocean. The giraffes and the chimpanzees were in a very white clinical setting, but it was a 'soft', not hard environment. All the animals looked quite peaceful. I don't know whether they (the Andromedans) have done something to them, but the animals don't seem to be distressed in any way.

We are moving on to the recreation area now, and we go up some stairs and emerge into a huge open space. There is a bridge in front of us with nothing underneath, like a huge cavern with hundreds of softly lit units all over the walls, above and below. The sides of this space go up and up for hundreds of feet, and as we cross the gantry we come into a space that is large with a friendlier atmosphere.

This is just like a scene from Star Trek! There are all kinds of different sectioned areas. Places where you can go and sit, and places to eat and drink things. There's one section that has lots of lounging couches in it, and people are lying on them wearing a kind of visor across their eyes. They are obviously viewing something within. Oh! She says its history! People can view events of their choice happening on any planet, in any time zone. I will describe one of the beings I see lying on a lounger bed. It's a very tall slender being, with blue grey skin, probably another Andromedan.

They all appear to be wearing an 'all in one' suit. It's almost like a second skin, because as I looked at them, the thought occurred to me that they hadn't got anything on at all. I thought I was just seeing the body, but as I looked closer, I can see that they are clothed. There don't appear to be any seams or joins of any description, just a total body covering.

Ann: Is it the same colour as their skin?

Elaine: It's not far off, maybe a bit more silvery.

Ann: Are their bodies very humanoid?

Elaine: Yes, two arms, two legs, and the chest area is indented with ridges of muscles. This goes right across the chest area without a dip in the middle.

Ann: Is there a shape to their torso, or is it straight down?

Elaine: It seems to be pretty much straight down, actually. They have hands the same as we have, but with very long fingers; much longer than we would have anyway. I am trying to see what their feet look like. Their suits end with soft boots that are all in one with the suit. I can't see any defined toes, only feet shapes, covered by these soft boots.

She is pulling me away from the loungers now. In another area I see planted areas dotted around, in the same way that we would have houseplants at home. This is the first time I have seen plants used in this way. This next section looks like a 'futuristic space age cafe'. I see a round 'smoked' glass case like a tube, and in it are lots of things that look like test tubes, with a variety of what I think are liquids in them. There is one in there that has beautiful dark royal blue liquid in, and it's glittering from within.

Ann: Is it the cocktail cabinet? (laughing)

Elaine: I don't think its quite cocktails! She says that it's a variety of their food, or more simply, liquid nutrients. There's a purple and a green one in there, and a flat glass dish with a tiny rim a round it in the bottom of the case. It has something rubbery looking in the bottom of it that's coloured a wonderful shade of blue. I ask her what it is and she answers, it's a plate. It's a plate with a non-slip surface! (And I thought it was something weird you could eat!)

Elaine: I can see and understand the tubes of liquid nutrient, but I wonder what they put on the plate? As if to answer me, she is showing me all kinds of soft fruit, and these are some of the weirdest fruit I've ever seen. There's one shaped like a starfish, and she says you must break it open to eat it. The inside is like clear jelly, with a consistency similar to an Aloe Vera plant.

She is taking me on a bit further now.

Oh, now we are going to see Andromedan children. (I assume that they are children, because they are small.) Some of them are as tall as my thigh height (Similar to a human three or four year old) ranging to 'teenagers' who are taller. There are many different sizes.

Although they all look similar at first impression, it is obvious if you really look carefully that they are all different with their own individual features. One comes forward who looks like a teenager. He has a silver suit on with some kind of padding at the top. It's wider at the shoulders, and he's wearing trousers. He has a small female child with him.

Ann: How can you tell the difference between male and female?

Elaine: I don't know, I can feel it, I suppose. I just know that he's a boy, and this smaller one is a girl. It's not as if they have any distinguishing body bumps that would tell me. Maybe I am being told telepathically. She is now telling me that these two are her children! I am honoured! I ask her, 'Do you have a husband?'

Andromedan: Not husband, as in your human terms, but I do have a male counterpart. We share the duties concerning the children. Others undertake the actual care of the children, from a very early age. Compared to humans in size and stature these look like children, but they are actually many years older than you would think. I will explain how they arrived, but it was many years ago.

When it is our particular turn to create children, we are selected. It is part of our life duty to create these children. The 'boy' you see here is fifty (in your earth terms) years old and the girl is thirty-five. And yet to you, she looks just like a seven or eight year old. The period of closeness that we share after creation with the beings that we create is in your Earth terms, five years. This is when we supervise and govern the way they begin their process of development. Someone else actually looks after them, but for the first five-year period (and she says please don't confuse your years with our time) we have special duties to perform.

What is in reality five months to us would be five years to you. We must go two or three times daily to attend the presence of the being we have created. This is for the giving of knowledge; I will show you how we do it. I touch with my hands to the child's head, and communicate with it telepathically.

When we created children at this period of time, one of my tasks was to endow all I have to the child; and then we went two or three times a day to do this. The child is cared for in every other way, and my special contribution is bonding and passing on of all that I have learnt. I totally endow all that I know for just this period of five months. We also share time, as in eating together, and doing things together. But it is only for this short period of time (for her). Then, to use your words, the children are then 'schooled' by someone else. They are taken to different departments to learn different things. When they come of a certain age, they are then free to walk around the ship, be curious, and see everything that goes on. But the bonding that we make when they are young is always there. So these that you see are my children, but they live their own lives. There is a whole bank of people that they look to for instructions. Until they are fully grown and old enough to graduate and become a member of the fleet with a specific task to do, they have to attend to their learning. It has a moderate comparison to Earth schooling.

Ann: So have her children always been on the ship?

Elaine: Yes.

Ann: Have they ever visited their home planet?

Elaine: No, she says they were created (and I'm told not to say born because she didn't give birth to them in our sense of the word) on the ship during her term of duty.

Andromedan: For Andromedans, it doesn't matter where we are, when our time comes to create, we do what is needed, and it happens.

Elaine: I am asking now where the male counterpart comes in, because I have only seen her going to pass on her knowledge. She shows me where her male counterpart is. He's in (using our standards) a very plush room. The older of the two children has gone there, and there are maybe 10 or so others gathered around him. I see a large viewing window open to the stars outside. He is teaching them about stars and galaxies, and all things outside the ship, not inside.

Ann: Is she willing to tell you how these children are created?

Elaine: I'll ask her. I am now seeing images of her, and I'm asking questions at the same time. I can see her lying down on a couch, and I see one whom we would class as a doctor. He has a test tube in his hand, with what must be the beginnings of the creation of a child inside. It's in a liquid, and it looks very strange! When her time to create is ready, he just presses his hands right up high on her stomach area, (not abdomen) an opening appears, the liquid is poured in, and then he brings the sides of the tissue back together again. He has what looks like a red laser light, and he uses this to seal the opening again. This beginning of the embryonic growth, stays within her for.......how long?......One week!.

Andromedan: One week is all that it needs for the embryo to absorb all my genetic chemistry and information, and all the nutrients it needs. There is something else that is very important. I will explain.

Elaine: She is showing me something fascinating. It's like an energy vortex that pools over her body. I can see all kinds of colours in it.

Ann: Is it something to do with the energy body of the embryo?

Elaine: It could be. It is energy that is taken from her. It's almost like she is giving it part of her soul to grow with. She says that the initial embryo needs to be inside of her for a period of a week, in order to become complete. Then they remove it, and place it in what she calls a growing chamber. I ask for how long?

Andromedan: Ten weeks for it to become the same size as your human babies. The older the children get, the slower the growing process becomes.

Elaine: For example, concerning the female child that I thought was seven or eight. She said it was thirty-five of our years old, and that the initial growth process is very fast. At that time the capacity inside to develop is very rapid, but the bodily growth is very slow. Now, I am going back to ask her about the test tube, because I want to know what is inside, where do they get it from, and how does the 'father' come into it? I sit quietly for a moment, whilst she shows me the whole process.

I have seen it... and I am in awe with the knowledge that this is a totally different concept to what we are familiar with. I am trying to understand what she has shown me. I will describe it as I see it.

When the time comes, I see the two of them standing face to face, as if they are glued together from the feet to the shoulders, with only their heads either side of one another. She tells me this part is a total joining of their energy, and she refers to levels of energy (what we call the chakras), so I can understand a little better. Then they totally merge into one being, 'energy wise'. I have asked her how long it takes, and she says, twenty-four of your hours. That's how long they are united in energy together in the same position.

And then what?

I see now.... she tells me that the soul or energy body of the child has to be the product of the two of them. So his (the male counterpart) energy has to be melded with hers. After the union, she then carries within her the necessary energy from the two of them. It's a very different energy to what they have inside their bodies at any other time. The combined energy has joined into this one creative thing, inside her body. Whatever it is that is in the test tube doesn't come from either of them. It's something... a chemical mixture...I don't know what it is, maybe DNA? I can only guess. But as soon as this mixture is placed inside of her, the united energy from both-plus all her body chemicals, then come together over a period of one week to form a new being. A new being that has both a physical and an energy form. Then it is removed, and put into a growing chamber to be taken care of.

Andromedan: Then begins the period of five weeks when I must go to it two or three times a day, and give it all that I have within me. It's a process that helps it to develop properly; then my task is completed.

Ann: When the baby is taken out of her, is it in a recognisable physical form, or is it contained within some other structure?

Elaine: She says yes, it has a physical form, even though it is tiny. It is fully formed, and all it needs to do then is grow.

(Wow, that's fascinating!)

Andromedan: ALL are required to do this, and the choice may be one child, or sometimes two, but usually no more than this. We have an equal balance amongst my people as to the choice of one child or two. I also meet with my counterpart occasionally, and we discuss the progression of our children.

Elaine: It seems that part of his job is also to be teacher to a lot more of them, not just his own.

Ann: So are there any tender feelings between the Andromedans?

Andromedan: Indeed! There is a unique feeling of love and bonding when we create another being. We look with love upon all others too, and there is a great deal of love and peace between all of us. But for those of us who have bonded together, we share a common concern over our 'own' children. It is not like a responsibility, it's an allocation. These children are ours by allocation, and as we concern ourselves with these two, others concern themselves with their children. But we all share. Your Earth reproduction is a totally different concept from ours.

Elaine: I understand that it's not a priority for them to be together the whole time. It's not as if they share the same sleeping quarters, or anything similar.

Andromedan: Regardless of the way you view it, there is always special love and regard for one that you have bonded with. The twenty-four hour period of unification of energy makes us like two halves of a whole, and there is always a greater attraction to the one that you have bonded with.

Ann: It sounds like there is no emotional possessiveness in their relationships.

Elaine: I don't think there is.

Ann: So there is love, but no feelings like you have to be with that person exclusively?

Andromedan: No, not at all; but it is rare for us ever to bond with more than one. One is chosen for genetic compatibility, and then that is it. Then life goes on.

Ann: Judging by the relative size and age of the children, the adults must have long life spans.

Andromedan: Yes, in our years, between seven and nine hundred years on average.

Ann: This throws a new light on our Old Testament, doesn't it!

Andromedan: I have shown you these things to illustrate that in comparison to Earth beings, we are 'normal'. We are not as different as some species. Granted, we are different, but we do have some similar structures to your civilisation.

This is a gift from me to you, that I show you our way. I would that we will always be friends, and that you understand our reasons for being involved with your planet, and with you.

Elaine: Now I have come back abruptly into the presence of all the other Extra-Terrestrials, and the one with the blue eyes is really smiling and beaming at me, and I know why. I was feeling his presence very strongly the other day, when I was in a 'liquid sound' pool. This is an experience I had, immersed in a warm pool of salt water with coloured lights playing over the surrounding walls and underwater sound.

He is saying, 'If you think that was good, you haven't seen anything yet!'

Whilst I was in the pool, I was thinking that although the experience was simply wonderful, it must be a poor man's version of what the Extra-Terrestrials can do. It was still wonderful, nevertheless.

So he is still smiling, and very happy.

Ann: It must be gratifying for them to see this kind of thing starting to happen now on Earth.

Elaine: Yes, he is very eager to tell me lots more things about sound and light in the future. If you recall, he comes from the planet with the unpronounceable name, sounding like a lot of musical tones all strung together. I am asking if there is anything more to be said tonight, and the Sirian has stepped forward. I haven't spoken to him for a while. He says there is more, but not now. The Arcturan is ready to go off on a mission, so we may not see him for a while, and the Lyran is there in the background, parenting, and being very loving, sending out wonderful vibrations of love and goodwill.

Sirian: I have a lot more teachings to give you, but those will come later.

Andromedan: I am always here for you. There are things that we will do together, but I cannot disclose them as yet. This is sufficient material for you both to work on now. As with the creation of my children, you must bring the energy together now and create the 'soul' of the book. We will be there anytime you need us, to answer any questions. There are a lot more beings from around the galaxy that would like to make themselves known to you, but we can do this at a later date.

Elaine: This was a most intimate thing she has shown me, and I am very grateful. We closed the session with much joy and wonder that we could be privy to such extraordinary information.

22
A Trip to Sirius ......

As an end to my story, I am including this last chapter to round off all the things I have been privileged to learn. These writings were given to me solely in January of 1992, I think as a preparation of the things that are happening now.

I was asked by a being from Sirius in 1993 to write this book, telling about various races of Extra-Terrestrials in and around the galaxy. New things entered my life that year, and the project was shelved. However, in the light of what has happened now, I feel it might be appropriate to include the following transcript. These are a series of 'parables' or short stories that give insight into ways of being. This information comes from The Sirian Being.

Elaine: I have arrived on a planet. It seems to have many clouds around it, and has a faint green glow in the atmosphere. All around me I see a beautiful landscape, and in the distance, I see strange cone shaped mountains. They are perfectly rounded, coming to a point at the tops. They have bands of colour around them, and it seems as if they are made of some fine material like sand.

I have gone on a little further, and there are lots of trees a bit like the Earth silver birch. Some of them have green leaves, but a lot have orange leaves. They are extremely tall, maybe a hundred feet high. There is a strange quality of bright and sparkly light all around the place, and I see that I have arrived on the surface of this planet in some kind of a valley. Everything seems to be very neat and tidy, and I see a stream flowing nearby. There are beautifully shaped white marble buildings in the distance, very 'futuristic'. All around me things are very big, including buildings I judge to be two or three hundred feet tall.

Maybe I am misjudging here, on second look, perhaps they are only one hundred feet tall, it's difficult to tell. There are pillars and curved domes; no angles on any of the buildings anywhere, so smooth and white. There is an open palazzo or courtyard in the centre of these buildings.

I can see a male being from Sirius dressed in some kind of a robe. It is wide across the shoulders with pleated folds of cloth falling gently down to the ground. His skin seems to be very pale, and I can see he doesn't have any hair. His head is big at the back with a large forehead and an indentation in the centre where the 'scalp' begins. His head seems to have a dip in the middle, and then be very rounded on either side. (see picture)

He carries a tall staff, and he is beckoning me to come forward and go with him. We go towards a large building where he says he will show me something. These buildings remind me of the Halls of Learning I have seen in our Earthly Spiritual realms.

I have seen the surface of this planet at other times, and I understand it to be Sirius. It doesn't matter that astronomically speaking Sirius is a large planet like a sun. I believe that there are many planets 'out there' that we know nothing about. Indeed, it wasn't too long ago (in the 1960s) that it was proved there is another planet behind Sirius. Maybe these suns have planets in orbit around them. Astronomers don't know yet. But I do understand that seemingly bare planets can hold life, and it is life on a different dimension to the one that we can readily see. Just because you can't see it, does not mean it doesn't exist!

Everything is so large; I can see that the place where I must look for information is very high, and not possible for me to reach. I am positive that the people on this planet are very tall. They are at least fourteen feet high when they are truly in their natural state. I think they can change their size to suit the occasion, or maybe use holograms for visitors like me so that we are the same size.

I see a podium with a book rest on it. On it is a book, and when I opened it, initially there's nothing there. Then as I look a moving picture or film of what ever it is I am to see appears on the page. It may be history, some facts of your present life, past lives, or whatever I want to see. I've seen this book before, and I know I can view my own personal 'akashic record' (history of all my past lives). I can choose any life from any page, and the appropriate picture will appear, then disappear when it's finished.

The Sirian individual who is guiding me is telling me that I can alter my size to accommodate the size of my surroundings, as I am not in my physical body. I am only using my mental or spiritual essence here.

He is asking me to close my eyes, and imagine becoming as big as they are. So I do, and I feel myself growing.

Now everything seems to be the right size! The podium and the buildings seem to be much better suited, although the tops of the buildings are still immensely high and all around there is still an air of spaciousness. The air is very warm here, and there is a quality of clearness and purity about everything. I don't think you could even get this feeling on the top of a mountain on Earth, it's so different.

Sirian: We have asked you to come here because there are certain principles, teachings and ways of doing things that need to come to Earth. You are not the only one who is doing this; there are many people all over the Earth who are receiving the same information.

It is necessary that we use as many 'channels' as we can, in order to create sufficient impact and enough recognition. You have only a few years left before changes will begin on Earth. Monetary structures and ways of doing things will alter by the late 1990s. Some of our people are already working with these things on Earth, over- shadowing people to influence them in a beneficial way. This includes scientists, researchers, engineers, and people who work on designing aircraft. The military in some countries have several of our people who are teaching them about methods of flight, fuel, and other things.

Elaine: What shall I do with the information once you have given it to me?

Sirian: Your first job is to see and memorise; then we will tell you later what you will do with it once it is learnt.

Elaine: He is taking me first to a long table. Everything seems to be made of white marble, and yet it's warm, not cold. Around the long table are other beings that look similar to him. Really, their foreheads are so huge and their eyes set so deeply, it's quite strange!

They ask me to sit down and eat with them. All they have on the table are natural fruits and vegetables on plates. There's lots of water in evidence, and as they drink, I see the water has a quality to it like everything else I've seen on this planet, very sparkly and light. I also see what looks like the juice of some of the fruits, in glasses.

They tell me everything is rich in vitamins and minerals and that it's mostly all they need to sustain them, but I think there are other things. I see very thin round biscuits like wafers. Unlike Earth biscuits, they're not cream or brown coloured; they're a silvery white colour. I am asked to sit down and eat with them, and I ask what the 'biscuits' are. He says they are made from different kinds of vegetables and fruit. He mentally shows me things that look like great big bright yellow gourds. Fat at the top and fat at the bottom like an hourglass, they are mashed down to make into biscuits. Apparently they are incredibly nutritious, containing all that people need, including natural minerals and salt. He says the custom is to eat once a day; and I have a feeling that their day is much longer than ours, maybe thirty-six or forty-eight hours, and that they convene to eat for sociability. They get together to talk, and at the same time they eat to take in all the necessary vitamins and minerals to sustain them.

But mostly they go about their business doing other things, as the regular 'ritual' of eating is not the same as it is on Earth.

At this point, a friend of mine who was giving some healing in another room disturbed me. She was using her voice (vocal tones) and also a Tibetan Bowl. The being from Sirius has just informed me that these are methods that they also used for healing. He comments that they don't use it so much on their own people now, as they have no need.

Sirian: In the past it was a very valuable tool in our elevation from one type of vibration to another. It took us a long time to perfect it. Musical tone alters the structure of your being if used in the right way.

Elaine: They use something else other than Tibetan bowls, I think, (because they obviously wouldn't have Tibetan things on this planet). They had other instruments that produced the same tones. Now he is showing me that they placed them on the body and made them ring, using the voice in combination with tones to affect some kind of a healing.

Sirian: Your energy on Earth can be compared to a big tangled ball of wool; things are not running smoothly and in line. They are jumbled and scattered all over the place. When you sing, or make tones, and you 'ring' sounds, the energy molecules in your body are all brought into beautiful patterns such as lines, circles and geometric shapes.

Elaine: I can see they make forms very similar to the experiments I did as a child with iron filings; or when you send frequency through metal and it forms into a pattern or a circle, as in the work of Hans Jenny.

Sirian: This is what happens in your body. With the correct patterns, you will function more efficiently and be more at ease with yourself; lighter, much more at peace, with a sense of well being.

Elaine: I think that would be wonderful! I now ask him to explain a little more about musical tone altering the structure of the body.

Sirian: Musical tones can be used to heal your body and rearrange your cell structure; to align your physical body make-up and alter internal patterns. You can use whatever methods you have available, either Tibetan bowls, or any musical instrument that will make clear tones from the octave. When you have these tones resonating throughout your body, sing them also. This will realign and reshape the molecules in the body. They will regroup in different numbers. For example: If one basic molecule has four or maybe six elements to its makeup, (like $C12$ $N4$ $H3$ $O12$) the number of molecules can regroup and begin to alter your physical internal make-up. This also allows a particle of light to come in; it also allows for 'The Knowingness' or recognition to come in. But whilst you are concentrating with the musical notes, you must especially focus your attention on every part of your physical and energy body. Fingers, toes, legs, internal organs; every single part of you is pervaded by your energy body. For you to truly 'know', you must know throughout all of you.

Elaine: I have asked him the question about possible incarnation from Sirius to Earth, and he has reminded me of a vision I saw once concerning music and light, and he says this is how I came once from Sirius to Earth using musical tones. In essence, my body was broken down into millions of particles with sound and coloured light, and I was then sent to Earth like a beam of light. You could compare it to a message down a telephone line, or even the transporter machine from 'Star Trek'. He tells me it's easy when you know how to do it. He says it is not necessary to have space ships from Sirius, although they do exist. This is because the higher beings from Sirius can do their work from a distance with their mental powers, but it most certainly helps if there is an equal link or a bridge from Earth to them with which they can work.

I can see one of their spaceships now, and it looks to me like a 'typical' silver disc. It's silver in colour and almost flat, with a slight dome on one side and very streamlined. I believe that their method of travel is almost instantaneous, and the way they travel is most strange.

They use their consciousness to facilitate travel; when they get to a place like Earth, they then utilise their combined consciousness to form denser bodies (not as dense as ours) in which to appear. So when they do appear, they are not as I see them now (about 14 feet tall with large heads), they take on a more appropriate and less 'frightening' appearance to present themselves to Earth people.

Some people here on Earth call them 'The Shining Ones', who are very fair and have very beautiful eyes, look very much like humans and work very strongly with telepathy. He tells me that there are different vibratory levels of being on Sirius; they are not all like him. People can take on a difference appearance, according to their level of awareness.

I think I understand this. For communication and work purposes, beings must adapt their bodily structure to suit the purpose. For those from Sirius who work on Earth, they must appear to be human and have a stronger compatibility with our Earth vibrations than those of the elders (or higher beings) on the planet.

It's very interesting to see how interplanetary incarnation works! Beings from Sirius have come to Earth, and there are some from Earth who have spent many lifetimes on Sirius; volunteering to come back to Earth to experience the cycle of growth here helped by their 'extra' added knowledge. This is in order that our awareness can be more complete. So whilst some Earth people could call Sirius a 'home base', we have been on Earth a lot longer than those who come to help us directly from Sirius now. Others have come from Sirius within the last century. They are the fair-haired, blue eyed, telepathic beings who are our planetary brothers, but on a different level.

He is asking me now if I would like to look into one of the books on the podium. So I replied, well yes, but I really don't know what I'm looking for, or what I am expected to see.

Sirian: What we want to teach you is difficult to put into words. So you must see the pictures for yourself, use your own words to describe them and then you will understand.

Elaine: Walking back to the podium, it feels very natural to be as tall as this, and it seems as if I have taken on a similar outward form to them. My brain capacity feels enormous, as if I could understand everything if I allowed myself to!

Sirian: We are going to show you with these stories how to re-tune your body.

Elaine: So, now I am standing on the steps in front of the podium, looking at the big white book. It's about the size of an old family bible. When I open the pages it becomes like a television screen, but with holographic figures on it, so that it actually feels like I am there in the picture.

The first thing I see is an Asian woman walking along a riverbank. The bank is covered in grass and daisies; the water is very blue, and every thing looks very cartoon-like in its perfection. As I look more closely, I can actually see fine details of the blades of grass and daisies. The woman is traditionally dressed in a long sari. She has long dark hair with flowers entwined in it, and is standing quite still now looking at the water. Now she walks up and down the bank a little. I look to the other side of the river, and I can see an elephant! The elephant makes loud trumpeting noises, and he too is walking up and down. It seems as if the elephant wants to get to the woman, and she wants to get to the elephant, but neither of them can get across the river. I have no idea what the significance of this is, but I will reserve judgement on it and just see!

Now I see a wooden bridge further down the river. It is clear to me that either the woman can go across to the elephant or vice versa. But they cannot meet in the middle, because the combined weight would be too much for the bridge; it would break and they would both fall in the water.

So, the elephant is at one side of the bridge, woman at the other, and neither moves. The woman fears if she starts to walk towards the elephant he will come towards her, and the elephant is uncertain as to what to do next. So they both wait. As they wait I feel a strong urgency; the elephant is swinging his trunk from side to side, his feet are going up and down continuously and the woman has a worried look on her face. She is trying to communicate with the elephant. She judges that if the elephant comes across the bridge, his weight will be too much. So she decides that she must run very quickly across the bridge; but using some kind of telepathy to make the elephant stay where he is. So, concentrating very hard, she makes in her mind a big shield to push the elephant back in case he comes forward. Now walking across the bridge with this mental screen in front of her, she pushes energy towards the elephant, and it backs off. She gets successfully across the bridge........and now what?

Now the elephant picks her up, puts her on his back, and off they walk. The first point I see is that she is now elevated to a higher position so can see much more of the landscape than she was able to before. As I think about the significance of this little story, I think I can begin to understand it now.

Take the woman as being an example of anyone who wants to get to a position of strength and advantage where they can see the overall picture of life. If they have found heightened awareness in their lives, it enables an overview of what is actually happening with a 'higher' perspective on personal and perhaps spiritual levels. I feel this is where most people would like to be.

In order to get there, they must find a pathway (the bridge) and cross it towards the advantage point (the elephant, or higher perspective). I think that if the advantage point comes towards them before they are ready, (as with possible contact from Extra-Terrestrials, or Spirit Guides), it could be too much to comprehend for the average person, and would break the bridge. The bridge represents the comprehension and mental sanity of the person. Too much all at once would confuse or destroy the sanity. So when ready, using his or her own mental powers, the person must form a barrier or shield (the will) to push forward, until he or she reaches that vantage point of strength and vision, where all is clear.

I interpret the hesitation in the beginning as the fear of death or disaster; (i.e. the elephant comes across the bridge, it breaks and you fall in the river and drown). This can be also seen as fear of being overwhelmed by new concepts, such as before-mentioned Extra-Terrestrial or Spiritual Guides.

I felt the impatience of the elephant to come towards her (contact from Extra-Terrestrials or Spirit Guides) but knowing that it would be dangerous to approach. Then seeing the mental preparation and determination of the girl as she walked across the bridge using self awareness as her mental shield, (no fear) to push her energy forwards. Facing her fears allowed her to gain the higher knowledge advantage point on the other side. This is my interpretation of this little story.

The Sirian has asked me to close the book and come and sit for a while, and discuss what I have seen. I think this is a very good way to teach me! When I see pictures of things I cant understand or don't know the reasons for, it's beneficial when the explanations come later, as it then makes very good sense to me. This way, I don't get 'in the way' with my own mind and my rationalisations!

Elaine: I ask him, how can people here on this Earth do what the woman did? Push forward with their minds, in order to get to a higher vantage point?

Sirian: Remove judgement, make the decision to face their fears, and take action. The biggest fear is that of change. It is always feels 'safer' to follow familiar patterns of behaviour in your life. If change doesn't occur, progress in self-awareness comes to a halt.

At this point, I take a break.

I think more explanation for this comes in the main part of the book.

I have resumed the mental connection now, and the first thing I do is to make my way back to the planet. I landed in the same place, on the bridge. I find myself carrying a shield with two symbols, one on either side. They are a triangle, a double spiral like a DNA helix, and in between are eight different coloured points of light, each representing a musical note. I am told to sing these notes as I walk across the bridge, and I have now come to the other side. I am not sure if I understand the significance of these symbols, but nevertheless, I have followed my intuition, and I feel that I can now go forward to meet the guide from Sirius again. Maybe singing the notes altered my vibrations?

He is once more asking me if I will grow, leave behind the earthly concept of my body, and become my light body, which I can feel. This is now tall enough to see the book. My body as it is now seems to be solid, in a physical shape, but very much taller and made of very sparkly light. My intelligence and reasoning are there, but I cannot feel anything else. I am also aware of an intermittent high-pitched note in my left ear. I don't know whether this has significance or not. I look at the guide in front of me, and he appears to be telling me a little about his body.

He says that they have a similar kind of nose to us, but not the same. He breathes mostly through his skin, and his ears are slightly different; with the mouth, the lips are not prominent, mostly inside. He is telling me that this is enough examination of himself, and we must now proceed with some work.

I want to talk to him again about the significance of the musical notes and the symbols from the shield, but he says I already know the reasons. The explanation was given earlier, concerning molecular changes in the physical structure, enabling vibrational and dimensional change. He says I must look in the book again, so I will.

I see now a picture of one of the cone shaped mountains. This mountain appears to be made of sand; it is soft but perfectly formed. I see a man at the top of the mountain, trying to come down. It's obvious to me that he can't walk down. If his feet touch the sand, he will sink. So he must lie flat, with as much of his body area touching the sand as possible. When he does this, he begins to slide, and comes down the mountain quickly and easily with little resistance. The larger the area of body that touches the surface of the sand, the easier his passage down the mountain is. If he stands, he will sink up to his knees and be stuck.

I pause for a moment, to allow the meaning of this to surface. I think what they are trying to show me is this: When you wish to contact and align with 'all knowing' and 'all understanding', then you must use every part of your body. By this, I mean every cell of your body must have the information, both energetically and physically. Not just the energy of the mind, at the crown centre or the third eye, but your complete energy body, from your feet to your head. When you bring the whole of yourself into line or contact with the 'source that knows', only then it will be integrated fully.

If you try just to use one part, i.e. mental understanding, or heartfelt feelings, you cannot understand the whole. It will not be integrated into every cell. In order to change or transmute, you must gather together your consciousness, and mentally allow it to flow like syrup throughout every single part of you.

Now I ask him, what are the things that we must know? What are the things that we must apply to every part of our body and to every cell?'

He replies: I must look in the book again.

Now he is showing me a picture of a blue sky and in the sky is an aeroplane. The aeroplane is flying directly towards the top of a mountain. The aeroplane flies into the mountain! The top of the mountain bends as if it were rubber, and the plane bounces backwards. Again, the plane flies at the mountain, it reacts like rubber, and the plane bounces back. Now the plane is motionless in the air, almost as if it were thinking, and the pilot has decided to rev up the engines. He turns up the fuel injection, the engine power, and anything else in the plane that can be speeded up. Everything is functioning to a 'higher degree.' Now he comes towards the mountain more slowly. As he reaches it, the plane is vibrating at such a high rate, that it passes through the top of the mountain as if the peak were invisible.

I think with this example, he is confirming to me that in order for us to achieve, not invisibility, but the ability to pass through matter, then we must do what I already believed we must do, and that is raise our vibrational frequency. But quite in what manner we must 'turn up our fuel' and 'expand our revs', I'm not quite sure. It's probably to do with diet and quality if life.

I know being attuned to your energy body is very important. The vibrations of the energy body are controlled from the emotions in the brain centre. Somewhere in the brain lies the conscious ability to raise our vibrations, and I think we can access this partly with visualisation, and a positive attitude towards all things. Diet too, is of maximum importance, perhaps eating raw foods such as vegetables and fruit, enabling gradual changes in the structure and content of our cells by what we eat. This is important. From my own understanding of this, and others may agree, raw fruit and vegetables, juice and pure water, occasional herbal teas, without the heaviness of meat, dairy produce and fat, (the more energetically dense foods) will bring about molecular and cellular changes in the body. This cannot be done too rapidly otherwise the body has a hard time adjusting. If it is introduced over a period of time, then it can be achieved.

He says that if you wish to go forward fairly quickly then this is the path that you should take. The cooking of food destroys part of the vital energy and the enzymes that are intrinsic to the food. There is a special quality about food in its natural state that we on Earth have been missing for a long time, because we consume it in its cooked form.

He says: 'On Earth you call it prana or vital energy. Here we call it "As is", or in other words, the fruit or the vegetable as it should be, as it is; natural, whole and complete.'

I have asked to look again at the book. I am standing in front of it now, and again I see a river. On the river is a swan; at first the swan attempts to swim against the flow of the river, and finds it difficult. She finds that her feathers are flattened smooth by the wind that blows against her. Her eyes water, and she cannot see, and it is difficult for her to breathe against the wind, and difficult for her to swim against the tide or flow of the river.

Then the swan is turning around, and the wind catches under her feathers, and they fluff out. Her eyes are protected, and she begins without any effort at all, to go rapidly downstream. She is heading towards a very steep drop, a waterfall. As she approaches the waterfall, she expands her wings, (the wings are a comparison to our consciousness), and takes off into the air. The wind takes her higher than she has ever been before. There is light rain, and it washes her clean, so she sparkles; it nourishes her, and the sun warms her. She flies higher and higher and becomes lighter and lighter. She can now stay in the air without any effort at all. She doesn't need to flap her wings; she is just riding the air. It's so beautiful. It's like being an angel.

I feel the significance of this has to do with the natural elements of wind, rain, and sunshine; also the simple lesson of allowing your life to go with the 'flow' (as with the river). When you go with the flow of life, all things are possible. You can attain great spiritual heights; i.e. reach your higher self and the angelic-like being which is within you. I feel he is saying to me that the elements of rain, sun and wind will be enough to sustain us, eventually. I am not sure how this would apply or work in reality, but I will think about it.

Sirian: These are enough teachings for now. To really learn anything, you must sit and contemplate, then digest and integrate it into your body. To 'know' these things totally, they must become a natural way of living in order to transform and transmute the whole.

The next day..........
Sirian: Come with me.
Elaine: I go forward again, this time to a circular white open temple. Inside there is a round white dais, and the roof over it is supported by very tall pillars, fifty or sixty feet tall. He takes me to the book on the podium, and I grow in size so I can see the pictures. I ask what must I learn today and he says, 'Open the book and you will see'.

In the top right hand corner of the book, I see snow capped mountains. This is a lovely peaceful scene that looks like a Swiss valley with tiny houses dotted around, like a postcard. I see inside the small and cosy houses; they are warm and glowing with lights on everywhere. Inside one of the houses I see quite a large ample woman, ladling out soup into bowls from a really old fashioned cauldron. I see a wooden table, with twelve places set. The first bowl is very tiny, and the bowls get gradually bigger until about the sixth or seventh place, and then the bowl becomes a plate, with mashed potato on it!

On the twelfth plate is a huge mountain of mashed potato! So it goes, around the table, from the smallest amount of soup to the largest plate of mash. I don't have any idea what this means!

I now see that the person sitting at the place with the biggest amount of food looks pretty sad, and he is thinking, 'Oh dear, do I have to eat all this again?'

The person with the smallest bowl thinks, why does everybody get more than I have? I wish I could change places!

Two extremes are present, wishing they could change places. In fact to a varying degree, everybody around the table wishes they had something other than what they have got. It's either too much, or not enough.

The one who sits at the head of the table with a medium-size bowl, is sitting eating soup quite happily, saying nothing.

There ensues an argument over who has what, and how much. Then the person with the medium bowl finishes his soup, carefully wipes his mouth, and puts the spoon down gently on the table. He gets up and quietly leaves, taking the bowl with him to wash and stack away. I also see that he has finished before everyone else. He has taken his time, but he is still finished and satisfied before the rest. In the mean time they are still fighting over what they've got and what they haven't got.

The story seems to have come to a standstill now, so I must think about it now, and find the greater meaning.

I feel I am being told...

'Do you see the disharmony that comes with having too much or too little? Only by having just enough, is real contentment present.

Just enough food is sustaining; if you always have desire for more, or believe you need less even, the extremes are as unbalanced as one another.

Contentment or peace of mind is illusive; dissatisfaction always unsettles the well-being and creates worry. This is quite a valuable lesson, to be content with just enough.

He says, enough is completion, because when you have more or less than enough, it can become a burden or a liability, and you become sick and tired of it, and you wish you had different. The most important point is not the actual quantity of *anything*, it's the emotions that go with any state that is not in balance.

He is talking in terms of money, food or possessions, and situations that apply to life in general. He has asked me to look at the book again for the last time, and the picture that has come up is this.

I am viewing a large indoor aquatic tank, and I see a big, solid olive-green fresh water fish that looks like a carp. I am looking at it through a glass observation window. The fish turns to face me, is startled, and blows bubbles out through its mouth. Because it blows bubbles this way, it shoots backwards. Then it swims back up to the glass; it seems to be expressing its freedom, in the fact that I'm on one side of the glass, and it's on the other. It seems quite cheeky, as if to say, 'You can't get me, and I can do what I want'.

In the meantime I am looking at it with curiosity. I see the scales and eyes; I note the way it functions and swims. I feel that I'd like to touch and talk to it saying, 'I'm not going to hurt you, why can't we be friends?' But this is interacting with the fish from my point of view. I must reverse it and see things from the fish's point of view. Does he want to be friends with me? If I were the fish, would I like it if he wanted to touch me? I am reminded that by saying I'd like to touch the fish, I am imposing my will. Because the glass is between us he has protection, and I can't impose my will no matter how much I want to. I think in some surreal way this shows me the situation between the Extra Terrestrials and the people of planet Earth.

People of planet Earth are like the 'fish', and the alien beings are like I was on the other side of the glass. If I wish, I can learn to relate instead of being afraid I would be under someone's control. Communication is needed so that both parties understand one another. Fear must be dealt with for progress to be made.

I think each and every one of us needs to think about the benefits and freedom gained from recognising, facing up to, and dealing with their fears. This is the most natural way towards Peace in our times, and progression of our growth and development. I feel the more we are open to help, the faster our progress will be. All of us from every corner of the earth, whether we are king, government, farmer or person in the street, needs to lay aside our judgement of each other and begin to see our fellow human beings with compassion and awareness.

Finally, we all need to recognise that we are personally responsible for our own actions and thoughts, not laying blame and judgement on others; and above all, it is for our highest good that we all remain open and unafraid to change.

***